Legal Literacy for Public School Teachers

Edited by Luke Stedrak and Jennifer Mezzina

EDUCATION LAW ASSOCIATION

No. 100 in the K-12 Series

© 2021 by the Education Law Association
(833) ELA-1954
EducationLaw.org

All rights reserved
Printed in the United States of America

ISBN-13: 978-1-56534-192-0

Education Law Association Publications

Founded in 1954, the Education Law Association is a nonprofit membership association focused on practical knowledge, scholarship, and interdisciplinary dialogue about legal and policy issues affecting education. ELA promotes interest in and understanding of the legal framework of education and the rights of students, parents, instructors, administrators, school employees, and other stakeholders, at both the PreK-12 and higher education levels of public and private schools.

Authors and editors who collaborate on ELA publications include many of the best-known experts in their fields: deans, professors of education or law, school administrators, and attorneys specializing in education law.

Whether you're doing research as an educational professional, attorney, or student—or you are a professor selecting high-quality and affordable text-books—help yourself succeed by choosing publications from ELA's bookstore at EducationLaw.org.

Notice to Readers

This book quotes directly from court cases in which strong profanity and words that some readers may find to be offensive are used.

Citations

Text and footnotes use *The Bluebook: A Uniform System of Citation*. For basic information on this system, visit guides.ll.georgetown.edu/bluebook.

Introduction

We Must Improve the Legal Literacy of Public School Teachers

John Hatcher III, Luke Stedrak, and Jennifer Mezzina

Introduction

School teachers are trained in pedagogy, child development, and subject areas, but they do not receive extensive training in school law. Having knowledge of school law enables teachers to better understand school policies and how to address them. *Legal Literacy for Public School Teachers* was derived primarily from the sixth edition of *The Principal's Legal Handbook*, an extensive reference guide for school principals. Chapters of *The Principal's Legal Handbook* were reworked to serve the needs of public school teachers, to help them understand how to navigate the legal challenges they encounter. *Legal Literacy for Public School Teachers* aims to support educators in developing a better understanding of school law, which will enable them to make sound, informed decisions in the classroom.

In a world of social media, cellphones, and online classes, the "walls" of a classroom can no longer be defined as physical structures. As the definition of a "schoolyard" is changing, and information is shared electronically, now more than ever it is imperative for school teachers to have a basic understanding of school law and how it applies to the school's authority to carry out disciplinary policies. Teachers' speech has become more publicly accessible through electronic means, and therefore is subject to broader scrutiny. Because they are employees of the school, teachers need to understand their rights and responsibilities in their communications. Furthermore, the actions of teachers in school also are no longer contained in the physical classroom. As students have access to recording devices via computers and cellphones, they have the means and ability to record and share a teacher's behavior in school. In this digital age, the school community has greater access to teacher speech outside of school, and schoolteachers have been dismissed based on their off-campus, online speech.[1] Such terminations could easily be avoided if teachers were to develop a basic understanding of their First Amendment rights as school employees.

During the COVID-19 pandemic starting in 2020, schools quickly had to find ways to extend the setting for education beyond the building, and teachers across the country were forced to shift their instruction from a physical structure to an electronic space.[2] The pandemic sparked a redefinition of "classroom," which now

---

1 Kimberly W. O'Connor & Gordon B. Schmidt, *'Facebook Fired': Legal Standards for Social Media–Based Terminations of K-12 Public School Teachers*, SAGE J. of Workplace Rights (2015). https://journals.sagepub.com/doi/full/10.1177/2158244015575636.
2 Young Zhao, *COVID-19 as a Catalyst for Educational Change*, PROSPECTS (June 11, 2020). https://link.springer.com/article/10.1007/s11125-020-09477-y#citeas.

can be defined as a traditional physical room inside a school building, or a "Zoom room" or "Google Meet room," or a place where instruction is delivered via video conferencing platforms. Now, more than ever, students are encouraged to interact with each other online, such as via Google Classroom, Blackboard, Moodle, and other learning management systems. As the "walls" of a school building have vastly expanded, it is even more imperative that teachers develop a basic understanding of school law, their rights, and the rights of students.

Teachers reach a diverse population of learners. Students may qualify for 504 plans or individualized education plans (IEPs) under federal law. Other students may be English language learners (ELL), or identify as transgender. It is imperative that teachers have a basic understanding of special education law so they understand the legal requirements for assessment, implementation, and their own responsibilities. Teachers who know more about special education will have a deeper understanding of their role in IEP team meetings, what needs to be considered when an administrator disciplines a student with a disability, and the legal responsibilities that schools have to provide students with a free appropriate public education (FAPE).

Legal Literacy for Public School Teachers is intended to serve as both a starting point for understanding school law and as a legal reference. This book will allow teachers to learn how the law applies to their responsibilities as educators. Although teachers are not expected to be attorneys, they are often the "first responders" to potentially problematic legal situations. Having a basic knowledge of school law will empower them to make informed, appropriate decisions—and, in turn, protect the rights of their students, as well as their own rights as public school employees.

In the nine chapters of *Legal Literacy for Public School Teachers*, written by noted experts in the field, readers will increase their awareness about school law and how it is relevant to daily decision making. Subjects addressed in this book include:

- keeping students and teachers safe in school and classroom settings
- basics of the American legal system
- teachers' rights and responsibilities under the First Amendment, related to speech and expression
- searches of lockers, cell phones, and other personal property in light of students' right to privacy
- sharing student records in an appropriate manner
- awareness of rules governing on- and off-campus social media content
- the primary aspects of special education assessment, placement, discipline, and the role that teachers play in providing FAPE to students with disabilities.

These topics will provide teachers with the tools to build their legal literacy, empowering them to act in the best legal interests of students, themselves, the school, and the community.

About the Editors

Luke J. Stedrak, Ed.D.

Luke Stedrak is Associate Professor and Hibernia National Bank Endowed Professor in the College of Education and Coordinator of the Educational Leadership Doctoral Program at Southeastern Louisiana University. His research focuses on the intersection of K-12 school finance and school law with an emphasis on constitutional and statutory rights of students, teachers, and administrators in K-12 public schools. He is nationally recognized in the fields of school finance and school law.

Jennifer Mezzina, Ed.D.

Jennifer Mezzina is Director of Data, State Reporting, and Compliance, Northern Valley High School District, Demarest, New Jersey, where she observes instruction and oversees the Teacher Mentoring Program, I&RS/MTSS Committee, and Local Professional Development Committee, as well as serving on the School Improvement Panel and District Evaluation Committee. She is the 504 Administrator and Affirmative Action Officer. Jennifer co-facilitates the district's Ad Hoc Anti-Racism Committee. Prior to becoming an administrator, she was a high school Spanish teacher.

Contributing Authors

Justin Bathon, Ph.D., J.D., Associate Professor, Director of Graduate Studies, Department of Educational Leadership Studies, University of Kentucky, Lexington, Kentucky

Watt Lesley Black, Jr., Ph.D., Clinical Professor, Department of Education Policy & Leadership, Southern Methodist University, Dallas, Texas

Kevin P. Brady, Ph.D., Associate Professor, Curriculum & Instruction, Director, UCEA Center for the Study of Leadership and the Law, University of Arkansas, Fayetteville, Arkansas

Jean B. Crockett, Ph.D., Professor, School of Special Education, School Psychology, and Early Childhood Studies, University of Florida, Gainesville, Florida

Janet A. Decker, J.D., Ph.D., Associate Professor, Educational Leadership & Policy Studies, Indiana University, Bloomington, Indiana

John S. Gooden, Ed.D., Coordinator, Doctoral Program in Educational Leadership, Policy, and Law. Alabama State University, Montgomery, Alabama

Mark A. Gooden, Ph.D., Christian Johnson Endeavor Professor of Education Leadership, Teachers College Columbia University, New York, New York

John Hatcher III, Ed.D., Assistant Professor, Department of Education Leadership & Technology, Southeastern Louisiana University, Hammond, Louisiana

W. Kyle Ingle, Ph.D., Professor & Assistant Department Chair, Educational Leadership, Evaluation, & Organizational Development, The University of Louisville, Louisville, Kentucky

Julie F. Mead, Ph.D., Professor Emerita, Educational Leadership & Policy Analysis, University of Wisconsin-Madison, Madison, Wisconsin

Jennifer Mezzina, Ed.D., Director of Data, State Reporting, and Compliance, Northern Valley High School District, Demarest, New Jersey

Allan G. Osborne, Jr., Ed.D., Principal (Retired), Quincy Public Schools, Quincy, Massachusetts

Mark A. Paige, J.D., Ph.D., Associate Professor, University of Massachusetts-Dartmouth, Dartmouth, Massachusetts

John Pijanowski, Ph.D., Professor of Educational Leadership, University of Arkansas, Fayetteville, Arkansas

James A. Plenty, Ed.D., Instructor and Conductor, MediaTech Institute, Houston, Texas

Charles J. Russo, J.D., Ed.D., Panzer Chair in Education, School of Education, and School of Law, University of Dayton, Dayton, Ohio

Luke Stedrak, Ed.D., Associate Professor, Department of Education Leadership & Technology, Southeastern Louisiana University, Hammond, Louisiana

Mitchell L. Yell, Ph.D., Fred and Francis Lester Palmetto Chair in Teacher Education, University of South Carolina, Columbia, South Carolina

Table of Contents

Chapter 1
Why Teachers Should Increase Their Legal Literacy
Janet R. Decker

Introduction 1
Why This Book Is Needed 2
Who Benefits from Reading This Book 4
How To Use This Book 5
Case List 6
Key Words 6
Takeaways 6
Practical Extension 7

Chapter 2
The American Legal System
Charles J. Russo and Allan G. Osborne, Jr.

Introduction 9
Sources of Law 9
    Generally 9
    Constitutions 10
    Statutes and Regulations 11
    Common Law 12
Judicial Systems 13
Legal Resources 15
Reading Legal Citations 16
Case List 16
Key Words 16
Takeaways 17
Practical Extension 18

Chapter 3
Freedom of Expression
Watt Lesley Black, Jr.

Introduction 19
Student Speech and the First Amendment 20
    The Material Disruption Standard: *Tinker v. Des Moines* 20
    On-Campus Student Speech That Is Lewd or Vulgar
        Is Not Protected: *Bethel v. Fraser* 22
    On-Campus Student Speech Promoting Illegal Drug
        Use Is Unprotected: *Morse v. Frederick* 23
    The Student Press and the School's Authority:
        Hazelwood v. Kuhlmeier 24

Student Speech Online, but Off-Campus 27
Participation in Patriotic Rituals 30
Clothing and Student Expression..31
Equal Access to School Facilities..32
Expression of Sexual Orientation and Gender Identity 34
Distribution of Printed Materials on Campus......................................36
Student Free Speech: Considerations for Best Practice.....................37
Teacher Speech and the First Amendment 38
   Teachers Speaking as Citizens on Matters of Public Concern:
     Pickering v. Board 39
   Unprotected Speech: Teachers Speaking as Employees
     on Matters of Private Interest..40
   Unprotected Speech: Teachers Speaking as Employees
     Pursuant to Job Duties...41
   Social Media and Other Online Teacher Expression........................42
   Teachers' Free Speech: Considerations for Best Practice 44
Case List..46
Key Words 47
Takeaways...48
Practical Extension..49

Chapter 4
Student Searches in Public Schools: Contemporary Legal Considerations for Educators
Kevin P. Brady, W. Kyle Ingle, and John C. Pijanowski

Introduction 51
Recent Examples of Student Searches in K-12 Settings
   in the National Media 51
The Legal Standard of Reasonable Suspicion...52
   Step I: Justification at Inception...53
   Step II: Scope of the Search 57
     Pat-Down Searches..60
     Student Strip-Searches 61
     Searches Off of School Grounds 67
Special Needs Doctrine...68
   Detection Dogs Used in School Searches...71
   Metal Detectors Used in School Searches 72
   Random Urinalysis Drug Testing..73
   Searches of Student Cellphones and Related Tech Devices 76
School Searches Involving School Resource
   Officers (SROs) and Law Enforcement...79
Student Seizures..81
Conclusion 84
Case List..84

Key Words 87
Takeaways 88
Practical Extension 89

Chapter 5
Student Records
Justin Bathon, John S. Gooden, and James A. Plenty

Introduction 91
FERPA Overview 91
FERPA Details 92
    Remedies & Enforcement under FERPA 92
    Definition of Educational Records 93
    Directory Information 95
    Personally Identifiable Information (PII) 96
    Other Educators & Law Enforcement 96
    Access by Custodial and Noncustodial Parents 97
    Students Reaching Age of Majority and Higher Education 98
    Records of Records 98
    Press Access and FERPA 98
    Technology Issues 99
Special Education Students 100
Protection of Pupil Rights Amendment 101
Recommendations for Practice 102
Case List 103
Key Words 104
Takeaways 104
Practical Extension 105

Chapter 6
Students' Speech Rights in an Online Era
Mark A. Gooden and Bradley W. Davis

Introduction 107
Legal Issues 108
    Student Speech 109
    Free Speech and the Internet 111
    Cyberbullying 114
    Threats 118
    Internet Use Policies 121
Conclusion 122
Recommendations for Practice 123
Case List 124
Key Words 125
Takeaways 126
Practical Extension 127

Chapter 7
Fundamentals of Federal Disability Law
Julie F. Mead

Introduction	129
Section 504 of the Rehabilitation Act of 1973	130
Americans with Disabilities Act	133
Individuals with Disabilities Education Act	135
Figure 7.1	137
Figure 7.2	144
Recommendations for Practice	144
Case List	145
Key Words	145
Takeaways	146
Practical Extension	147

Chapter 8
IEPs, Least Restrictive Environment, and Placement
Jean B. Crockett and Mitchell L. Yell

Introduction	149
Legal Issues	150
Defining Special Education and the Purpose of the IDEA	150
IEPs: Prescribing an Appropriate Education	153
Determining the Extent of Educational Benefit	158
Implementation of a Student's IEP	166
Selection of Educational Methodologies for Particular Students	166
COVID-19 and FAPE	169
LRE: Utilizing the Principle of the Least Restrictive Environment	170
Placement: Determining Appropriate Educational Settings	172
Changing Placements and Protecting Individual Rights	178
Suspension and Expulsion	180
Recommendations for Practice	181
Case List	184
Key Words	185
Takeaways	186
Practical Extension	186

Chapter 9
Disciplining Students with Disabilities
Mark A. Paige

Introduction	189
Discipline and the IEP	190
General Disciplinary Authority and Short-Term Removals	191

    Long-Term Removal: More than Ten Days in Total over Time............191
    Long-Term Removal: Change of Placement 192
    Duties of School District when Change of Placement Occurs...............194
    Discipline Other than Out-of-School Suspension 197
    Interim Alternative Educational Setting: 45-Day Removal 197
    Non-identified Students and Child Find.. 199
    Referral to Law Enforcement and Judicial Authorities 200
    Restraint and Seclusion... 201
Recommendations for Practice 202
Case List.. 205
Key Words 204
Takeaways... 205
Practical Extension.. 205

Chapter 1

Why Teachers Should Increase Their Legal Literacy

Janet R. Decker

If you are a teacher who never completed a School Law course, or took one many years ago, you are in good company. Most teacher preparation programs do not require future teachers to learn about the legal rights of students and school employees; however, research has shown that current teachers believe that future teachers should be taught about school law.[1] Of course, teachers are not expected to have in-depth legal knowledge, but they are the first people called upon to respond to a variety of legal dilemmas. For example, when teachers have students with disabilities in their classrooms, they must adhere to the many legal rights and protections guaranteed under a myriad of laws such as the Individuals with Disabilities Education Act (IDEA). Teachers also must be careful not to violate students' constitutional rights. For instance, they must be cognizant of students' Fourth Amendment rights when conducting searches and students' First Amendment rights when censoring student expression or clothing. Teachers also need the legal acumen to know how to persuade others to make the changes that they believe are needed in education. Overall, when teachers are legally literate, they avoid legal violations and become empowered to advocate on behalf of themselves, their students, and their schools.

The Education Law Association's *Legal Literacy for Public School Teachers* pools the experience and expertise of scholars and practitioners into one valuable resource. The authors of the following chapters are experts in school law from across the U.S. They represent the diverse membership of the Education Law Association, which includes practicing attorneys, education law professors, school leaders and teachers, and many others.[2] Founded the same year as the U.S. Supreme Court decision *Brown v. Board of Education* (1954), the Education Law Association has become the leading professional organization in education law. Today, the Education Law Association fosters its mission of providing "unbiased information…about current legal issues affecting education and the rights of those involved in education in both public and private K-12 schools, universities, and colleges."[3] In addition to offering publications,

---

[1] Janet R. Decker, Patrick Ober, & David Schimmel, *The Attitudinal and Behavioral Impact of School Law Courses*, 14 J. OF RES. ON LEADERSHIP EDUC., 160 (2017).
[2] Education Law Association, *Our Mission*, https://educationlaw.org/about-ela/mission (last visited Feb. 28, 2021).
[3] *Id.*

the Education Law Association holds an annual conference to discuss the practical legal challenges schools are facing.

Importantly, many of the authors of this book have been PK-12 teachers at some point in their careers. Although they are now education law scholars and attorneys, they understand how to translate the law to inform professionals who do not have a legal background. Each chapter highlights the most critical issues and provides practical recommendations.

Why This Book Is Needed

When educators are legally literate, they are "able to spot legal issues, identify applicable laws or legal standards, and apply the relevant legal rules to solve legal dilemmas."[4] The research about legal literacy is limited; however, two national studies identified that principals and teachers lack legal knowledge. According to Militello, Schimmel and Eberwein, a majority of principals were misinformed or uninformed about students' and teachers' legal rights.[5] Schimmel and Militello found in a similar study that most teachers were receiving their "information or misinformation about school law [from] other teachers who were similarly uninformed."[6]

Although often overlooked as a group in need of legal training, current and future teachers benefit from reading this book. Most legal dilemmas originate where teachers are present (e.g., classrooms, playgrounds, gym class, sporting events). Oftentimes, it is the teachers instead of the administrators who must first respond to legal issues. For example, teachers must make immediate decisions, such as whether to follow a student's individualized education program (IEP), whether to discipline a student for controversial speech, or whether to search a student. Teachers who are never taught about the law may unintentionally violate students' legal rights. Plus, the law allows teachers to recognize their rights as employees. Legally literate teachers know what to do when they believe their constitutional rights have been violated, their contracts have not been followed, or other employment issues occur.

While teachers are not expected to be lawyers, they must respond to legal dilemmas on a daily basis. It is difficult for teachers because many are fearful of the law, causing them to "fail to act when they should and overreact when

---

[4] Janet R. Decker & Kevin Brady, *Increasing School Employees' Special Education Legal Literacy*, 36 J. OF SCH. PUB. REL. 231, 231 (2016).

[5] Matthew Militello, David Schimmel & H. Jake Eberwein, *If They Knew, They Would Change: How Legal Knowledge Impacts Principals' Practice*, 93 NAT'L ASS'N SECONDARY SCH. PRINCIPALS BULL. 27 (2009).

[6] David Schimmel & Matthew Militello, *Legal Literacy for Teachers: A Neglected Responsibility*, 77 HARV. EDUC. REV. 257, 257 (2007).

they should not."[7] As Schimmel and Militello explain, "...too many teachers view the law as a source of fear and anxiety—an invisible monster lurking in the shadows of the classroom, hallways, or playground, waiting to ensnare any educator who makes an innocent mistake."[8] Although avoiding lawsuits is often cited as a reason why teachers should be legally literate, teachers should also recognize that they need to understand legal principles because they must interpret and apply the law to school policies and procedures.[9] For example, a school may have a dress code policy that the teachers are to enforce; yet, the teachers must also recognize when disciplining students for their clothing could be discriminatory or in violation of students' free expression rights. Stated differently, teachers need to be legally literate because it is a requirement of their daily responsibilities. Therefore, using this book allows teachers to become more confident and better decision makers who know how to protect the legal rights of students and school employees.[10]

Furthermore, teachers often want to advocate about the problems that they observe in schools, but in order to do so they must understand the law and the legal system. Once educators learn about how legislation and case law influence their daily lives, "they become empowered to influence education policy within and outside their classrooms, buildings, and districts."[11] When educators understand the law, McCarthy states that they become skilled at embracing "concepts such as fundamental fairness and the protection of minority interests and counteract the belief that the scales of justice are tilted against them."[12] Legally literate teachers become empowered to advocate on behalf of themselves, as well as their students, colleagues, schools, and districts.

Because research documents that teachers typically lack legal literacy, this book is necessary. It will help the reader become better informed about students' and teachers' basic legal rights and be able to solve a wide variety of legal dilemmas. Ultimately, the book allows teachers to practice preventive law and avoid legal problems from arising in the first place.

---

[7] Janet R. Decker, *Legal Literacy in Education: An Ideal Time to Increase Research, Advocacy, and Action*, 304 Educ. L. Rep. 679, 680 (2014); *See also,* David Schimmel & Matthew Militello, *The Risks of Legally Illiterate Teachers: The Findings, the Consequences and the Solutions*, 6 U. Mass. Roundtable Symp. L. J. 37 (2011); David Schimmel, Matthew Militello & Suzanne Eckes, *Principals: An Antidote to Educational Malpractice*, Educ. Wk., June 8, 2011, at 24, 24–25. Barry L. Bull & Martha M. McCarthy, *Reflections on the Knowledge Base in Law and Ethics for Educational Leaders*, 31 Educ. Admin. Q. 613, 621 (1995).

[8] Schimmel & Militello, *supra* note vi at 257-258.

[9] Barry L. Bull & Martha M. McCarthy, *Reflections on the Knowledge Base in Law and Ethics for Educational Leaders*, 31 Educ. Admin. Q. 613, 627 (1995).

[10] Decker, *supra* note vii.

[11] *Id.* at 681.

[12] Martha McCarthy, *The Marginalization of School Law Research: Missed Opportunities for Educators*, 331 Educ. L. Rep. 564, 584 (2016).

Who Benefits from Reading This Book

As illustrated by its title, *Legal Literacy for Public School Teachers* was written with teachers in mind; however, many others will benefit from reading it.

Other School Staff. Importantly, school employees besides teachers would benefit from increasing their legal literacy. For instance, school counselors, nurses, instructional aides, office staff, and school psychologists may need to respond to legal dilemmas similar to those faced by teachers. If school personnel are assigned to recess or cafeteria duty that lacks sufficient supervision, these staff need the legal acumen to recognize that as a legal vulnerability. Ignorance of the law is not a justifiable defense when a school is sued; therefore, all school employees should be trained in the basics of school law.

School Leaders. Administrators of all levels—including superintendents, directors of human resources, principals, special education directors, technology directors, curriculum coordinators, assistant principals, deans, and others—must know how the law relates to a variety of issues that they encounter. While educational leadership preparation programs may provide superintendents and principals with some legal training, many other school leaders have never completed a school law course. Some of the situations in which their roles require them to analyze the law include when technology directors must follow federal student privacy laws, when deans must ensure that disciplinary policies and practices do not have a discriminatory impact on students, and when special education directors must navigate the complicated maze of disability law.

Attorneys. School or parent attorneys could use the book to research a specific topic, such as collective bargaining or discipline of students with disabilities. They can quickly access the most recent precedent by reviewing the relevant chapter. Because the chapters are shorter in length and more general in scope than law journal articles, attorneys—and particularly, attorneys who are new to practicing school law—will discover that the book is a particularly handy reference.[13]

Instructors/Professors of Education Courses. Instructors/professors who are responsible for preparing future teachers and school leaders will also benefit from this book. They may opt to use the book as a textbook in their School Law, Ethics, Special Education Leadership, Personnel, and other courses. It is also possible to use this book as a research tool. Professors could reference it when their research relates to the recent court cases, or when drafting literature reviews.

---

[13] Jay P. Heubert, *The More We Get Together: Improving Collaboration Between Educators and Their Lawyers*, 67 Harv. Educ. Rev. 531, 558 (1997).

Others Involved in Education. In addition to other school staff, administrators, attorneys, and instructors/professors, the book could benefit others with a variety of roles in education. Each chapter is written in a straightforward manner, where legal issues are translated for someone who is not familiar with the law. Therefore, school board members, as well as those who work at nonprofit educational organizations or federal/state educational agencies, will benefit from increasing their legal literacy. Additionally, parents may find the book useful—especially parents of children with disabilities. The book informs a variety of other professionals who need to know about school law.

Anyone affiliated with education will find that increasing their legal knowledge allows them to make fewer mistakes, which also means less legal vulnerability and time wasted on avoidable legal violations. In addition to avoiding lawsuits, legally literate individuals are better able to ensure that students' and school employees' legal rights are protected, and they are more empowered to advocate to improve the current education system.

How To Use the Book

Although this book could be read from cover to cover, it could also be used as a training tool, reference guide, supplemental textbook, or a research tool:

- **Training Tool.** Teachers and other school employees could meet to discuss and review the book one chapter at a time. School leaders could use examples from the book to share at faculty meetings. Alternatively, human resource directors could use the book when developing in-service training for school employees.

    Example: Students have formed a Christian Club that meets after school, and teachers wonder if this is legal. They could consult the chapter on religion to analyze how they should respond.

- **Reference Guide.** If a legal issue occurs, the book can be consulted to identify what steps should be taken next.

    Example: A teacher searches a student's backpack because she believes the student stole money from another student. The student claims the teacher violated the law. The teacher could read the chapter about search and seizure to analyze whether her actions were in violation of the Fourth Amendment.

- **Supplemental Textbook.** Instructors/professors in teacher preparation programs could assign pre-service teachers readings so the teachers learn about the legal issues they will face.

    Example: An instructor of an Introduction to Special Education course could assign the section about the law and students with disabilities.

- **Research Tool.** Those who are studying school law could use the book to inform their research.

    Example: A professor researching student speech could apply the relevant court decisions to a current project by reviewing the section on students and the law.

In sum, *Legal Literacy for Public School Teachers* allows teachers and others to increase their legal literacy. By doing so, they can become more confident to handle a myriad of legal dilemmas that arise in schools on a daily basis.

Case List

Brown v. Bd. of Educ., 347 U.S. 483 (1954)

Key Words

education law
Education Law Association
education policy
educational leadership
in-service training
legal literacy
litigation
professional development
research

Takeaways

1. Public school teachers regularly are faced with potential legal dilemmas in the classroom; however, most teacher education programs do not include a school law component.
2. For example, teachers should understand and consider students' First Amendment rights in the classroom.
3. Public school teachers should be encouraged to develop their "legal literacy" and to understand both the rights of students and the rights of teachers in school.
4. School law should be taken into consideration when designing and carrying out school policies. Having an understanding of school law empowers teachers to make informed decision in the classroom. Educators should develop a basic understanding of the legal issues so they are equipped to face on-the-job dilemmas, such as:
5. Under what circumstances is it appropriate to censor student speech in a school-issued publication or speech?
6. Under what circumstances might students be disciplined for their speech outside of school, such as on social media?
7. What is a teacher's legal responsibility in the classroom to implement an individualized education program or Section 504 plan?
8. What rights to privacy to students have in the classroom or elsewhere in school?
9. Under what circumstances might school personnel have the authority to search a student's backpack or person?

Practical Extension

1. Consider your current role as an educator. What do you hope to gain from reading this book? What questions do you have regarding your own rights as an educator and school employee? What questions do you have regarding the rights of your students?
2. Consider a scenario from this chapter, or one that you have encountered.
   a. What pitfalls might an educator encounter without a knowledge of school law?
   b. How might having a knowledge of school law help the educator navigate the dilemma?

Chapter 2

The American Legal System

Charles J. Russo and Allan G. Osborne, Jr.

Introduction

Pursuant to the Tenth Amendment of the United States Constitution, education is a function of the states rather than the federal government.[1] Even so, before any discussion of legal issues arising in the context of public education can take place, it is important to understand the legal framework under which American schools operate on both the federal and state levels. Accordingly, this introductory chapter examines the sources and types of laws in the American legal system. The chapter also reflects on how these various types of laws interact as they impact the daily operations of public schools.

Sources of Law

Generally

There are four sources of law in the United States: constitutions, statutes, regulations, and judicial decisions. These sources of law exist at both the federal and state levels.

A constitution is the fundamental law of a nation or state.[2] A statute, on the other hand, is an act of a legislative body, or a law enacted by Congress, a state legislature, or other elected body.[3] All statutes must be consistent with the controlling constitutions within their jurisdiction. Many statutes are accompanied by implementing regulations or guidelines written by officials in the agencies responsible for their execution and enforcement. Regulations are usually more specific than the statutes they are designed to implement because they interpret and expand on legislative intent as to how laws should work in practice.

The many judicial opinions interpreting constitutions, statutes, and regulations comprise a body of law known as case, judge-made, or common law.

---

[1] *San Antonio Indep. Sch. Dist. v. Rodriguez*, 411 U.S. 1, 35, 93 S. Ct. 1278, 36 L.Ed.2d 16 (1975), wherein the Justices refused to intervene in a school finance dispute from Texas, the majority ruled that "[e]ducation, of course, is not among the rights afforded explicit protection under our Federal Constitution. Nor do we find any basis for saying it is implicitly so protected."

[2] B. A. GARNER, BLACK'S LAW DICTIONARY (8th ed.) (2004).

[3] *Id.*

Relying heavily on the notion of binding precedent—that a ruling of the highest court in a jurisdiction is binding on lower courts in that jurisdiction—case law provides insight into how judges apply constitutions, statutes, and regulations to different factual situations. Cases from other jurisdictions, known as persuasive precedent, have no binding effect on courts outside of their jurisdictions. More specifically, this means that decisions of courts in one jurisdiction are not binding in the other jurisdictions, but may have some influence on how other courts may interpret laws, as judges may look to see how other jurists have dealt with the same or similar issues. As an applied example, this means that decisions of the United States Supreme Court are binding on all American courts, while orders of the Supreme Court of Ohio are binding only in Ohio and are persuasive in all other jurisdictions.

Constitutions

Simply put, the Constitution of the United States is the law of the land. Consequently, all federal statutes and regulations, state constitutions, state laws and regulations, and ordinances of local governmental bodies, including school board policies, are subject to the Constitution as interpreted by the United States Supreme Court and other courts. Still, only a limited number of sections of the U.S. Constitution are implicated directly in school-related cases. For the most part, the amendments protecting individual rights, such as the First, Fourth, Fifth, and Fourteenth amendments, are the sections of the Constitution impacting the operation of the schools most significantly.

The U.S. Constitution specifies the four duties of the federal government, and, by extension, of state governments. Article I, Section 8, identifies the first, or *enumerated*, powers—those exclusively within the purview of the federal government. These include the duty "to provide for the common Defence [sic] and general welfare of the United States ... [t]o regulate Commerce with foreign Nations, and among the several States ... [t]o coin Money, and regulate the value thereof ... [t]o promote Post Offices ..., [and] [t]o constitute Tribunals inferior to the Supreme Court."

The second set of powers are *implied*, meaning they are reasonably necessary to carry out the express duties of the federal (or a state) government. For example, in providing for the national defense, the federal government has the implied authority to create the Department of Defense and subordinate offices necessary to carry out its duties, such as draft boards during times of war.

According to the Tenth Amendment, the third set of powers, *reserved*, are those not delegated to the federal government by the Constitution, or prohibited by it, to the states or to the people. For the purposes of practitioners and students of education law, the most important reserved power is education. This is because—despite its coverage of a wide area of powers, duties, and limitations, as noted—the U.S. Constitution is silent with regard to education, thereby rendering it a responsibility of individual states.

An example of the final power, *concurrent*, meaning it is shared by both the federal and state governments, is taxation.

Along the same line, state constitutions are the supreme laws in their jurisdictions, with which all state statutes, regulations, and ordinances must conform. State constitutions typically deal with many of the same matters as their federal counterpart, but typically provide greater detail when addressing education. In operation, insofar as state constitutions can grant their citizens greater, but not fewer, rights than the U.S. Constitution, they are supreme within their boundaries.

Statutes and Regulations

As pointed out, under the Tenth Amendment to the Constitution, education is reserved to the states.[4] Yet, Congress has the authority to enact laws under the General Welfare Clause of Article I, Section 8, by offering funds for purposes it believes will serve the public good. For example, Congress enacted a series of statutes that forever altered the landscape of public education, starting with the Civil Rights Act of 1964,[5] which subjects public school systems to its antidiscrimination in employment provisions.

Federal statutes often make funds available to state and local governments conditioned on their acceptance of specific requirements for the use of the money. As discussed below, when states accept federal funds, educational officials are bound by whatever conditions Congress has attached to the legislation. If challenged, federal courts must be satisfied that the conditions pass constitutional muster.

In 1987, Congress expanded its authority by defining a "program or activity" as encompassing "all of the operations of [an entity] any part of which is extended Federal financial assistance."[6] This broad general prohibition against discrimination covers "race, color or national origin,"[7] "sex,"[8] and "otherwise qualified handicapped individuals,"[9] categories that have become increasingly important in school settings. For instance, in order to receive funding for students who qualify for special education under the Individuals with Disabilities Education Act (IDEA)[10]—originally enacted in 1975 as the Education for All Handicapped Children Act—states, through their local educational agencies or school boards, must develop detailed procedures to identify and assess children with disabilities before serving them by offering all qualified students free appropriate public educations in the least restrictive environment.

Another key example of federal involvement in education occurred when Congress superseded its most recent reauthorization of the Elementary and Secondary Education Act of 1965, the controversial No Child Left Behind Act

---

[4] *See* Epperson v. State of Ark., 393 U.S. 97, 104, 89 S. Ct. 266, 21 L.Ed.2d 228 (1968).
[5] 42 U.S.C.A. § 2000e–2a.
[6] Civil Rights Restoration Act, 20 U.S.C.A. § 1687.
[7] 42 U.S.C.A. § 2000d.
[8] 20 U.S.C.A. § 1681.
[9] 29 U.S.C.A. § 794.
[10] 20 U.S.C.A. §§ 1400 *et seq.*

in 2002,[11] by enacting the Every Student Succeeds Act (ESSA) in late 2015.[12] The ESSA retains much of the NCLB, but eliminates some of its more controversial elements such as adequate yearly progress standards, while returning additional power to states.

Regulations promulgated by the U.S. Department of Education and other administrative agencies grant the executive branch the means to implement statutes by carrying out their full effect. That is, while statutes set broad legislative parameters, regulations allow administrative agencies to provide details to satisfy the requirements of the law. Regulations, which are presumptively valid, generally carry the full force of the law unless courts interpret them as conflicting with the legislation.

Most of the laws impacting public schools are statutes enacted by state legislatures. Although, as indicated previously, state legislatures are subject to the limitations of federal law and of state constitutions, they are relatively free to establish their own systems of education. The law is well settled that state and local boards of education, administrators, and teachers have the authority to adopt and enforce reasonable rules and regulations to ensure the smooth operation and management of schools. State and local rules and regulations are thus subject to the same constitutional limitations as statutes passed by legislative bodies. Accordingly, if it is unconstitutional for Congress or state legislatures to enact laws violating the free speech rights of students, it is impermissible for teachers to do so by creating rules applicable only in their classrooms. It is also important to note that legislation—or rule-making on any level, whether federal or state—cannot conflict with higher authorities such as constitutions.

Common Law

The duty of the courts is to interpret the law. When there is no codified law, or if statutes or regulations are unclear, courts apply common law. Common law is basically judge-made law, meaning that the courts may interpret the law in light of new or changing circumstances. The collective decisions of the courts make up the body of common law. When disputes involve legislation, the duty of the courts is to uncover, as best they can, the intent of the legislative bodies that enacted statutes.

To the degree that judicial decrees establish precedent, judges provide a measure of certainty and predictability because in basing their judgments on the collected wisdom of earlier litigation, they do not have to "re-invent the wheel" whenever new, or seemingly new, legal issues arise. Consequently, when judges consider novel points of law, they often look to see how other jurists have addressed the same or similar issues in other jurisdictions, but are not obligated to follow those judgments. In this way, judges have considerable

---

[11] 20 U.S.C.A. §§ 6301 *et seq.*
[12] P.L. 114-95, Dec. 10, 2015, 129 Stat. 1814.

weight in terms of providing guidance on how statutes and regulations are to be applied to everyday situations.[13]

Judicial Systems

The federal courts and most state judicial systems have three levels. The lowest level in the federal system consists of trial courts, known as district courts. Each state has at least one federal district court, while more populated states, such as California and New York, have as many as four. Federal district courts are the basic triers of fact in legal disputes; they review evidence and render decisions based on the evidence presented by the parties to disputes. Depending on the situations, trial courts may review the records of administrative hearings that have been conducted, hear additional evidence, and/or hear the testimony of witnesses.

Parties not satisfied with the judgments of federal trial courts case may appeal to the federal circuit courts of appeals within which their states are located. For example, a decision handed down by a federal trial court in New York would be appealed to the Second Circuit, which, in addition to New York, includes Connecticut and Vermont. There are thirteen federal judicial circuits in the United States, eleven of which are numbered and two of which are housed in Washington, D.C.

Parties displeased with the orders of circuit courts may seek further review from the United States Supreme Court. Due to the sheer volume of cases appealed each year, the Supreme Court accepts less than one percent of the disputes in which parties seek further review. Cases typically reach the Supreme Court in requests for a writ of *certiorari*, which literally means "to be informed of." When the Supreme Court agrees to hear appeals, it grants writs of *certiorari*. At least four of the nine Justices must vote to grant *certiorari* in order for cases to be heard.[14] Denying a writ of *certiorari* has the effect of leaving lower court orders unchanged,[15] but is of no precedential value beyond the parties to the litigation.

The states and territories have judicial systems similar to the federal scheme, except that the names of their courts vary. In most states, there are also three levels of courts: trial courts, intermediate appellate courts, and courts of last resort. It is important to take great care with the names of state courts. For instance, the highest court in most states is named the supreme court. Yet, in New York, the trial court is known as the Supreme Court, while the state's highest court is called the Court of Appeals, typically the name of intermediate appellate court in most other jurisdictions.

---

[13] For a discussion of the role of judges in educational disputes, see Charles J. Russo, *The Courts and Education Law: What Role Should Judges Play?*, 13 INT'L J. EDUC. L. AND POL'Y 7 (2017).

[14] The so-called "Rule of Four" is a long-standing judicial custom even though Congress may have been mindful of it in enacting the Judiciary Act of 1925. Earlier, Congress created *certiorari*, or discretionary review, in 1890 in 26 Stat. 826, Sections 4–6.

[15] GARNER, *supra* n. 2.

When courts render their judgments, their opinions are binding precedent within their geographic jurisdictions and are persuasive elsewhere. It is important to keep in mind that the term "jurisdiction" can refer to either the types of cases that courts can hear, such as appeals generally, or in specific areas of the law, such as family or juvenile matters, or to the geographic areas over which they have authority. In referring to the to the geographic areas over which courts have authority, this means, for instance, that judgments of the federal district court for Massachusetts are binding only in Massachusetts. The federal district court in Rhode Island might find a decision of the Massachusetts court persuasive, but it is not bound by its order. Nonetheless, a ruling of the First Circuit Court of Appeals is binding on all states within its jurisdiction, while the lower courts in those states must rule consistently. A decision by the Supreme Court of the United States is, of course, enforceable as binding precedent in all fifty states and American territories on issues of federal law.

As indicated, the complex American judiciary operates at both the federal and state levels. The most common feature of these systems is three-tiered systems consisting of trial courts, intermediate appellate panels, and courts of last resort, most commonly named supreme courts.

Trial courts have general jurisdiction, meaning there are typically few limits on the types of cases they may hear. Trial courts rely on the case specifics, apply the law to the circumstances, and generally are presided over by a single judge or justice.

Intermediate state appellate courts, often known as courts of appeal, review cases when the parties to disputes are dissatisfied with the judgments of the lower courts. Appellate courts are ordinarily not triers of fact; rather, these judicial panels review the lower courts' applications of the law. In rare cases, appellate panels may reject the factual findings of lower courts if they are convinced that they were clearly erroneous. Appellate courts usually consist of a panel of judges. By way of illustration, at the federal level, appeals are usually heard by panels of three judges. In unusual circumstances, a party in a federal court can petition a circuit court for an *en banc* appeal—literally, "in the bench"—meaning that all justices in the circuit participate in the oral arguments and decision.

Finally, disputes may be appealed to courts of last resort. At the federal level, this is the Supreme Court. The Supreme Court has discretion to review rulings of lower federal courts and state high courts involving federal constitutional, statutory, or regulatory issues.

Because education is a state function and federal courts exist for federal matters, state courts resolve most educational disputes. Disagreements must be tried in state courts unless there are substantial federal questions, such as the denial of equal educational opportunities to children of color in *Brown v. Board of Education*.[16] Put another way, although *Brown* involved the delivery of public education, because the children in the suit had the right to equal protection

---

[16] 347 U.S. 483 (1954).

under the Fourteenth Amendment—thus, a substantial federal question was involved with a matter of state law—it was properly subject to the jurisdiction of a federal trial court. The presence of federal questions, such as the right to freedom of speech under the First Amendment and/ or protection from unreasonable searches and seizures under the Fourth Amendment, is why cases involving these topics are often litigated in federal trial courts. When federal courts examine cases involving both state and federal law, they must follow interpretations of state law made by the state courts within the jurisdictions in which they are seated, because there is no such thing as federal common law.

Legal Resources

The written opinions of most courts are generally available in a variety of published formats. The official versions of Supreme Court opinions are in the United States Reports, abbreviated U.S. The same opinions, with additional research aids that make it easier to locate specific points of law in the opinions, are published in the Supreme Court Reporter (S. Ct.) and the Lawyer's Edition, now in its second series (L. Ed. 2d).

Opinions of federal circuit courts of appeal are published in the Federal Reporter, now in its fourth series (F.4th); cases that are not selected for publication in F.4th appear in the Federal Appendix (cited as Fed. Appx. or Fed. App'x), but are of limited precedential value. Federal district court cases are published in the Federal Supplement, now in its third series (F. Supp. 3d).

State court cases are published in a variety of publications, most notably West's National Reporter system, which divides the country up into seven regions: Atlantic, North Eastern, North Western, Pacific, South Eastern, South Western, and Southern. Most education-related cases are also republished in West's *Education Law Reporter*, a specialized series that ordinarily includes peer-reviewed articles on point.

Before being published in hardbound volumes, most judgments are released in what are known as slip opinions, a variety of looseleaf services, and electronic sources. In addition, many commercial services publish decisions in specialized areas. For example, special education cases, as well as the outcomes of due process hearings, are reproduced in a looseleaf format in the *Individuals with Disabilities Education Law Reporter* (IDELR), published by LRP Publications.

Statutes and regulations are also accessible in a variety of formats. Federal statutes appear in the United States Code (U.S.C.), which is the official version, or the United States Code Annotated (U.S.C.A.), published by West Publishing Company. Agency regulations of the United States appear in the Code of Federal Regulations (C.F.R.). Copies of education statutes and regulations can be downloaded via links on the U.S. Department of Education's website. Legal materials are also available online from a variety of sources, most notably WestLaw and LexisNexis. State laws and regulations are commonly available online from the websites of their states.

Reading Legal Citations

Legal citations are fairly easy to read. The first number indicates the volume number where the case, statute, or regulation is located, followed by the abbreviation of the book or series in which the material is published. The second number indicates the page on which a case begins or the section number of a statute or regulation; if a second number is present, it refers to the page on which a quote is published.

Other than the Supreme Court, which specifies just the year, the last parts of citations identify the names of the courts and the years in which the disputes were resolved. For example, in *Board of Education of the Hendrick Hudson Central School District v. Rowley*, the Supreme Court's first case interpreting what is now known as the IDEA, the federal trial court for the Southern District of New York initially ruled in favor of the parents and their daughter, 483 F. Supp. 528 (S.D.N.Y., 1980). The Second Circuit then affirmed the trial court's order, 632 F.2d 945, (2d Cir. 1980), but the Supreme Court reversed in favor of the board, 458 U.S. 176, 102 S. Ct. 3034, 73 L.Ed.2d 690 [5 Educ. L. Rep. 34] (1982). This means that the official version of the Court's opinion, rendered in 1982, appears in volume 458 of the United States Report, starting on page 176; the other citations read similarly.

The IDEA, 20 U.S.C. §§ 1400 *et seq.* (2018) appears in Title 20 of the United States Code beginning with section 1400. The IDEA's regulations, 34 C.F.R. §§ 300.1, are published in Title 34 of the Code of Federal Regulations, starting with section 300.1.

Case List

Bd. of Educ. of the Hendrick Hudson Cent. Sch. Dist. v. Rowley
Brown v. Bd. of Educ.
Epperson v. Arkansas
San Antonio Indep. Sch. Dist. v. Rodriguez

Key Words

appellate court
binding precedent
certiorari
circuit court of appeals
Civil Rights Act of 1964
common law
constitution
court of last resort
district court

Education for All Handicapped Children Act
Elementary and Secondary Education Act of 1965
en banc
enumerated powers
equal educational opportunity
equal protection
Every Student Succeeds Act (ESSA)
federal court system
Fourteenth Amendment
implied powers
Individuals with Disabilities Education Act (IDEA)
judicial decision
legal citations
legal resources
No Child Left Behind Act (NCLB)
persuasive precedent
regulation
source of law
statute
supreme court
Tenth Amendment
trial court
U.S. Department of Education

Takeaways

1. The four sources of law are constitutions, statutes, regulations, and judicial decisions.
2. The United States Constitution is the law of the land.
3. While there are amendments to the U.S. Constitution that impact education (First, Fourth, Fifth, and Fourteenth), the Constitution does not specifically grant authority over education to the federal government.
4. According to the Tenth Amendment to the U.S. Constitution, any power that is not given to the United States federal government, through the Constitution, is reserved for state government. Education is not a power included in the U.S. Constitution; therefore, states have the autonomy and authority to make laws, policies, and regulations regarding education specific to their state.
5. Federal acts, such as the Individuals with Disabilities Education Act (IDEA) and Every Student Succeeds Act (ESSA), provide broad-strokes legislation that impacts public schools; however, states have the autonomy to create state education legislation, provided it meets the parameters of the federal legislation.

6. Common law, which is judge-made law, provides insight as to how courts interpret constitutions, statutes, and legislation.
7. The judicial system is a hierarchical system. There are federal courts and state courts. Federal courts have three levels, as do most state courts. The decisions made in the higher court systems (such as the U.S. Supreme Court) are binding; they dictate to lower courts how to interpret law.
8. Most court cases involving education are determined at the state level. A few, such as *Brown v. Board of Education*, are determined at a federal level.

Practical Extension

1. How does the structure of the American legal system impact public education?
    a. What role does the federal government play in public education?
    b. What role does the state government play in public education?
    c. How does the judicial system impact public education and policy?
2. Describe the impact that *Brown v. Board of Education* has had on public education and educational policy. What other Supreme Court cases have impacted public school policies?

Chapter 3

Freedom of Expression

Watt Lesley Black, Jr.

Introduction

For more than 175 years, it was assumed that the United States Constitution did not protect the speech of public school students. Students who challenged school censorship during those years were required to prove that there was no rational basis for the censorship. The task was nearly impossible, and the rare student who went to court almost always lost.[1] The legal landscape for students changed significantly in 1969, when the Supreme Court decided *Tinker v. Des Moines*, holding that the students do enjoy First Amendment protection inside the public schools.[2]

As for teachers, the idea that they and other public employees forfeited their rights in exchange for their jobs became the legal basis to deny them constitutional free speech protection for the better part of the 20th century. In an 1892 case dealing with a police officer who was fired for engaging in controversial political speech, Oliver Wendell Homes wrote, "The petitioner may have a constitutional right to talk politics, but he has no constitutional right to be a policeman."[3] It wasn't until 1968 that the Supreme Court issued its landmark decision *Pickering v. Board of Education*, extending free speech rights to public school teachers.[4]

But, for both students and teachers, these newly won speech rights were not absolute—they were balanced against the state's rights as an educator and employer. Because the state has a legitimate interest in ensuring discipline, safety, and efficiency in the schools, the Court crafted holdings in *Tinker* and *Pickering* that allowed for both students and teachers to be legally subjected to discipline for speech when it is sufficiently disruptive. Over the last fifty years, the Court has further limited the speech rights of both students and teachers.[5]

---

[1] John E. Nichols, *The Pre-*Tinker *History of Freedom of Student Press and Speech*, JOURNALISM AND MASS COMMC'NS Q., Vol. 56, No. 472733, December 1979.
[2] Tinker v. Des Moines, 393 U.S. 503 (1969).
[3] McAuliffe v. Mayor of New Bedford, 155 Mass. 216, 220 (1892).
[4] Pickering v. Bd. of Educ., 391 U.S. 563 (1968).
[5] *See* Bethel Sch. Dist. No. 403 v. Fraser, 106 S. Ct. 3159 (1986); Hazelwood Sch. Dist. v. Kuhlmeier, 108 S. Ct. 562 (1988); Morse v. Frederick, 551 U.S. 393 (2007); Connick v. Myers, 461 U.S. 138 (1983); and Garcetti v. Ceballos, 547 U.S. 410 (2006).

This chapter is designed to help teachers understand the scope and limits of their students' and their own First Amendment speech rights. Section I reviews Supreme Court precedent related to the First Amendment rights of public school students, highlights emerging student speech issues, and advances critical considerations for practice. Section II outlines Supreme Court precedent related to the First Amendment speech rights of public school teachers, discusses emerging issues around teacher speech and the Internet, and forwards key considerations for practice.

Student Speech and the First Amendment

When the Supreme Court decided *Tinker*, it signaled a change in the relationship between the student and the school. The legal doctrine of *in loco parentis* (meaning "in place of parents") had traditionally dictated that when a student was at school, the school authorities functioned as if they were the student's parent, with the same rights and responsibilities. *Tinker v. Des Moines* chipped away at this theory and opened the door to a new era in which students had constitutionally protected rights that the school must respect. This section will outline the critical Supreme Court precedent that shapes student free speech rights, highlight how that precedent has been applied to numerous speech-related issues that have arisen in the public school context, and offer some critical considerations for practice.

The Material Disruption Standard: *Tinker v. Des Moines*

In *Tinker v. Des Moines*, the Court ruled in favor of a group of students who wore black armbands to school as a means of symbolic protest against American involvement in the Vietnam War. "In our system, state-operated schools may not be enclaves of totalitarianism," wrote Justice Abe Fortas. "School officials do not possess absolute authority over their students."[6] But, the Court also recognized that students' First Amendment rights in the school environment must be subject to certain restrictions that wouldn't apply to the general public.[7] A student who "materially disrupts class work" or causes "substantial disorder or invasion of the rights of others," Justice Fortas reasoned, may legally be subjected to discipline by the school.[8]

In 1969, extending even limited First Amendment protection to the speech of public school students was a controversial proposition. Justice Hugo Black warned in his dissenting opinion that the decision would usher in an era of "permissiveness" in the public schools.[9] The majority realized that protecting unpopular student expression might result in conflict, but insisted that the First Amendment required school systems to take that risk.[10] As Justice Fortas

---

[6] *Tinker*, 393 U.S. at 511.
[7] *Id*. at 506.
[8] *Id*. at 513.
[9] *Id*. at 525.
[10] *Id*. at 508.

explained, "our history says that it is this sort of hazardous freedom—this kind of openness—that is the basis of our national strength ... independence and vigor."[11]

Under the *Tinker* standard, school officials may discipline a student for speech that interferes with the rights of others or causes substantial or material disruption. Speech, however, cannot be prohibited merely because teachers or administrators are fearful or concerned about possible disruptions. As the Court stated, "undifferentiated fear or apprehension of disturbance is not enough to overcome the right to freedom of expression."[12] Restriction of such expression is only acceptable under *Tinker* when the prediction of a disruption is based on evidence and not merely intuition. Neither a teacher nor principal may prohibit a particular opinion merely "to avoid the discomfort and unpleasantness that always accompany an unpopular view."[13]

When there is evidence to suggest that a disruption is likely, however, the school does not have to wait for the disruption to actually happen in order to limit speech. In 2009, the Fifth Circuit upheld a Texas high school's disciplinary action against two female students who carried purses at school bearing the image of the Confederate flag.[14] The school had a history of racial conflict. At an athletic event against a predominately African American school, a group of students displayed the Confederate flag.[15] This not only caused conflict at the event, but also prompted complaints to the state's athletic governing body, which considered levying sanctions against the school.[16] Because of documented past disruptions associated with the Confederate flag, the court ruled that it was reasonable for the school to foresee disruption if students were allowed to display the image.[17]

In a 2012 case, a federal appeals court upheld the suspension of a fifth-grade student who wrote on a school assignment that he wished "to blow up the school with the teachers in it."[18] Other students in the class saw what he had written and at least one, according to the teacher, was disturbed by the comment.[19] The student had a history of misbehavior, including two other occasions in which he had turned in school assignments that contained imagery that school officials found disturbing.[20] The court upheld the suspension, holding that there was adequate evidence for the school to reasonably forecast substantial disruption. In these situations, the judge wrote that "courts have

---

[11] *Tinker*, 393 U.S. at 508–09.
[12] *Id.* at 508.
[13] *Id.* at 509.
[14] A.M. v. Cash, 585 F. 3d. 214 (2009).
[15] *Id.* at 218.
[16] *Id.* at 219.
[17] *Id.* at 224.
[18] Cuff v. Valley Cent. Sch. Dist., 2012 U.S. App. LEXIS 6024 (2d Cir. 2012).
[19] *Id.* at 4.
[20] *Id.* at 2.

allowed wide leeway to school administrators disciplining students for writings . . . threatening violence."[21]

Courts have sometimes disagreed over the importance of a student's age in relation to his or her expressive rights under *Tinker*. In a 1996 decision, a Seventh Circuit judge opined that "age is a critical factor in student speech cases" and the Court "has not suggested that fourth-graders have the free expression rights of high school students."[22] In contrast, in a 2011 Fifth Circuit decision, the court wrote, "It should be clarified today that the student speech rights announced in *Tinker* were in the elementary school context."[23] Ultimately, while the *Tinker* principles may apply more broadly in secondary schools, it is safe to assume that the First Amendment also applies to elementary schools—at least until the Supreme Court rules otherwise.

On-Campus Student Speech That Is Lewd or Vulgar Is Not Protected: *Bethel v. Fraser*

The Supreme Court carved out an exception to *Tinker* in 1986, when it ruled that students who engage in speech that is vulgar or offensive may be disciplined by school officials.[24] In *Bethel v. Fraser*, a high school senior was punished for giving a speech at a school assembly that employed "an elaborate, graphic, and explicit sexual metaphor."[25] The Court ruled that school officials have broad authority to punish students for using "offensively lewd and indecent speech" in classrooms, assemblies, and other school-sponsored educational activities, even if the speech does not cause disruption and is not legally obscene. In addition, *Bethel* held that administrators have the discretion to define and determine what constitutes vulgar and offensive speech.[26]

A 2013 decision by the Third Circuit, however, would suggest that the teacher's authority in this regard is not absolute. In *B.H. v. Easton Area School District*, the Third Circuit ruled against a school that had categorically banned the wearing of "I ♥ Boobies" bracelets that were part of a popular breast cancer awareness campaign.[27] In holding that the categorical ban of the bracelets violated the First Amendment rights of students, the court distinguished *plainly*

---

[21] *Id.* at 11.
[22] Muller by Muller v. Jefferson Lighthouse Sch., 98 F.3d 1530 (7th Cir. 1996).
[23] Morgan v. Swanson, 659 F.3d 359, 385-386 (5th Cir. 2011). *Morgan* includes a thoughtful discussion of this issue.
[24] *Bethel*, 478 U.S. at 677. Courts have never protected student speech or writing that is legally obscene. However, educators must remember that language is not legally obscene merely because it contains offensive, vulgar, or "dirty" words. To be legally obscene, material must violate three tests developed by the Supreme Court: (1) it must appeal to the prurient or lustful interest; (2) it must describe sexual conduct in a way that is "patently offensive" to community standards; *and* (3) taken as a whole, it "must lack serious literary, artistic, political, or scientific value." *See* Miller v. California, 413 U.S. 15 (1973).
[25] *Id.*
[26] For more on *Bethel*, see David Schimmel, *Lewd Language Not Protected: Bethel School District v. Fraser*, 33 EDUC. L. REP. 999 (1986).
[27] B.H. v. Easton Area School District, 725 F.3d 293 (3d Cir. 2013).

lewd speech from what it called *ambiguously* lewd speech. While plainly lewd speech can only be reasonably interpreted as lewd, the court described "ambiguously lewd speech" as expression that could reasonably be interpreted as lewd, but also has a reasonable alternative, non-lewd meaning.[28] Only speech that is plainly lewd, according to the court, can be categorically restricted. Ambiguously lewd speech may be protected if it could plausibly be interpreted as commentary on a "social or political matter."[29] The Third Circuit's decision suggests that school authorities should be cautious about invoking *Bethel* as a disciplinary authority when students engage in speech that has social or political meaning, even in cases where the speech might be provocative in nature.[30]

On-Campus Student Speech Promoting Illegal Drug Use Is Unprotected: *Morse v. Fredrick*

In 2007, the Supreme Court created a second exception to *Tinker* when it held that nondisruptive student speech has no First Amendment protection if it can be interpreted to promote the use of illegal drugs. *Morse v. Frederick* involved an Alaska student who unfurled a banner at a school event that said "BONG HiTS 4 JESUS."[31] The offending conduct occurred when school officials had allowed students to go outside and observe the Olympic Torch parade as it passed by the school. The student claimed that the banner was nonsensical, and that his intent was merely to attract the attention of the television news cameras.[32] The principal believed that the message on the banner encouraged the use of marijuana. A divided Court agreed with the principal.

The Court ruled 6-3 that the state has an "important, perhaps compelling interest" in discouraging the use of illegal drugs among students.[33] The requirements of the First Amendment, the Court reasoned, do not include forcing school officials to tolerate student speech that they deem contributes to such danger.[34] Accordingly, school officials may "restrict student expression that they reasonably regard as promoting illegal drug use."[35]

A significant concurring opinion by Justices Alito and Kennedy emphasized the narrowness of the majority opinion and suggested that not all student messages advocating illegal activity can be punished if they comment on political or social issues and do not cause disruption. For example, these justices said they would protect student views that criticized the war on drugs

---

[28] *Id.* at 297.
[29] *Id.* at 308.
[30] The Third Circuit's interpretation of *Bethel v. Fraser* is particularly interesting since the offending speech, by high school senior Mathew Fraser, was given for the purposes of nominating a classmate for a high office in student leadership. It thus had an inherently political interpretation in addition to the "lewd" one. Nevertheless, the Court supported Bethel schools' disciplinary action against Fraser.
[31] Morse v. Frederick, 551 U.S.393, 407 (2007).
[32] *Id* at 401.
[33] *Id.* at 407.
[34] *Id.* at 410.
[35] *Id.* at 409.

or advocated the legalization of marijuana. Thus, *Morse* reaffirmed *Tinker* and perhaps expanded the rights of students to criticize current laws and promote controversial political or religious views. Interestingly, the Third Circuit drew heavily on *Morse* in its *B.H. v. Easton Area School District* decision, in which it ruled that the "I ⌧ Boobies" bracelets were protected speech because they spoke to an issue of social importance, even though some might reasonably interpret the bracelets as inappropriate or lewd.

The Student Press and the School's Authority: *Hazelwood v. Kuhlmeier*

In 1986, the U.S. Supreme Court ruled in *Hazelwood v. Kuhlmeier* that the First Amendment offers little protection to student journalists writing in school-sponsored newspapers. The case involved a St. Louis high school principal who objected to two stories in a student newspaper. The principal was concerned that readers might be able to identify an anonymous student featured in a story about teen pregnancy.[36] Additionally, there were references in the article to sexual activity and birth control that the principal deemed to be inappropriate for younger students at the school.[37] In a story about the impact of divorce on students, a student criticized her father, who had been given no opportunity to respond.[38]

The Court ruled that a curricular newspaper was not a public forum and that "school officials were entitled to regulate the contents ... in any reasonable manner."[39] Critical in the Court's analysis was the fact that the district's curriculum guide clearly established that the newspaper was part of the curricular program, that the journalism teacher exercised great control over "almost every aspect of production and publication," and that the principal routinely exercised prior review of the paper.[40] In short, the school had not "by policy or by practice" converted the paper to an open forum that would allow "indiscriminate use" by the student journalists, or the student body in general.[41]

The Court explained that when a student expressed personal, controversial views on school grounds, the First Amendment protects such views and the principles of *Tinker* apply. However, in school-sponsored publications or theatrical productions that are part of the school curriculum, educators may exercise greater control and set higher standards for student speech. In a curricular publication, educators have broad discretion to prohibit articles

---

[36] Hazelwood Sch. Dist. v. Kuhlmeier, 484 U.S. 260 (1988).
[37] *Id.* at 263.
[38] *Id.*
[39] *Id.* at 270. The Court noted that, in this case, the paper had not been converted to an open forum by "policy or practice" and was thus closed. If the school had adopted a policy of allowing the paper to function as an open forum, or had, by practice, allowed students to publish whatever they wished without prior review or oversight, the school might cede the legal authority to control the content of the paper.
[40] *Id.* at 268, 269.
[41] *Hazelwood*, 484 U.S. at 270.

that are "ungrammatical, poorly written, inadequately researched, biased or prejudiced, vulgar or profane, or unsuitable for immature audiences."[42] Neither teachers nor administrators violate the First Amendment by "exercising editorial control over the style and content of student speech in school-sponsored expressive activities so long as their actions are reasonably related to legitimate pedagogical concerns."[43]

Hazelwood has also been used to bolster the school's ability to censor advertisements that appear in school newspapers, event programs or yearbooks.[44] A divided federal appeals court ruled in favor of the Nevada principal who refused to print an advertisement by Planned Parenthood not only in the school newspaper and yearbook, which were published as part of the curriculum, but also in the athletic programs, which were not.[45] According to the court, schools retain the right to disapprove of ads that might carry a school-sponsored message to readers and put their imprimatur on one side of a controversial issue.

Courts generally defer to the judgment of school professionals in terms of identifying what is a legitimate pedagogical concern, affording perhaps too much latitude to school officials who might seek to censor school-sponsored student expressive activity for subjective or personal reasons.[46] That the school has the legal authority to strictly regulate school-sponsored student expressive activity does not mean it is always in the best academic or social-emotional interests of students to do so. Further, student journalists who face censorship can easily publish online and reach a much wider audience than they might have otherwise, so to the extent the censorship was based on a desire to suppress information that might embarrass the school or administration, it's a decision that is likely to backfire.[47] It is the best interest of all involved for students, teachers, administrators to work together to carefully consider whether there is educational justification before censoring newspapers, plays, or other school-sponsored expression.[48]

---

[42] *Id.* at 271.
[43] *Id.* at 273.
[44] Planned Parenthood v. Clark Cnty. Sch. Dist., 941 F.2d 817 (9th Cir. 1991).
[45] *Id.* Note that in *Hazelwood,* 484 U.S. at 273, the Supreme Court ruled that school officials could control school-sponsored publications without specific written regulations. But it declined to decide whether such regulations "are required before school officials may censor publications not sponsored by the school." Since several federal appeals courts have required that schools have written due process safeguards in reviewing underground publications, such regulations continue to be required in the absence of a Supreme Court ruling to the contrary.
[46] Jordan, Samuel P., 70 Univ. of Chicago L. Rev. 1555, 1570. Fall 2003.
[47] Steve Inskeep, *Student Journalists Launch Website After They Say School Censored Their Paper,* NPR, February 1, 2018, https://www.npr.org/2018/02/01/582338663/student-journalists-launch-website-after-they-say-school-censored-paper.
[48] At the time the *Hazelwood* case was decided, newspapers were not digitally produced and last-minute edits were difficult. In 2020, the technology is such that corrections can be made up to the very last minute—thus truly "pedagogical" concerns should be more easily addressed without resorting to censoring entire stories.

As of September 2020, fourteen states had enacted "New Voices" laws, which strengthen the rights of student journalists.[49] In California, the Education Code states, "Students of the public schools shall have the right to exercise freedom of speech and of the press ... whether or not such publications ... are supported financially by the school."[50] As a result, a California court ruled in favor of a student who wrote a controversial article in a school newspaper. In explaining his decision, the judge stated, "The broad power to censor expression in school-sponsored publications for pedagogical purposes recognized in [*Hazelwood v.*] *Kuhlmeier* is not available to this state's educators."[106] In Massachusetts, the law states, "The right of students to freedom of expression in the public schools of the Commonwealth shall not be abridged provided that such right shall not cause any disruption or disorder."[51] Similarly, Colorado law protects freedom of expression and prohibits prior restraint in student publications, regardless of whether such publication is school-sponsored.[52]

In New Jersey, a state superior court ruled in favor of a student whose movie reviews for the school-funded extracurricular newspaper were censored because they reviewed R-rated films that the principal considered "inappropriate for junior high students." Judge Francis stated that if he were to decide the case under the United States Constitution, he would be compelled to declare that the school's action was constitutional under the test laid down by the United States Supreme Court in *Hazelwood*. However, he ruled that the school violated the student's rights under the New Jersey Constitution, which is "more expansive than the First Amendment" and "indicates that free speech is an affirmative right."[53]

Finally, *Hazelwood* does not give the school control over the style and content of non-school-sponsored newspapers that students may choose to publish on their own. Students may be required to submit such publications to administrators for review before distributing hard copies of their publication on campus, as long as the purpose of the prior review is "to prevent disruption and not to stifle expression."[54] Generally, the *Tinker* material disruption standard governs the distribution of such publications, which usually cannot be prohibited unless administrators have evidence to forecast that it will cause

---

[49] Student Press Law Center website, available at https://splc.org/new-voices/. Arkansas, California, Colorado, Illinois, Iowa, Kansas, Maryland, Massachusetts, Nevada, North Dakota, Oregon, Rhode Island, Vermont, and Washington had enacted "New Voices" laws as of September 14, 2020.

[50] CAL. EDUC. CODE § 48907 (1991).

[51] General Laws of Mass., Ch. 71, § 82 (1991).

[52] COLO. REV. STAT. § 22-1-120(1) (1990).

[53] Desilets v. Clearview Reg'l Bd. of Educ., Superior Court of N.J., Gloucester Cnty. No. C-23-90, May 7, 1991. Art. I, ¶ 5 of the New Jersey Constitution states: "Every person may freely speak, write, and publish his sentiments."

[54] Shanley v. Northeast Indep. Sch. Dist., 462 F.2d 960 (5th Cir. 1972).

substantial disruption or interfere with the rights of others.[55] Students cannot be punished merely for writing content that is controversial, sensitive, unpopular, or critical of the school administration or policies.

Student Speech Online, but Off-Campus

Modern communicative technology has made it possible for students to easily and broadly disseminate their speech. Students have often harnessed this power to engage in civic activism, but, sadly, some have also used it to tease, harass, or threaten members of the school community. Up until 2021, the Supreme Court had yet to hear any cases dealing with the question of whether or not the school has authority to discipline students for off-campus electronic speech. In April 2021, the Court heard oral arguments in *Mahanoy Area School District v. B.L.*, a case involving a high school cheerleader who was suspended from the squad after a profane social media post.[56] In the years leading up to the Supreme Court's decision to weigh in on this question, however, school administrators had been forced to rely upon the federal circuits for practical guidance. This section will briefly outline themes that have emerged from lower federal court decisions before briefly addressing the *Mahanoy* case.

Neither *Bethel v. Fraser* nor *Frederick v. Morse* seems to apply to student speech that originates off campus and not at a school-sponsored event.[57] The school has no authority to discipline students who engage in lewd or vulgar speech unless the speech occurs on campus or at a school activity. The same is true of the *Morse* exception for student speech that might be interpreted as advocating for the use of illegal drugs.

Federal appeals courts have, however, consistently applied the principles of *Tinker* to cases involving off-campus electronic student speech, although they have developed multiple "threshold tests" to help them identify the circumstances under which analysis of off-campus speech under *Tinker* would be appropriate. In two different decisions,[58] the Second Circuit determined that school officials have the authority to discipline students for off-campus electronic speech if it is a "reasonably foreseeable risk that the [speech] would come to the attention of school authorities"[59] or otherwise "reach" campus.[60]

---

[55] *See* Shanley v. Northeast Indep. Sch. Dist, 462 F.2d 960 (5th Cir. 1972) and Boucher v. Sch. Bd. of Greenfield, 134 F.3d 821 (7th Cir. 1898). Note also that in *R.O. v. Ithaca City School District*, 645 F.3d 533, 543 (2d Cir. 2011), the Second Circuit applied *Fraser* rather than *Tinker* in order to uphold administrators who prohibited distribution of an "underground" paper that featured cartoon stick figures in sexual positions. Students published the drawings in an underground paper after a faculty advisor censored them from the school-sponsored newspaper.

[56] As of May 11, 2021, the Court had not announced a decision in *Mahanoy Area School District v. B.L.*

[57] *See* Watt Lesley Black, Jr. and Elizabeth A. Shaver, *The First Amendment, Social Media and Public Schools: Emergent Themes and Unanswered Questions*, 20 Nev. L. J. 1, 50 (2019).

[58] Wisniewski *ex rel.* Wisniewski v. Bd. of Educ. of Weedsport Cent. Sch. Dist., 494 F.3d 34, 35 (2d Cir. 2007); Doninger v. Niehoff, 527 F.3d 41, 44 (2d Cir. 2008).

[59] *Doninger*, 527 F.3d at 50, citing *Wisniewski*, 494 F.3d at 39-40.

[60] *Doninger*, 527 F.3d at 48, citing *Wisniewski*, 494 F.3d at 40.

The Eighth Circuit subsequently adopted the Second Circuit's test of reasonable foreseeability.[61] Similarly, the Fourth Circuit, in *Kowalski v. Berkeley Co.*, developed a "nexus test" in which it sought a close connection (or nexus) between a student's speech and the school's pedagogical interest.[62]

In 2015, the Fifth Circuit Court of Appeals developed a test of "intentional direction."[63] The case involved a student who wrote and recorded a rap song and posted it publicly on YouTube in which he directed threatening verbiage at school employees. In an *en banc* decision, the majority held that the school may impose discipline on a student under *Tinker* if the student "intentionally directs" off-campus speech at "the school community," and the speech is "reasonably understood by school officials to threaten, harass, and intimidate a teacher."[64] In *Wynar v. Douglas County School District*,[65] the Ninth Circuit held that the school could legally discipline a student who had sent "a string of increasingly violent and threatening instant messages … bragging about his weapons, threatening to shoot specific classmates, intimating that he would 'take out' other people at a school shooting on a specific date, and invoking the image of the Virginia Tech massacre."[66] "When faced with an identifiable threat of school violence," the court reasoned, "schools may take disciplinary action in response to off-campus speech."[67]

In 2020, the Third Circuit became the first and only federal appeals court to hold that *Tinker* does not extend to off-campus student speech. In *B.L. v. Mahoney Area School District*, a high school student who failed to make her varsity cheer team posted a photograph of herself on Snapchat with the caption, "Fuck school fuck friends fuck cheer fuck everything."[68] After being made aware of the post, the cheerleading sponsor removed the student from the junior varsity cheer team. The Third Circuit ruled in favor of the student, holding that "*Tinker* does not apply to off-campus speech—that is, speech that is outside school-owned, -operated, or -supervised channels and that is not reasonably interpreted as bearing the school's imprimatur."[69] Additionally, the court took issue with the school district's argument that the student, by agreeing to the cheer team rules, had waived her First Amendment rights: "No doubt, for the government to condition participation in a beneficial program on a waiver of First Amendment rights raises serious constitutional concerns, particularly

---

[61] Kowalski v. Berkeley Cty. Sch., 652 F.3d 565 (4th Cir. 2011); D.J.M. *ex rel.* D.M. v. Hannibal Pub. Sch. Dist. #60, 647 F.3d 754 (8th Cir. 2011); S.J.W. *ex rel.* Wilson v. Lee's Summit R-7 Sch. Dist., 696 F.3d 771 (8th Cir. 2012).
[62] *Id.* at 573.
[63] Bell v. Itawamba Cty. Sch. Bd., 799 F.3d 379 (5th Cir. 2015) (en banc).
[64] *Id.* In a decision issued in 2016, the Fifth Circuit, quoting *Bell*, stated that the decision whether to apply *Tinker* in any particular case is "heavily influenced by the facts in each matter." Brindson v. McAllen Ind. Sch. Dist., 832 F.3d 519, 533 n.7 (5th Cir. 2016).
[65] 728 F.3d 1062.
[66] *Id.* at 1064–65.
[67] *Id.*
[68] B.L. v. Mahoney Area Sch. Dist. 964 F.3d. 170 (3d Cir. 2020).
[69] *Id.* at 189.

where the government "seek[s] to leverage [benefits] to regulate speech outside the contours of the program itself."[70] The Mahanoy Area School District appealed the Third Circuit's decision and the Supreme Court granted certiorari in January of 2021. Oral arguments were heard at the end of April of 2021. At the time of this writing, however, the Supreme Court has yet to issue a decision.[71]

The Third Circuit's decision in the *Mahonoy* case stands in contrast with its 2011 en banc decision, *J.S. v. Blue Mountain School District*, in which the court was divided over the issue of whether *Tinker* could be applied to off-campus student speech, and ultimately "assumed without deciding" that it did.[72] The court held in favor of a middle school student who had been disciplined for creating a fake—and unflattering—social media profile of her principal on social media. Even assuming *Tinker* could be applied off-campus, the court reasoned, the school district had not shown that the student's speech was substantially disruptive under *Tinker*.[73]

Prior to the Supreme Court's involvement in 2021, with the exception of the Third Circuit,[74] it had become safe to assume that *Tinker* standard could be applied to off-campus speech under certain conditions. While federal circuit courts had adopted different frameworks to address school administrators' ability to review student online expression and impose discipline, there was almost uniform agreement that schools could legally sanction students who engaged in threatening speech that is directed to or otherwise reaches the school community.[75] Even in deciding that *Tinker* does not apply to off-campus speech, the Third Circuit left open the possibility that when students threaten the school community, school discipline may be legally warranted, noting that when students engage in speech that can be "reasonably understood as a threat of violence or harassment targeted at specific students or teachers," it "would no doubt raise different concerns and require consideration of other lines of First Amendment law."[76] Whether or not the school may legally discipline students for online disparaging speech directed at teachers or other school employees

---

[70] *Id.* at 192.
[71] The Supreme Court website, available at https://www.supremecourt.gov/search.aspx?filename=/docket/docketfiles/html/public/20-255.html.
[72] J.S. *ex rel.* Snyder v. Blue Mountain Sch. Dist., 650 F.3d 915, 925 (3d Cir. 2011).
[73] *Id.* at 928.
[74] The Third Circuit comprises New Jersey, Pennsylvania, and Delaware.
[75] *C.L.M.*, 2016 WL 894450 at *4; McKinney v. Hunstville Sch. Dist., Civil Action No. 5:18-cv-5067, 2018 WL 5078112 (D. Ark. Oct. 17, 2018) (student who posted a picture on Instagram of himself wearing a trench coat and holding an AR-15 rifle was constitutionally subject to school discipline); N.Z. v. Madison Bd. of Educ., 94 N.E.3d 1198 (Ohio App. 2017) (students who had participated in social media postings on a messaging app called "Kik" were subject to school discipline for having discussed the possibility of a school shooting (a "Klebold surprise," named after one of the Columbine shooters, Dylan Klebold); A.N. v. Upper Perikomen Sch. Dist., 228 F. Supp. 3d 391 (E.D. Pa. 2017) (student subject to school discipline for an Instagram video posting of a school shooting, with a caption that read "See you next year, if you're alive"); R.L. v. Cent. York Sch. Dist., 183 F. Supp. 3d 639 (school authority existed over a student's Facebook post that made reference to a bomb having been placed at school);
[76] *B.L.*, 964 F.3d. at 190.

is less certain and would depend largely upon the circuit involved, as well as the particular circumstances of the case.

Participation in Patriotic Rituals

In the 1943 ruling *West Virginia v. Barnette*, the Supreme Court held that requiring students to recite the Pledge of Allegiance in public schools violates their First Amendment rights.[77] Though the complaint was based upon free exercise of religion rather than free speech, the Court opined that the compulsory flag salute also violated the free speech provision of the First Amendment.[78] As Justice Robert Jackson eloquently explained, "If there is any fixed star in our constitutional constellation, it is that no official, high or petty, can prescribe what shall be orthodox in politics, nationalism, religion, or other matters of opinion or force citizens to confess by word or act their faith therein."[79] So, in addition to the right to speak freely, the First Amendment also protects a student's right to remain silent, if speaking would violate the student's conscience.

All fifty states have statutes requiring mandatory flag salutes in public schools.[80] Thirty-two of those states have constructed their statutes in ways that align with the Court's guidance in West Virginia, allowing students the unilateral right to opt out of the pledge.[81] Fifteen states, however, have statutes that either specifically require parental permission for a student to opt out of the pledge, or are unclear.[82] The Texas Education Code, for example, provides that "on written request from a student's parent or guardian, a school district or open-enrollment charter school shall excuse the student from reciting a pledge of allegiance."[83]

In 2007, the Eleventh Circuit Court of Appeals upheld a similar Florida statute requiring parental permission in order for students to be exempted from the pledge.[84] But the constitutionality of such a requirement still remains in question. In September 2018, Texas Attorney General Ken Paxton intervened in a Houston area case,[85] making it clear that, under his interpretation of the state law, "school children cannot unilaterally refuse to participate in the pledge."[86] While not ruling on the constitutionality of the statute itself, the United States

---

[77] W.Va. State Bd. of Educ. et al. v. Barnette et. al., 319 U.S. 624 (1943). A group of Jehovah's Witnesses objected to the compulsory flag salute on First Amendment "Free Exercise" grounds.
[78] *Id.* at 634,635.
[79] *Id.* at 642.
[80] Scott Bomboy, *Can Schools Require Students to say the Pledge of Allegiance?*, THE HILL, February 26, 2019. Available at https://thehill.com/opinion/education/431719-can-schools-require-students-to-say-the-pledge-of-allegiance.
[81] *Id.*
[82] *Id.*
[83] TEC, §25.082.
[84] Frazier v. Winn, 435 F.3d 1279 (11th Cir. 2007).
[85] Oliver v. Klein Indep. Sch. Dist., 2020 U.S. District Lexis 51421, S.D. Tex (2020).
[86] Emma Platoff, *Attorney General Ken Paxton defends Texas law requiring students to stand for Pledge of Allegiance*, THE TEXAS TRIBUNE, September 25, 2018. Available at https://www.texastribune.org/2018/09/25/ken-paxton-texas-law-student-stand-pledge-allegiance-/.

District Court for the Southern District of Texas was unequivocal in its declaration that "a public school student's First Amendment right to abstain from the Pledge of Allegiance is well, long, and clearly established."[87]

Parental permission statutes, such as the one in Texas, raise an issue of what happens when a parent's rights collide with those of the students, and can place teachers between the proverbial rock and a hard place. As a matter of best practice, a teacher should never compel a student to stand or otherwise participate in the pledge if he or she has expressed a philosophical or religious objection to doing so.[88] Under *Tinker*, of course, a student who is disruptive during the pledge recitation may be disciplined. Similarly, under both *Barnette* and *Tinker*, students who refuse to stand or participate in the playing of the national anthem should not be subject to discipline, so long as their protest does not cause a material disruption.

Clothing and Student Expression

Students often wear clothing emblazoned with text or images that express particularized viewpoints, some of which may be upsetting to certain members of the school community. Courts have heard numerous cases concerning controversial texts or symbols on clothing throughout the country. In most cases, judges have applied the principles of *Tinker* and ruled that students should not be punished for wearing such clothing unless there is evidence that the message would substantially disrupt discipline or interfere with the rights of others.

Just before the Iraq War in 2003, a high school student from Michigan wore a T-shirt with a picture of President Bush above the caption "International Terrorist." Administrators banned the shirt because it was "inappropriate" and might be disruptive. Since there was no evidence that the T-shirt caused or was likely to cause substantial disruption, a federal court ruled that the ban violated the student's First Amendment rights.[89] In Virginia, a middle school student was prohibited from wearing a National Rifle Association T-shirt that depicted three silhouettes holding firearms above the words "Shooting Sports Camp."[90] Administrators said the shirt violated the school's dress code that prohibited "messages related to weapons." The judge noted that the school certainly could prohibit messages that were violent, threatening, indecent, libelous, or disruptive. But, in this 2003 decision, the message conveyed on the NRA T-shirt was seen by the court as nonviolent, nonthreatening, and nondisruptive. Similarly, another federal appeals court ruled in favor of a student who was suspended under the school's racial harassment policy for wearing a T-shirt inscribed with "redneck" jokes.[91] While past racial conflicts would justify banning any provocative racial message, it did not justify banning this T-shirt, since administrators had no evidence it might threaten disruption.

---

[87] *Oliver*, U.S. District Lexis *51421* at 37.
[88] Lipp v. Morris, 579 F.2d 834 (3d Cir. 1978).
[89] Barber v. Dearborn Pub. Sch., 286 F. Supp. 2d 847 (E.D. Mich. 2003).
[90] Newsom v. Albemarle Cnty. Sch. Bd., 354 F.3d 249 (4th Cir. 2003).
[91] Sypniewski v. Warren Hills Reg'l Bd. of Educ., 307 F.3d 243 (3d Cir. 2002).

Whether or not some extremely provocative T-shirts are protected is an open question. The Ninth Circuit upheld school district discipline of a student for wearing a T-shirt that said, "BE ASHAMED, OUR SCHOOL HAS EMBRACED WHAT GOD HAS CONDEMNED" on the front and "HOMOSEXUALITY IS SHAMEFUL Romans 1:27" on the back.[92] In *Harper v. Poway*, the Ninth Circuit ruled that the T-shirt could be banned since *Tinker* permits schools to restrict speech that "collides with the rights of other students to be secure and to be let alone."[93] The court emphasized that its ruling was limited to "injurious speech that strikes at the core identifying characteristics" of students who are members of minority groups that have been historically subject to verbal abuse.[94] Upon appeal, however, the Supreme Court refused to rule on the merits of the case, instead vacating the Ninth Circuit's decision and remanding the case to the district court with instructions to dismiss the complaint as moot since the student had already graduated from the school system.[95]

A year after the Supreme Court vacated the Ninth Circuit decision in *Harper*, the Seventh Circuit ruled in favor of a student who wore a T-shirt to school with the phrase "Be Happy, Not Gay" emblazoned on it.[96] School administrators argued that the shirt violated a school rule banning "derogatory comments that refer to race, ethnicity, religion, gender, sexual orientation, or disability."[97] The court described the message on the shirt as "only tepidly negative," suggesting that "derogatory" or "demeaning" were inaccurate characterizations of the phrase.[98] Further, the court added that it was "highly speculative" that the shirt would even have a "slight tendency to provoke" a disruptive reaction within the school.[99] In holding for the student, however, the Seventh Circuit distinguished between a message such as "Be Happy, Not Gay," and one that might be characterized as unprotected fighting words, such as "homosexuals go to hell."[100]

Equal Access to School Facilities

The Federal Equal Access Act prohibits public secondary schools with open forums from denying equal access to student groups on the basis of the

---

[92] Harper v. Poway Unified Sch. Dist., 445 F.3d 1166 (9th Cir. 2006).
[93] *Id.* 1177, quoting from *Tinker*, 393 U.S. at 508.
[94] *Id.* at 1178.
[95] Harper v. Poway Unified Sch. Dist., 549 U.S. 1262 (2007).
[96] Nuxoll v. Indian Prairie Sch. Dist., 523 F.3d 668 (7th Cir. 2008).
[97] *Id.* at 670.
[98] *Id.* at 676.
[99] *Id.*
[100] *Id.* at 671.

"religious, political, philosophical, or other content" of their speech.[101] In the 1990 case, *Westside v. Mergens*, the Supreme Court upheld the constitutionality of the Equal Access Act and held that a school establishes an open forum if it recognizes any noncurricular student groups on campus.[102] A student group is considered "noncurricular" if it does not directly relate to courses regularly taught in the school. "Access" includes not just the ability of a student group to meet on school premises, but also all of the "recognition and privileges afforded to other groups at school, including, for example, the right to announce club meetings in the school newspaper, on bulletin boards, or over the public address system."[103]

A school may avoid the mandates of the Equal Access Act by banning all noncurricular student groups, thus closing their forum. Once a school has noncurricular clubs operating on campus, however, shutting them down may prove difficult. The U.S. Department of Education has warned that a closed forum policy is insufficient if it does not match the school's actual practices.[104] This difficulty is clearly demonstrated in the 1993 Third Circuit case, *Pope v. East Brunswick Board of Education*.[105] From 1988 through 1991, Donna Pope was a student at East Brunswick High school, where she regularly met with an informal Bible group in the school cafeteria on Wednesday mornings.[106] The school "tolerated" the group's meetings, but did not officially recognize them.[107] In the aftermath of the passage of the Equal Access Act and *Mergens* decision, East Brunswick established a new policy that classified all groups as curricular-related, the goal of which was to close the forum.[108] Though a number of noncurricular-related student groups ceased to exist as a result of the policy change, other clubs somehow survived, including Students Against Drunk Drivers, Students Against Violating the Environment, and the Key Club.[109] Although the school argued that these groups were related to the curriculum, the Third Circuit viewed them as noncurricular in nature, thus opening the forum in practice.[110] The district, despite the fact that its written policy had

---

[101] 20 U.S.C. § 4071. While the federal Equal Access Act applies only to secondary schools, some states have passed "religious viewpoints anti-discrimination acts" that push equal access provisions down to the elementary school level. These laws also strengthen protections for students who wish to express their religious viewpoints in the academic setting or at school functions, and require school districts to adopt policies that create limited open forums at events where students are speaking. Such laws exist in Texas, Tennessee, and Virginia.

[102] Board of Educ. of Westside Cmty. Sch. v. Mergens, 496 U.S. 226 (1990).

[103] U.S. Department of Education, *Legal Guidelines Regarding the Equal Access Act and the Recognition of Student-Led Noncurricular Groups*, at 2. Available at http://findit.ed.gov/search?utf8=%E2%9C%93&affiliate=ed.gov&query=%22equal+access+act%22+, last accessed October 5, 2016.

[104] *Id.* at 4.

[105] Pope v. E. Brunswick Bd. of Educ., 12 F.3d. 1244 (3d Cir. 1993).

[106] *Id.* at 1246.

[107] *Id.*

[108] *Id.* at 1247.

[109] *Id.*

[110] *Pope*, 12 F.3d.at 1253.

established a closed forum, was found to be in violation of the Equal Access Act by refusing to recognize and grant equal access to Pope's student Bible Club.[111]

Neither may schools avoid the mandates of the Equal Access Act by broadening the definition of "curriculum-related" to the point where it "would render the act meaningless."[112] The Eighth Circuit provides an example with *Straights and Gays for Equality v. Osseo Area School District No. 279*, in which the Maple Grove High School attempted to differentiate between "curricular" and "noncurricular" student groups, affording greater access and recognition to groups it deemed related to curriculum.[113] The school defined cheerleading and synchronized swimming as curricular-related, while the Straight and Gays for Equality (SAGE) group was designated noncurricular-related.[114] The Eighth Circuit held that neither the synchronized swimming nor the cheerleading class related directly to any particular classes or to the body of classes as a whole.[115] Further, membership in either of these two organizations was not required for any class, nor did students receive academic credit as a result of participation.[116]

Schools may exclude groups that "are directed, conducted, controlled or regularly attended by nonschool persons," and require student groups to have school employees present at group meetings for custodial purposes.[117] Teachers who act as "custodial" sponsors may monitor, but should not participate in or lead student activity. Custodial sponsorship does not mean that the school supports the group's message.[118]

Finally, schools retain the authority to ban groups that are unlawful, or that would otherwise materially and substantially interfere with the orderly conduct of educational activities.[119] The disruption, however, must be attributable to the student group itself and not to those who may oppose its formation. School officials must not exercise a "heckler's veto" by suppressing a student group based on the disruptive reaction of others.

Expression of Sexual Orientation and Gender Identity

Increasingly, students are making First Amendment claims based upon expression related to sexual preference or gender identity. The Court specifically noted that *Tinker* should not be read to inhibit the school's authority to enforce rules related to student dress and grooming.[120] However, the Superior Court

---

[111] *Id.* at 1254.
[112] U.S. Department of Education, *Legal Guidelines Regarding the Equal Access Act and the Recognition of Student-Led Noncurricular Groups*, at 3.
[113] Straights and Gays for Equality v. Osseo Area Sch. Dist. No. 279, 471 F.3d. 908, 910 (8th Cir. 2006).
[114] *Id.*
[115] *Id.* at 912.
[116] *Id.* at 913.
[117] U.S. Department of Education, *Legal Guidelines Regarding the Equal Access Act and the Recognition of Student-Led Noncurricular Groups*, at 2.
[118] *Id.* at 2, 3.
[119] *Id.* at 3.
[120] Tinker v. Des Moines, 393 U.S. 503, 508 (1969).

of Massachusetts ruled in 2000 that a student who dressed in a non-gender-conforming manner was engaging in expressive speech.[121] Further, courts have ruled that certain conduct, such as attending school dances with a same-sex partner or engaging in limited public displays of affection, contain expressive elements that may place them within the ambit of the First Amendment.[122] Schools may regulate dress, grooming and conduct, but should take care to do so in a way that is viewpoint-neutral. A federal judge in California, for example, upheld a school's disciplinary action against a student who repeatedly engaged in same-sex public displays of affection, because the evidence showed that the school had responded to such displays in a consistent manner, without regard to whether the students involved were of the same or opposite sex.[123]

Students may not be subjected to discipline for expressing pro-lesbian, gay, bisexual, transgender, or questioning viewpoints. A 2008 case from the Florida panhandle is illustrative. When high school senior Jane Doe reported being bullied as a result of her sexual orientation, her principal shamed her, outed her to her parents, and warned her to stay away from the younger students on the campus.[124] When the student body became aware of the principal's treatment of Jane, a number of students expressed their support for her by inscribing "Gay Pride" or "GP" on their bodies, and donning clothing with symbols and other messages supportive of gay rights."[125] The principal responded by launching an investigation of what he called the "gay pride movement" at the school, which resulted in a categorical ban on any pro-LGBTQ expression.[126] Ultimately, eleven students who had worn clothing or accessories that advocated for equal treatment of the LGBTQ community were suspended for participating in what the school board called an "illegal organization."[127] A federal district judge ruled that the students' expression was nondisruptive under *Tinker*, and chastised the school for what he deemed "an outright ban on speech by students that is not vulgar, lewd, obscene, plainly offensive, or violent, but which is pure, political, and expresses tolerance, acceptance, fairness, and support for not only a marginalized group, but more importantly, for a fellow student."[128]

When considering the expressive rights of LGBTQ students, it should be noted that they have benefitted greatly from the Equal Access Act. Principals may not deny access to LGBTQ student organizations because of "general moral

---

[121] Doe v. Yunits, 2000 Mass. Super. Lexis 491 (2000). The Superior Court ruled in favor of a transgender 15-year-old who was disciplined for dressing as a female. The ruling was based upon the free speech provisions in Article XVI of the Massachusetts Declaration of Rights.
[122] *See* Fricke v. Lynch, 491 F. Supp. 381 (D. R.I. 1980) and Nguon v. Wolf, 517 F. Supp. 2d 1177 (C.D. Cal. 2006).
[123] *Nguon*, 517 F. Supp. 2d. 1177.
[124] Gillman v. Sch. Bd. for Holmes Cnty., Fla., 567 F. Supp. 2d 1359, 1361 (N.D. Fla. 2008).
[125] *Id.* at 1362.
[126] *Id.* at 1363.
[127] *Id.*
[128] *Id.* at 1371.

disapproval or on assumptions about the content of speech at group meetings."[129] If a school has established an open forum, LGBTQ student groups must be given access to school facilities and treated equally to any other noncurricular groups that are recognized at the school.

Distribution of Printed Materials on Campus

A number of controversies have involved student distribution of religious or political publications. Policies prohibiting distribution of such materials usually have been struck down. A Colorado case, for example, involved students who were suspended for giving out a Christian newspaper, *Issues and Answers*, in violation of a policy prohibiting distribution of "material that proselytizes a particular religious or political belief." The administrators argued that they had the authority to prohibit distribution of such controversial publications, but the judge disagreed and explained, "Because students have a right to engage in political and religious speech," school policies that prevent students from discussing issues they feel are important inhibit their individual development and "defeat the very purpose of public education in secondary schools."[130]

Similarly, a federal court ruled against a Massachusetts high school that punished members of a Bible club for distributing candy with a religious message.[131] Administrators claimed the controversial message violated the school's "responsible" speech code and its policy prohibiting student distribution of any printed material without administrative approval. However, the court ruled that the school could not totally prohibit students from distributing literature during noninstructional time that does not cause disruption, and it held that the policy giving administrators discretion to suppress any speech they feel is not responsible is unconstitutionally vague. In a 2011 decision, the Fifth Circuit ruled against principals who barred elementary students from distributing religious-themed candy canes and pencils with religious messages such as "Jesus is the Reason for the Season." The court concluded that the principals violated the students' First Amendment rights by discriminating against student speech solely on the basis of its religious viewpoint.[132]

Content-neutral policies that simply regulate the time, place, and manner in which students can distribute printed material usually are upheld. In another Colorado case that concerned *Issues and Answers*, students challenged school rules that prohibited distribution of newspapers in hallways. Since distribution was allowed in other locations within the school, and since the restrictions were applied equally to all students, were designed to maintain order, and were not based on the viewpoint of the publication, the court concluded that the policy did not violate student freedom of

---

[129] U.S. Department of Education, *Legal Guidelines Regarding the Equal Access Act and the Recognition of Student-Led Noncurricular Groups*, at 4.
[130] Rivera v. E. Otero Sch. Dist., R-1, 721 F. Supp. 1189, 1194 (D. Colo. 1989).
[131] Westfield High Sch. L.I.F.E. Club v. City of Westfield, 249 F. Supp. 2d 98 (D.C. Mass. 2003).
[132] Morgan v. Swanson, 659 F.3d 359 (5th Cir. 2011).

expression.¹³³ And, in a New Jersey case, a federal court allowed an elementary school to prohibit a first-grade student from distributing pencils with religious messages to his classmates during a school-sponsored, in-class party.¹³⁴ The judge gave several reasons for supporting the school: the party was part of the curriculum; there were legitimate concerns that allowing the distribution during class time might lead young, impressionable students to think that the school endorsed the religious message; and the school allowed the student to distribute his gifts before and after school, as well as during recess.

Student Free Speech: Considerations for Best Practice

Four Supreme Court decisions—*Tinker, Bethel, Hazelwood,* and *Morse*—provide the constitutional framework for analysis of student expression disputes in the public schools. What emerges from these and more recent rulings is a sense that the First Amendment applies broadly to a student's personal views and narrowly in areas that are considered part of the curriculum. Teachers who wish to balance respect for student speech rights against their responsibility to maintain safety, order, and discipline should consider the following:

1. Teachers and principals may not impose discipline on students for expressing their personal opinions about controversial political, religious, social, or educational issues, even if their views are unpopular and in conflict with the ideas of most students, parents, teachers, and administrators. When a student speaks or writes as an individual, such expression is protected by the First Amendment and cannot be restricted unless it causes substantial disruption or interferes with the rights of others.

2. Teachers and principals may impose discipline on a student who speaks *at school or at a school event* in a way that is deemed lewd or vulgar, without regard to whether it is disruptive. Such speech is not protected under the First Amendment, according to the Supreme Court in *Fraser*. Teachers and principals should, however, be cautious about disciplining students for speech that has social or political meaning, even if may possibly be interpreted as lewd or vulgar.

3. Teachers and principals may impose discipline on a student who speaks *at school or at a school event* in a way that is construed to advocate the use of illegal drugs. Such speech is not protected under the First Amendment, according to the Supreme Court in *Morse*. Teachers and principals may not, however, impose discipline on students for advocating for changes in existing drug laws or policies.

4. Teachers and principals may censor a curricular-based student newspaper or other school-sponsored student expression, when the decision is reasonably related to legitimate pedagogical concerns, according to the Supreme Court in *Hazelwood*. But, just because a decision to censor may

---

¹³³ Hemry by Hemry v. Sch. Bd. of Colo. Springs, 760 F. Supp. 856 (D. Colo. 1991).
¹³⁴ Walz v. Egg Harbor Twp. Bd. of Educ., 187 F. Supp. 2d 232 (D. N.J. 2002).

be legally defensible does not mean that it is educationally sound. Whenever possible, teachers and administrators should work with students to address legitimate pedagogical issues rather than censoring. If the school converts the paper (by policy or practice) to a limited public forum, it may no longer exercise its discretion to censor under *Hazelwood*. Because authority to censor school-sponsored student speech under *Hazelwood* is limited in some states, teachers and principals should be aware of relevant state statutes, regulations, judicial opinions, and district policies before developing school rules or imposing punishments that restrict school-sponsored student expression.

5. Teachers and principals may not impose discipline on students who wear clothing with controversial text or imagery unless it disrupts education or interferes with the rights of others under the *Tinker* Standard. Schools may enforce content-neutral clothing policies—for example, a ban on all clothing bearing text.

6. Teachers should never require students to participate in or stand during the pledge of allegiance, nor should they require a student to stand during the playing of the national anthem. According to the Supreme Court in *West Virginia v. Barnette*, the First Amendment also protects the right to abstain from participation in patriotic rituals. Students who disrupt during these exercises legally may be disciplined.

7. Teachers and principals should not prevent a student from distributing private materials because they advocate a particular religious, political, or social view. Policies that regulate the time, place, and manner for distributing materials in the schools are constitutional, as long as they are viewpoint-neutral and not overly restrictive.

8. While most federal circuits that have heard cases have applied *Tinker* to off-campus speech (with the exception of the Third Circuit), they have not done so uniformly, and the results have not always favored the school. In order to subject students to discipline for off-campus speech, administrators need significant evidence of a material and substantial disruption or invasion of the rights of others. Speech that is threatening to members of the school community generally will meet the required standard of disruption. Disparaging speech directed at a teacher or administrator may not be sufficiently disruptive enough to justify discipline, particularly if the speech is clearly a parody.

Teacher Speech and the First Amendment

With *Pickering v. Board of Education* in 1968, the Court extended First Amendment protection to public school teachers—and dispensed with the antiquated notion that teachers voluntarily forfeit their rights in exchange for the "privilege" of teaching.[135] Section II of this chapter will highlight the key Supreme Court decisions that impact the First Amendment speech rights of public school teachers, and highlight how lower courts have applied these precedents to situations in practice.

Teachers Speaking as Citizens on Matters of Public Concern: *Pickering v. Board*

Marvin Pickering, a public high school teacher, wrote a letter to the editor of a local paper that was critical of the school board's use of funds from a bond election.[136] The board, believing that he had cast aspersions on their "motives, honesty, integrity, truthfulness, responsibility and competence," terminated him.[137] Pickering filed suit in federal court, arguing that the board's actions were illegal retaliation for exercise of his First Amendment speech rights.

The Court held that public school teachers have a First Amendment right to speak as citizens on matters of public concern, but the state also has an interest as an employer in providing government services with basic efficiency. Accordingly, the Court sought to balance the state's interests against the educator's right to speak. When a teacher's speech begins to disrupt the orderly operations of the school, the Court explained, then the balance may tilt in favor of the employer.[138] So how does a teacher know when his or her speech is disruptive enough to merit workplace discipline?

In examining Pickering's letter, the Court posed several specific questions. First, had Pickering revealed confidential information?[139] Second, did he knowingly or recklessly include false information?[140] Third, did the letter undermine superior/subordinate relationships? And fourth, did the letter disrupt school business or interfere with Pickering's ability to function effectively in the job?[141] The Court answered all of these questions negatively; thus, Pickering's firing was unconstitutional. Had the answer to any of these questions been yes, however, Pickering's termination would have been legally justified, even though his speech was considered protected.

For a public school teacher, the key takeaway is that even though the teacher has a First Amendment right to speak as a citizen on a matter of public concern, that right has limits. Teachers may still legally be subjected to workplace discipline if their speech sufficiently disrupts school business. Teachers who plan to speak out should weigh their words carefully against the questions embedded in *Pickering*, which will be referred to in this chapter as the *Pickering* Balancing

---

[135] Pickering v. Bd. of Educ., 391 U.S. 563 (1968).
[136] *Id.* at 575.
[137] *Id.* at 567.
[138] *Id.* at 568.
[139] *Id.* at 567. Pickering's letter contained no confidential information.
[140] *Pickering*, 391 U.S. at 567. Pickering's letter did contain inaccurate information, but there was no evidence that he had knowledge that the information was false, or that he acted recklessly.
[141] *Id.* The Court noted that, with the exception of the board and superintendent, Pickering's letter elicited little or no reaction from the community.

Test. The table below incorporates the test into a series of simple questions that a teacher may use to analyze content before they decide to share it publicly.

Table 1: *Pickering* Balancing Test

If I say or write what I am thinking right now, could I...

1. Divulge confidential information?
2. Knowingly or recklessly spread false information?
3. Undermine or damage important workplace relationships?
4. Disrupt school business?
5. Disrupt my own ability to continue to function effectively in the job?

Unprotected Speech: Teachers Speaking as Employees on Matters of Private Interest

While the *Pickering* Court recognized the right for teachers to speak as citizens on matters of public concern, in *Connick v. Myers* it held that not all expressive activities of public employees merit First Amendment protection.[142] Sheila Myers worked as an assistant district attorney in New Orleans. Upset by her boss's decision to transfer her to another section of the criminal court, she distributed a survey to approximately fifteen coworkers, soliciting input on office morale, confidence in supervisors, and whether there should be an official "grievance committee."[143] The survey did not go over well with District Attorney Harry Connick, who terminated Myers as a result.[144]

The Supreme Court viewed Myers's survey as fundamentally different from Pickering's letter to the editor. Rather than addressing matters of public concern, it focused on matters almost exclusively of private interest.[145] Unlike Pickering, who wrote his letter as a private citizen, the Court felt that Myers was speaking in the capacity of an employee when she distributed the work-related survey throughout her office.[146] The majority opinion explained that "when a public employee speaks not as a *citizen* upon matters of *public concern*, but instead as an *employee* upon matters of *personal interest*, absent the most unusual circumstances, a federal court is not the appropriate forum in which to review the wisdom of a personnel decision taken by a public agency allegedly in reaction to the employee's behavior."[147]

---

[142] Connick v. Myers, 461 U.S. 138 (1983).
[143] *Id.* at 140, 141.
[144] *Id.* at 141.
[145] *Id.* at 154. It is important to note that, while Myers was speaking in the capacity of an employee, she was not actually doing her job when she was speaking.
[146] *Id.* at 154.
[147] *Id.* at 147 (emphasis added).

Before engaging in any public speech, a teacher should consider whether he or she is speaking in the capacity of a citizen or an employee—and whether the content of the speech addresses a matter of public concern or private interest. According to the Court, we must examine the "content, form, and context of a given statement."[148] For example, the content of Sheila Myers's survey dealt primarily with private workplace complaints, which were of no interest to the general public.[149] Myers's speech was in the form of a survey sent directly to coworkers. The context within which her survey was distributed was an ongoing grievance with her boss. Rather than Myers seeking to blow the whistle on incompetent or corrupt practices within the district attorney's office, the Court viewed her as a disgruntled employee, upset about her impending transfer, hoping to "gather ammunition for another round of controversy with her superiors."[150] As such, Myers's survey was unprotected speech, and the Court upheld her termination.

Unprotected Speech: Teachers Speaking as Employees Pursuant to Job Duties

In the 2006 decision *Garcetti v. Ceballos*, the Court was forced to grapple with a type of speech that was notably different from both Pickering's letter and Myers's survey.[151] Richard Ceballos was a deputy assistant district attorney in Los Angeles County. As "calendar deputy," Ceballos reviewed the work of other attorneys in the office at the request of defense attorneys.[152] While acting on one such request, Ceballos felt that there were significant inconsistencies surrounding a state affidavit that could adversely affect the prosecution of the case. As a result, he forwarded a recommendation that the case be dropped.[153] Ceballos's recommendation was not well-received by his superior, Gil Garcetti, who stripped him of his title as calendar secretary, transferred him to another courthouse, and denied him a promotion.[154]

Ceballos filed a suit in federal court, alleging that Garcetti's actions were retaliation for his exercise of his First Amendment speech rights. The Court disagreed, pointing out what it viewed as a critical difference between this case and the others it had decided. When Ceballos forwarded his recommendation to his superiors, he was neither speaking in his capacity of a private citizen on a matter of public concern, like Pickering, nor was he speaking as an employee on a matter of private interest, like Myers. Making such recommendations was officially part of his responsibilities as a calendar deputy. As such, he was speaking as an employee *pursuant to his job duties*. In other words, he was actually doing his job when he forwarded the recommendation.

---

[148] *Id.* at 147.
[149] *Id.* at 154.
[150] *Id.*
[151] Garcetti v. Ceballos, 547 U.S. 410 (2006).
[152] *Id.* at 413.
[153] *Id.* at 414.
[154] *Id.* at 414, 415.

The Court held that "when public employees make statements pursuant to their official job duties, the employees are not speaking as citizens for First Amendment purposes, and the Constitution does not insulate their communications from employer discipline."[155] Rather than being a victim of illegal retaliation over the exercise of constitutionally protected speech, the Court viewed Ceballos an employee simply receiving consequences for poor performance—in this case, making recommendations that his supervisors may have perceived as "inflammatory or misguided."[156]

Social Media and Other Online Teacher Expression

The trilogy of *Pickering*, *Connick* and *Garcetti* provide the framework for all cases involving the free speech rights of public school teachers. But each of these cases occurred prior to the explosion of social media and other forms of online communication, so in order to understand how they are applied to cases involving online teacher speech, we must look to decisions in the lower federal courts.

When teachers (or other public employees) engage in controversial speech online, many times they are sharing an opinion on a matter of inherent public concern, such as politics, police brutality, or immigration. But, because *Pickering* articulates such a broad concept of disruption, teachers have been largely unsuccessful in their First Amendment challenges.[157] Often, these cases turn on whether the speech interferes with an employee's ability to continue to function effectively in the job. For example, when Natalie Monroe blogged about profane and insulting commentary that she wished to add to students' report cards, the Third Circuit Court of Appeals held that, by directing such invective at the very people she was supposed to serve, she had rendered herself unable to continue effectively in the job.[158] And, in *Craig v. Rich Township High School District*, the Seventh Circuit upheld the firing of a high school guidance counselor/girls' basketball coach who self-published (and marketed online) a book for women that was full of misogynistic and racist stereotypes.[159] Due to the nature of the book's content, the court concluded that members of the community would rightfully lose confidence in his fitness to counsel or coach their children.

Less frequently, teachers have faced consequences for online expression because their speech failed to pass the *Connick* test of public concern. In two very early cases involving teachers on social media, federal district courts ruled that content on teachers' MySpace pages did not meet the test of public concern,

---

[155] *Id.* at 421.
[156] *Id.* at 423.
[157] *See* Watt Lesley Black and Elizabeth Shaver, *The First Amendment, Social Media, and the Public Schools: Emergent Themes and Unanswered Questions*, 20 Nev. L. J. 1 (2019).
[158] Munroe v. Cent. Bucks Sch. Dist., 805 F.3d 454, 473–474 (3d Cir. 2015).
[159] *See* Craig v. Rich Twp. High Sch. Dist. 227, 736 F.3d 1110 (7th Cir. 2013); *see also* Duke v. Hamil, 997 F. Supp. 2d 1293 (a deputy police chief was demoted after posting an image of a confederate flag with the caption "time for a second revolution" the morning after President Obama's reelection).

and therefore the speech was unprotected.[160] In 2017, the Second Circuit ruled that a member of the New York City Teaching Fellows (NYCTF) was speaking as an employee on a matter of private concern when she posted critical comments on Facebook about the master's program associated with the NYCTF, thus upholding her dismissal from the program.[161]

In other cases, however, courts have sidestepped the *Connick* test, even when the speech in question didn't seem to touch on a public concern. For example, in the 2009 case *Richerson v. Beckon*, the Ninth Circuit "assumed without deciding" that a teacher's "highly personal and vituperative" blog posts about her employers and coworkers touched on matters of public concern.[162] And, when the aforementioned Natalie Monroe blogged that she'd like to add comments to student's report cards such as "frightfully dim," "lazy asshole," and "utterly loathsome in all imaginable ways," the Third Circuit court "reluctantly assumed" that she was blogging on matters of public concern, that is, the work ethic of today's youth and the value of hard work in general.[163] As mentioned above, her blog subsequently failed the *Pickering* Balancing Test.

Under *Garcetti v. Ceballos*, when teachers speak "pursuant to their job duties," their speech is not protected. In October 2014, the United States District Court for the Northern District of West Virginia decided the case of Courtney Austin, the director of the Preston County Animal Shelter, holding that she was speaking pursuant to her job duties when she created and administered a shelter Facebook page.[164] Austin only used the page for shelter business and posted as "Preston County Animal Shelter" rather than in her own name.[165] The Facebook page was listed in shelter information as its official website.[166] These factors led the court to conclude that she was speaking in the capacity of an employee "pursuant to her job duties," and, as such, had no claim under the First Amendment.

Courtney Austin's case is instructive for teachers who use social media in furtherance of their job duties. For example, a fine arts director who maintains a social media page for the band, orchestra, or choir should be aware that what the educator posts on the site is likely to be considered pursuant to job duties, and therefore not protected speech. Consider the case of Katie Nash, who worked as the "Social Media Coordinator" for the Frederick County schools

---

[160] *See* Spanierman v. Hughes, 576 F. Supp. 2d 292 (D. Conn 2008), in which an English teacher interacted with students on his page in a way that his employers found personal and inappropriate; and Snyder v. Millersville Univ., 2008 U.S. Dist. LEXIS 97943 (E.D. Penn. 2008), in which a student teacher who criticized her supervising teacher and posted a picture of herself wearing a pirate hat with the caption "Drunken Pirate" was removed by her university from her student teaching assignment.

[161] Odermatt v. N.Y.C. Dep't of Educ., 694 F. App'x 842 (2d. Cir. 2017).

[162] Richerson v. Beckon, 337 F. App'x 637, 638 (9th Cir. 2009).

[163] *Munroe*, 805 F.3d 454, 473–474 (3d Cir. 2015).

[164] Austin v. Preston County Commission, Civil Action No. 1:13-cv-135, 2104 U.S. Dist. LEXIS 146041 at *3 (N.D. W.Va., Oct. 14, 2014).

[165] *Id.* at *16.

[166] *Id.* at *16-17.

in Maryland. When a student tweeted at the district (in anticipation of a possible snow day) "close school tammarow PLEASE," Nash responded, "But then how would you learn to spell 'tomorrow?'"[167] Nash was fired a week later.[168] She didn't legally challenge her firing. Based upon the *Garcetti* "pursuant to work duties" standard, it would have been hard to argue that her termination was unconstitutional.

The "pursuant to job duties" standard also means that teachers should be cautious about what they write in their work emails and texts. While this type of electronic speech is much less likely to reach an unintended audience than social media posts, it can sometimes go public as a result of a mistaken "reply all," an unauthorized "forward," as well as in litigation or open records requests. Work emails or texts are highly likely to be viewed as pursuant to job duties and, therefore, unprotected. Recently, the Tenth Circuit ruled that a city planner was speaking pursuant to his job duties when he sent an email to the city attorney raising concerns about suspected corruption directly related to a city project with which he was involved.[169] Additionally, a federal district court in New York ruled that a teacher who sent a series of internal emails expressing concerns about student discipline, conduct of district employees, district policies, lack of support, and alleged violations of law/policy, was speaking pursuant to her job duties.[170]

Teachers' Free Speech: Considerations for Best Practice

Public school teachers are citizens and do not forfeit their First Amendment expression rights in exchange for their jobs. However, even when speaking as a citizen on a matter of public concern, a teacher may face workplace discipline if that speech is disruptive under *Pickering*. Further, when a teacher speaks as an employee (either pursuant to job duties or on a matter of personal interest), such speech is no longer protected by the First Amendment.

A teacher should contemplate the following questions before engaging in potentially controversial public speech. Applying this framework prior to engaging in public speech will reduce the chances that a teacher will speak out in a way that results in workplace discipline—but there are no guarantees:

1. **Is what I'm about to say/write actually part of my job duties?**
   Speech pursuant to or in furtherance of job duties is unprotected speech under *Garcetti v. Ceballos*. A teacher who answers this question with a "yes" should think carefully about whether to speak/write, because it may result in workplace discipline. If the answer is "no," then move to question 2.

---

[167] *Id.*
[168] *Id.* This was despite Nash's response receiving 1400 likes and 1100 retweets, as well as the student who posted the original misspelled tweet taking no offense.
[169] Knopf v. Williams, 884 F.3d 939 (10th Cir. 2018).
[170] Agyeman v. Roosevelt Union Free Sch. Dist., 254 F. Supp. 3d. 524 (E.D.NY. 2017).

2. **Am I speaking as a citizen on a matter of inherent public concern?**
   Under *Pickering v. Board of Education*, a teacher who speaks as a citizen on a matter of public concern is protected by the First Amendment as long as the speech isn't disruptive to the school. A teacher who answers "yes" to this question may skip to question 4 to analyze the disruptive potential of the speech. A teacher who answers "no," or is unsure how to answer to this question, should proceed to question 3.

3. **Am I speaking as an employee?**
   According to *Connick v. Myers*, a teacher who speaks as an employee on a matter of private interest is not protected by the First Amendment. In order to understand the status of speaking as an employee, a teacher should consider the following questions:
   (a) Am I about to say/write something that protects or promotes my personal interests as an employee?
   (b) Am I about to say/write information about a workplace complaint or grudge?
   (c) Am I about to say/write information that can be linked back to my employer in a harmful way (i.e., have I identified myself as a school employee)?
   A teacher who answers any one of the previous three questions with a "yes" should think carefully about whether to speak/write. It is likely that such speech could be viewed as that of an employee on a matter of personal interest, and therefore unprotected. A teacher who answers "no" to the previous three questions should proceed to question 4, in order to consider the disruptive potential of the speech using a set of questions based upon the *Pickering* Balancing Test.[171]

4. **Am I about to say/write...**
   ...anything that could be disruptive to my school, my school district, or to my ability to continue to effectively function in my job?
   ...any information that is confidential or is untrue?
   ...anything that could harm working relationships with my superiors, colleagues, students, or parents?
   ...anything that could cause community members to reasonably question my fitness to teach, such as content that might be interpreted as insensitive in terms of race, religion, sex, or gender?

   A teacher who answers "yes" to question 3a, 3b, or 3c should not speak/write. This speech is likely going to be disruptive in a way that would expose the teacher to workplace discipline. A teacher who answers "no" to the above questions may likely speak/write without facing workplace discpline.*

   Teachers who work through these questions must do so earnestly and with an ability to honestly assess their speech from the viewpoints of their employers

---

[171] These recommendations are largely based upon Watt Lesley Black, Jr., *When Teachers Go Viral: Balancing Institutional Efficacy Against the First Amendment Rights of Public Educators in the Age of Facebook*, 82 Mo. L. Rev. (2017).

and others within the community. This framework will not protect individuals who are unable to do so.

Case List

Austin v. Preston Cnty. Comm'n
Agyeman v. Roosevelt Union Free Sch. Dist.
A.M. v. Cash
B.H. v. Easton Area Sch. Dist.
B.L. v. Mahoney Area Sch. Dist.
Barber v. Dearborn Pub. Sch.
Bell v. Itawamba
Bethel v. Fraser
Blue Mountain Sch. Dist. v. J.S.
Bd. of Educ. of Westside Cmty. Sch. v. Mergens
Boucher v. Sch. Bd. of Greenfield
Connick v. Myers
Craig v. Rich Twp. High Sch. Dist. 227
Cuff v. Valley Cent. Sch. Dist.
D.J.M. v. Hannibal Pub. Sch. Dist.
Desilets v. Clearview Reg'l Bd. of Educ.
Doe v. Yunits
Doninger v. Niehoff
Frazier v. Winn
Frederick v. Morse
Fricke v. Lynch
Garcetti v. Ceballos
Gillman v. Sch. Bd. for Holmes Cnty., Fla.
Harper v. Poway Unified Sch. Dist.
Hazelwood Sch. Dist. v. Kuhlmeier
Hemry by Hemry v. Sch. Bd. of Colo. Springs
Knopf v. Williams
Kowalski v. Berkeley Cnty. Schs.
Leeb v. DeLong
Lipp v. Morris
Miller v. California
Morgan v. Swanson
Morse v. Frederick
Muller by Muller v. Jefferson Lighthouse Sch.
Munroe v. Cent. Bucks Sch. Dist.
Newsom v. Albemarle Cnty. Sch. Bd.
Nguon v. Wolf
Nuxoll v. Indian Prairie Sch. Dist.
Odermatt v. N.Y.C. Dep't of Educ.
Oliver v. Klein Indep. Sch. Dist.

Pickering v. Bd. of Educ.
Planned Parenthood v. Clark Cnty. Sch. Dist.
Pope v. E. Brunswick Bd. of Educ.
R.O. v. Ithaca City Sch. Dist.
Richerson v. Beckon
Rivera v. E. Otero Sch. Dist., R-1
Shanley v. Northeast Indep. Sch. Dist.
Snyder v. Millersville Univ.
Spanierman v. Hughes
Straights and Gays for Equality v. Osseo Area Sch. Dist. No. 279
Sypniewski v. Warren Hills Reg'l Bd. of Educ.
Tinker v. Des Moines
Walz v. Egg Harbor Twp. Bd. of Educ.
West Virginia State Bd. of Educ., et al. v. Barnette, et al.
Westfield High Sch. L.I.F.E. Club v. City of Westfield
Wisniewski v. Bd. of Educ.

Key Words

cell phones
censorship
clothing
clubs
computers
content-neutral
controversial messages
curricular vs. noncurricular
cyberbullying
derogatory
distribution of materials
electronic student speech
Federal Equal Access Act
fighting words
First Amendment
freedom of press
freedom of speech
gender expression
heckler's veto
illegal drug use
in loco parentis
LGBTQ
Marketplace of Ideas
material and substantial disruption
matters of conscience
National Anthem

off-campus speech
online student speech
open forum
Pledge of Allegiance
political
protest
religious
religious viewpoints antidiscrimination act
right to remain silent
school library
school newspaper
school-sponsored
sexual orientation
state law
student expression
student rights
student-sponsored
threatening
vulgar or lewd speech

Takeaways

1. Students and teachers retain First Amendment rights in school; however, those First Amendment rights are not unlimited.
2. *Tinker v. Des Moines* afforded students First Amendment protection and *Pickering v. Board of Education* extended First Amendment rights to school teachers.
3. Educators should consider the *Tinker* Standard when considering school policy or disciplining students for speech: (1) Does the speech cause a substantial disruption? (2) Does the speech interfere with the rights of other students or the orderly operation of the school? (3) Can one reasonably predict that the speech would cause a substantial disruption or interfere with the rights of others in school?
4. Courts have applied the decision in *Tinker v. Des Moines* and determined that schools may discipline students for online speech when there is both nexus to the school and the speech causes or foreseeably would cause a substantial disruption in school, or interferes with the rights of others.
5. School officials have authority to discipline students for on-campus speech that is lewd or offensive in nature (*Bethel v. Fraser*), as well as for nondisruptive speech at school-sponsored events that references illegal drugs (*Morse v. Frederick*).
6. School administrators have the authority to censor student speech in school-sponsored publications (*Hazelwood v. Kuhlmeier*); however, some states have laws that limit the school's ability to censor student publications.

School officials should collaborate with students to ensure that student publications are educationally sound.
7. Student dress is a form of student expression; therefore, administrators and teachers should not discipline students for clothing with controversial messages unless it disrupts education or interferes with the rights of others under the *Tinker* Standard.
8. Although teachers retain First Amendment rights, as employees their rights are more limited than the rights of students. Teachers need to consider whether they are speaking as a matter of public concern, and if their speech is disruptive. When teachers speak as an employee, their speech is no longer protected by the First Amendment.
9. Teachers should use caution when speaking about their school, students, or controversial topics.

Practical Extension

1. A parent contacts the principal and shares a screenshot of a social media post in which another student in the school has written disparaging remarks on social media about her child. What should the principal take into consideration when determining how to proceed?
2. A student comes to class with a political T-shirt during an election year. Some students in class have expressed they are uncomfortable because they do not like the candidate on the T-shirt. How should the teacher proceed?
3. A teacher is upset at the quality of students' work. If the teacher posts online that their students have "gone downhill" this year and are "lazy" and "playing too many video games," is this speech protected?

Chapter 4

Student Searches in Public Schools: Contemporary Legal Considerations for Educators

Kevin P. Brady, W. Kyle Ingle,
and John C. Pijanowski

Introduction

The freedom from unreasonable searches and seizures is legally guaranteed to all adult citizens under the Fourth Amendment of the United States Constitution. The Fourth Amendment provides a right to privacy against "unreasonable searches and seizures" that also extends to students in public schools.[1] Public school employees are considered state officers and are legally bound by the Fourth Amendment. However, today's school officials are not held to the same warrant and probable cause requirements expected of law enforcement officials to establish a legally viable search. Instead, the constitutionality of searches in public schools is guided by considerations of reasonableness in relationship to maintaining safe schools. A continuing challenge of the reasonableness standard for conducting searches in public schools is attempting to properly balance a student's legal expectations of privacy with school officials' need to maintain a safe and orderly student learning environment.[2] Although teachers do not have authority or responsibility for conducting searches, it is important for them to understand the current legal boundaries and implications of failing to be aware of students' Fourth Amendment constitutional rights.

Recent Examples of Student Searches in K-12 Settings in the National Media

Tragic, high-profile instances of gun violence in U.S. schools, such as the 2018 school shooting that occurred at Marjory Stoneman Douglas High School in Florida, serve as an ongoing impetus for sacrificing student privacy in pursuit of student safety. One need not look long or hard for incidences of student searches in K-12 schools that led to contemporary media reporting.

---

[1] The Fourth Amendment reads, in pertinent part, "The right of the people to be secure in their persons, houses, papers, and effects, against unreasonable searches and seizures, shall not be violated..." U.S. Const. Fourth Amendment.

[2] *See* Lawrence F. Rossow & Jacqueline A. Stefkovich, SEARCH AND SEIZURE IN THE PUBLIC SCHOOLS (4th ed. 2014).

These incidences, whether reasonable or not, bring unwanted media attention to local schools, districts, and the educators involved—not to mention costs associated with subsequent investigations, legal proceedings, opportunity costs associated with responding to media inquiries, and time spent on duties other than teaching and administration. Of course, there is also the potential for cost associated with settlements or rulings against the school district in civil actions. For example, four black middle school girls in upstate New York were strip-searched by school personnel for suspicions of drug possession because they were observed as acting "hyper and giddy." The event led to angry protests and statements from the district that it would engage a third-party firm to investigate, as well as district counterclaims that there was no evidence that administrators actually strip-searched the girls. The district's school board countered that the incident was the result of "misinformation" spread by social media, and that the students and parents were overreacting to having to remove outerwear in order to expose their arms for the purpose of taking vital signs (e.g., blood pressure and pulse rates).

Even the COVID-19 international pandemic and subsequent switch to online instruction for a majority of K-12 students in the United States did not prevent controversial educator decision making, angry parents, and negative media coverage for the local school and district. For example, a Colorado vice principal called a 12-year-old boy's mother at their home to inform her that a police officer was on the way to her house in response to his teacher reporting that her student was observed playing with a toy gun during a virtual art class. This resulted in the boy receiving a five-day suspension from school, a juvenile record with the county sheriff's department, and a disciplinary record in his school for bringing a "facsimile of a firearm to school"—even though he was in his own home doing a virtual class. The "gun' was painted black and green and had the words "Zombie Hunter" visible on the side of what was obviously a toy.[3] Similarly, a teacher in a Louisiana public elementary school reported a 9-year-old fourth-grader to school administrators after noticing a BB gun in the boy's bedroom during online instruction. Initially, the young boy was expelled, but was subsequently suspended for six days for committing a "violation of weapons in the classroom setting."

The Legal Standard of Reasonable Suspicion

Prior to the United States Supreme Court's landmark decision in *New Jersey v. T.L.O.*,[4] the legal relationship between students and parents was con-

---

[3] See J. Peiser (September 8, 2020). A Black seventh-grader played with a toy gun during a virtual class. His school called the police. *Washington Post*. Retrieved from https://www.washingtonpost.com/nation/2020/09/08/black-student-suspended-police-toy-gun/.
[4] New Jersey v. T.L.O, 469 U.S. 325, 105 S. Ct. 733, 83 L.Ed.2d 720 (1985).

trolled by the legal principle of *in loco parentis* (in place of parents).[5] If school officials believed they were acting "in the place of parents," students did not have any legal expectation of privacy. In 1985, the United States Supreme Court established the standard of reasonable suspicion as the legal basis for a public school administrator's search of a student. In *New Jersey v. T.L.O.*,[6] an assistant principal sought evidence to confirm a teacher's statement that a student had been smoking in a restroom. After questioning the student and hearing her denials, the vice principal searched the student's purse and discovered a pack of cigarettes and rolling papers. Knowing that rolling papers were often used with marijuana, the school administrator continued to search the purse, discovering a hash pipe, empty plastic baggies, $40 in cash, an index card with names and amounts of money owed, and a small bag of marijuana. The marijuana was turned over to police. When the student was subjected to a delinquency proceeding, she sought to have the marijuana excluded from evidence on the grounds that the school administrator's search violated the student's Fourth Amendment rights.

Based on the *T.L.O.* ruling, determining the reasonableness of any search in a public school environment requires a two-pronged inquiry. First, the school official must consider whether the search was justified at its inception, given the totality of the circumstances that led to the suspicion of the student. The Court reasoned that the initial search was justified because the assistant principal had testimony from a reliable source that the student had violated school rules by smoking on school grounds, and the purse was an obvious place for the student to keep cigarettes. The second inquiry is whether the search was reasonable in its scope. The scope of the search is deemed acceptable "when the measures adopted are reasonably related to the objectives of the search and not excessively intrusive in light of the age and sex of the student and the nature of the infraction."[7] Although the search was intended to confirm the student was in possession of cigarettes, the discovery of the rolling papers justified the continued search of the purse. Therefore, the search of the high school student in *New Jersey v. T.L.O.* met the reasonableness standard.

Step I: Justification at Inception

The search of a student is justified at its inception "when there are reasonable grounds for suspecting that the search will turn up evidence that the student has violated or is violating either the law or the rules of the school."[8] Courts typically interpret the "justified at incep-

---

[5] Translated from Latin, the *in loco parentis* doctrine states: The parent may also delegate part of his parental authority, during his life, to the tutor or the schoolmaster of his child; who is then *in loco parentis*, and has such a portion of power of the parent committed to his charge, viz. that of restraint and correction, as may be necessary to answer the purposes for which he is employed (12 WILLIAM BLACKSTONE, COMMENTARIES *453).
[6] 469 U.S. 325, 105 S. Ct. 733, 83 L.Ed.2d 720 (1985).
[7] *Id.* at 342.
[8] *Id.* at 341-42, 105 S. Ct. 743, 83 L.Ed.2d 735.

tion" prong of the reasonableness standard as school officials having individualized suspicion of a particular student's wrongdoing,[9] and the courts have often upheld multiple ways to achieve this legal standard, including use of informant information[10] or consent of the party to be searched.[11] The courts have generally accepted information from other students as successfully meeting the reasonable suspicion standard.[12] For example, two 1998 cases illustrate how the use of detailed information from another student can help establish justification at the inception of a search. In an Indiana case, a rash of school locker thefts and the discovery that the master locker combination book was missing led to an investigation in which a student informant specifically identified a student as having the locker combination book in a blue bookbag. Once in the school office, the bookbag was searched, the combination book was discovered, and the student was charged with theft. Finding that the search of the bookbag was reasonable, a state appeals court emphasized that the search was justified at inception because school officials established individualized suspicion based on the testimony of a student informant, who provided specific identification of the student and detailed information concerning where the book could be found.[13]

During the same year, a New Hampshire assistant principal received an anonymous phone call in which the caller said that a particular student at the high school would be carrying drugs to school that day. The caller identified the student by name, and the assistant principal knew of the student as a result of reports from teachers that implicated the student in a previous drug transaction at the school. The administrator was also aware that the student had been arrested for drug possession in another state. The student, who reported late for school that day, was called into the principal's office and told to turn his pockets inside out. The contents of his pockets included a pipe and rolling papers. The principal then required the student to open his backpack, which held several bags of marijuana and an unloaded semi-automatic pistol. The Supreme Court of New Hampshire held that the totality of circumstances justified the search. The telephone tip, which specifically identified the student, and the existing

---

[9] Chandler v. Miller, 520 U.S. 305 (1999).
[10] *But see* Phaneuf v. Fraikin, 448 F.3d 591 (2d Cir. 2006) in which the federal appeals court noted that while the student informant made the tip "face-to-face," claimed that her knowledge was based on a "direct conversation" with the plaintiff, and gave "relatively specific" information, her tip was nevertheless inadequate because there was no concrete evidence of her reliability, and the defendants had failed to make any effort to "investigate, corroborate, or otherwise substantiate [the tip] prior to ordering the strip-search." *Id.* at 598.
[11] State v. M.W.H., 246 Ore. Ct. App. 421, 267 P.3d 165 (Ore. Ct. App. 2011).
[12] *Id.*
[13] S.A. v. State, 654 N.E.2d 791 (Ind. Ct. App. 1995). *See also* C.B. v. Driscoll, 82 F.3d 383 (11th Cir. 1996) *reh'g en banc denied* (1996) in which reliance on a student informant resulted in the discovery of a lookalike drug that was located in a student's coat pocket.

knowledge detailing the student's prior drug involvement, were enough to establish individualized suspicion for the search.[14]

In addition to information from other students, most courts have upheld the validity of school searches involving anonymous tips implicating another student or students. An anonymous tip can satisfy the reasonable suspicion test if the information is considered detailed and the allegation itself is reasonable given existing conditions at the school during the time. In a Michigan case, the search of a student's vehicle was initiated by an anonymous tip received by a local "crime stoppers" organization involving the selling of illegal drugs at a high school.[15] The anonymous tip identified four students, including the defendant, who were selling drugs at the high school. The level of detail provided in the anonymous tip was extensive, including each of the students' names, their grades at the high school, the vehicles they drove, and the specific drugs being sold. When the anonymous tip from the local agency was provided to the high school, a police officer acting as a school resource officer verified that the vehicle identified by the tipster was owned by the defendant. The assistant principal was also aware that the identified student previously had drug-related problems at the local junior high school. According to the court, both the anonymous tip and corroborating evidence from the high school's assistant principal were sufficient to initiate a search of the student's truck parked in the school's parking lot.

A generalized hunch of wrongdoing, however, usually is insufficient evidence of reasonable suspicion.[16] An observation that a male student was not "acting himself," together with an inference that "something was not right," would not justify a search unless additional information were adduced that would permit a reasonable inference of misconduct.[17] Yet, a student's demeanor and conduct may be a factor that contributes to individualized suspicion, especially in cases of alleged drug or alcohol use.[18] In a Pennsylvania case, a teacher reported that a student was sleeping in class, had glassy eyes, and complained of nausea. After the teacher reported her concerns to the assistant principal, the student's parents were contacted and the student, consistent with district policy, was transported by bus to a local hospital, where a urine screen

---

[14] State v. Drake, 139 N.H. 662, 662 A.2d 265 (N.H. 1995). *But see, In re* J.N.Y., 931 A.2d 685 (Pa. Super. Ct. 2007), in which an anonymous tip that could not be corroborated did not provide reasonable suspicion.

[15] People v. Perreault, 781 N.W.2d 796 (Mich. 2010).

[16] *See T.L.O.*, 469 U.S. 346, 105 S. Ct. 745, 83 L. Ed. 2d 737, in which the U.S. Supreme Court held that reasonable suspicion must be something other than "an inchoate and unparticularized suspicion or hunch."

[17] A.N.H. v. State, 832 So. 2d 170 (Fla. Dist. Ct. App. 2002). *See also,* A.H. v. State, 846 So. 2d 1215 (Fla. Dist. Ct. App. 2003) in which search of a student's wallet was not supported by sufficient facts when the sole basis for the search was that a teacher had difficulty understanding the student and advised the administrator that the student might be "on something."

[18] *See* Rinker v. Sipler, 264 F. Supp. 2d 181, 188 (M.D. Pa. 2003), in which a search was justified at inception on the basis that a school administrator and a security officer observed that the student "looked stoned, smelled of marijuana, and was somewhat incoherent."

yielded a positive result for marijuana use. Although the parent challenged the district's policy requiring urine screening as a violation of privacy, the federal district court found the district policy constitutional and held that the search met the current legal standard for reasonable suspicion.[19] A few years earlier, when an Alaska high school student was confronted for creating a disturbance in the school library, a school security officer noticed that the student swayed and bumped into objects as he walked, his eyes were glassy, and his face was flushed. Discovering the student was evasive in responding to questions and had improperly parked his automobile on school grounds, an assistant principal undertook a search of the automobile and discovered two grams of cocaine. A state appeals court ruled the search was constitutional, noting that evidence of individualized suspicion was initially established given the student's disorientation, and finding that the improperly parked automobile added to a suspicion that the student was using drugs.[20]

A complex issue for contemporary educators, as well as the courts, is whom to search when there is misconduct among a group of students, but no individualized suspicion of a particular student. For example, school officials in a Hawaii high school observed a student and her companion leave school grounds without authorization and cross the street to an area called "The Tunnel," a culvert system off school grounds where students were known to gather to smoke cigarettes and marijuana. An assistant principal and school security officer (SRO) followed the students into the area, detected the odor of burning marijuana, and observed four students congregating near a grate. All four students exited when directed to do so, and two students were found to be carrying purses. The two students who were carrying purses were subjected to searches, and marijuana was found when the students emptied the contents of their purses on the school principal's desk. The Hawaii Supreme Court considered the totality of the circumstances and found credible evidence supporting the searches since the students were violating specific school policies by being in a restricted area, as well as school officials detecting the odor of marijuana.[21]

In a similar situation involving a student who was caught in possession of knives, a school administrator responded to a complaint from a private citizen that students were congregating in a cul-de-sac on the way to school to smoke cigarettes. The school administrator found a group of twenty students in a haze at that location, many of whom made furtive gestures as if discarding cigarettes. After ordering the students to a room at school, the administrator had each one searched. In the course of this search, knives were found. One student objected, on the basis that the search was not based on individualized suspicion, and brought a civil suit against the school administrator; however, the federal appeals court affirmed a lower court's rejection of the suit, finding

---

[19] Gutin v. Washington Township Bd. of Educ., 467 F. Supp. 2d 414 (D. N.J. 2006).
[20] Shamberg v. State, 762 P.2d 488 (Alaska Ct. App. 1988).
[21] In Interest of Doe, 77 Haw. 435, 887 P.2d 645 (Haw. 1994).

that there was nothing improper in the administrator's action.²² By contrast, years later, a New Mexico appellate court ruled on a comparable set of facts in which students from "smokers' corner" were all subjected to a pat-down search upon their return to campus. The court suppressed evidence after it determined that school officials did not have reason to suspect that any particular student was in possession of contraband.²³

Finally, in addition to considering individualized suspicion, it is essential that public school administrators have a general notion of "what" they are searching for. In a case from Illinois, after a 45-minute interrogation, a school official finally asked a student to empty his pockets "to further see just who he was ... ."²⁴ The appellate court ruled that school officials were acting on a hunch that something more was wrong, but the initial reason for detaining the student dissipated during the interrogation. In summary, it is not sufficient to go on a "fishing expedition" for evidence just because a school administrator assumes a student may possess an object.

Step II: Scope of the Search

Once the totality of circumstances supports reasonable suspicion to initiate a search, a school official, in making a determination about how far the search should go, must balance the student's expectation of privacy against the legitimate need to maintain a safe learning environment in the school. As the *T.L.O.* Supreme Court decision emphasized, "[a] search will be permissible in scope when the measures adopted are reasonably related to the objectives of the search and not excessively intrusive in light of the age and sex of the student and the nature of the infraction."²⁵

As a general rule, the closer the search is to the person, the more evidence a school official must provide in order to establish a reasonable basis for the scope of the search. For instance, judges grant little expectation of privacy as it relates to school-owned property, such as a school locker, particularly when school board policy or state statute makes it clear that lockers are the property of the school and subject to inspection at any time.²⁶ However, an expectation

---

[22] Smith v. McGlothlin, 119 F.3d 786 (9th Cir. 1997). *See* People v. Alexander B., 220 Cal. Ct. App. 3d 1572, 270 Cal. Rptr. 342 (Cal. Ct. App. 1990,) in which a school search was reasonable where suspicion focused on a group of five or six students, rather than one student alone.

[23] State v. Gage R., 243 P.3d 453 (N.M. Ct. App. 2010).

[24] People v. Pruitt, 278 Ill. App. 3d 194, 209, 662 N.E.2d 540, 550 (Ill. App. Ct. 1996).

[25] 469 U.S. 341-42, 105 S. Ct. 743, 83 L.Ed. 2d 735.

[26] *See In re* Patrick Y., 358 Md. 50, 746 A.2d 405 (Md. Ct. Spec. App. 2000); Commonwealth v. Cass, 551 Pa. 25, 709 A.2d 350 (Pa. 1998); and *In re* D.E.M., 727 A.2d 570 (Pa. Sup. 1999). *But see* State of Iowa v. Jones, 666 N.W.2d 142 (Iowa 2003), in which the court recognized that students have a legitimate expectation of privacy in the contents of their school lockers, but ruled that the discovery of marijuana as part of an end-of-year school locker clean-out search was reasonable.

of student privacy would apply in the case of a student's vehicle,[27] but even that particular instance of an expectation of privacy has been diminished when the student's vehicle is located on school grounds,[28] and school policy makes clear that students must register their cars and vehicles may be routinely searched.[29] A student's bookbag,[30] purse, or cellphone[31] carries an expectation of privacy, requiring evidence of reasonable suspicion, but touching the outside of the bookbag or purse would be less intrusive than opening and examining the contents.[32] A minor medical examination, in the form of a vital signs check involving limited contact, would be sufficiently invasive to require reasonable suspicion of drug use, usually manifest in the student's uncharacteristic behavior

---

[27] *See* Commonwealth v. Williams, 749 A.2d 957 (Pa. Sup. 2000), in which school security officers violated the Fourth Amendment when they searched a student's car parked on a city street off school grounds.

[28] The Supreme Court of New Jersey ruled that a school administrator need only satisfy the lesser reasonable grounds standard rather than the probable cause standard to search a student's vehicle parked on school property. State v. Best, 987 A.2d 605 (N.J. 2010).

[29] Myers v. State of Indiana, 839 N.E. 2d 1154 (Ind. 2005), *cert. denied*, Myers v. State of Indiana, 126 S. Ct. 2295 (2006). *See* People v. Williams, 339 Ill. App. Ct. 3d 956, 791 N.E.2d 608 (Ill. App. Ct. 2003), in which a school security officer's search of a student's car was permissible based on a student's testimony that a gun was in the car; Covington Cnty. v. G.W., 767 So. 2d 187 (Miss. 2000), in which a vehicle search was justified because informants advised school officials that the student had been observed drinking beer at his vehicle while it was parked on school grounds and school administrators discovered beer cans when the car was inspected; and F.S.E. v. State, 993 P.2d 771 (Okla. Crim. App. 1999), in which a school official's search of a student's vehicle was justified because the vehicle was parked on school grounds, the school administrator smelled marijuana on the student, and the student alleged that a stranger had left a marijuana cigarette in the car.

[30] *In re* Murray, 136 N.C. App. 648, 525 S.E.2d 496 (N.C. Ct. App. 2000), in which the school administrator had a reasonable suspicion to search a student's bookbag based on a reliable informant's tip that the student had something in the bag that "he shouldn't have" and on the student's initial evasiveness in stating he did not have a bookbag; Greenleaf *ex rel.* Greenleaf v. Cote, 77 F. Supp. 2d 168 (D. Me. 1999), in which a student's tip that four students had discussed drinking alcohol at school provided a reasonable suspicion justifying a requirement that a student shake out her bookbag in order to discover evidence of alcohol possession.

[31] Klump v. Nazareth Area Sch. Dist., 425 F. Supp. 2d 622 (E.D. Pa. 2006).

[32] Matter of Gregory M., 184 A.D.2d 252, 585 N.Y.S.2d 193 (N.Y. App. Div. 1992). In this case, a school security officer patted down the exterior of a student's bookbag when the metallic thud of the bookbag on the desk alerted the officer to the possibility of a weapon. The outline of a gun led the officer and a school administrator to search the bag, and they discovered a handgun. In a subsequent juvenile court proceeding, the court ruled that the search was reasonable and the weapon was properly admitted in evidence.

and evasiveness.[33] In addition, requiring students to remove caps or jackets to permit examination of pockets appears permissible, particularly when there is a reasonable suspicion that the student is in possession of a weapon or drugs.[34]

The final question concerning the scope of a search is, "when is a search over"? Should a school administrator stop the search once they have found what they were looking for, or can they continue under the premise that there could be additional contraband? In 2009, a New Mexico appellate court noted that it was legally permissible to continue a search after the student handed over cigarettes and a lighter because the school principal believed the student may have additional cigarettes or related contraband beyond that which was already voluntarily relinquished by the student.[35] A similar legal rationale guided a federal court, the Eighth Circuit Court of Appeals, in a case in which a student was subjected to a search by school resource officers while attending a shop class at a local body shop. On the way to that location, the supervising teacher observed a student using a folding knife, but did not know that the student had borrowed the knife from another student to open an orange juice can. After searching the bus, school resource officers asked if any of the students had a knife, and the student who had brought the folding knife on the bus handed it over. Thereafter, all the students were subjected to a pat-down search; the student who had used the knife on the bus was discovered to be in possession of an expandable baton and was subject to additional discipline.

The federal Eighth Circuit Court of Appeals ruled that the search was justified at inception on the basis of reasonable suspicion.[36] The court determined that the search off school grounds did not elevate the standard beyond reasonable suspicion because the nature of the administrator and teacher's supervisory responsibilities for the students dictated the Fourth Amendment standard. The school resource officers were justified in continuing the search, even though a knife had been discovered, because they had no way to verify that the confiscated knife was the one that had been seen earlier, and they were aware that the student who handed over the knife had not been seen previously

---

[33] *See, e.g.,* Ineirghe v. Bd. of Educ. of E. Islip, 2007 U.S. Dist. LEXIS 61841 (E.D.N.Y. 2007) (nurse's examination and salvia drug test were warranted when student had been found in parking lot during school hours in violation of school rules, exhibited anxious behavior, continued to wipe his eyes and nose during questioning); Hedges v. Musco, 204 F.3d 109, 117 (3d Cir. 2000) (nurse's vital signs examination, a urinalysis, and a blood test did not constitute unreasonable searches when the student had exhibited uncharacteristic behavior consistent with drug use); and Bridgman v. New Trier High Sch. Dist., 128 F.3d 1146, 1149 (7th Cir. 1997) (medical assessment was reasonably calculated to uncover further evidence of suspected drug when the student was "giggling and acting in an unruly fashion," "had dilated and bloodshot eyes," and provided "flippant" answers).

[34] *See In re* L.A., 21 P.3d 953 (Kan. 2001), in which removing a student's cap to check the headband was justified by an informant's tip that the student was hiding marijuana in the headband; and D.B. v. State, 728 N.E.2d 179 (Ind. Ct. App. 2000), in which the minimally intrusive pat-down of a student's clothing was justified by evidence the student had been smoking in a school bathroom and was unresponsive to questioning.

[35] State v. Jonathon D., 2009 LEXIS 402 (N.M. Ct. App. 2009), *cert. denied* (N.M. 2009).

[36] Shade v. City of Farmington, Minn., 309 F.3d 1054 (8th Cir. 2002).

with a knife. Given these facts, the school resource officers had reason to believe that there was another knife in the possession of one of the student participants.

Pat-down Searches

Concerns for safety in the school setting justify the use of pat-down searches.[37] Judges generally grant substantial flexibility to those conducting such searches, especially when weapons are suspected to be in the possession of students.[38] In a representative case involving the use of a frisk for a weapon, a school security officer in a New York high school observed a youth entering the school within a restricted area and demanded identification. When the student failed to produce identification, the officer sought to escort the youth to the school principal's office. As he took the youth's elbow, the school resource officer testified that his hand brushed against a metal object in the student's waistband. An immediate pat-down resulted in the recovery of a pistol. The court reasoned that the school resource officer was justified in frisking the student based on his suspicion that the student was carrying a weapon.[39]

Even if a pat-down is regarded as highly intrusive, judges have largely affirmed these searches when weapons are implicated. In a case from Wisconsin, several informants told the school principal that a 14-year-old was carrying a weapon on school grounds. The principal called the school security officer; the officer interviewed one of the informants, who corroborated the story. After identifying the student, the officer and a school administrator removed the suspected student from class. The officer explained to her that they had received information that she may have a weapon. He did a quick pat-down search of her jacket and had the student empty and display the contents of her backpack. She was then taken to an office, where the officer initiated a second pat-down. In this search, which included visual inspection of her waistband, the officer discovered and removed a nine-inch knife. The Supreme Court of Wisconsin ruled that the pat-down search was justified in scope despite its highly intrusive nature.[40]

---

[37] *See, e.g.,* C.S. v. State, 735 N.E.2d 273 (Ind. Ct. App. 2000), in which a pat-down by a school resource officer was justified by concern for her safety in removing a student from a classroom.

[38] *See, e.g., In re* Randy G., 18 Cal. App. 3d 1023, 96 Cal. Rptr. 338 (Cal. Ct. App. 2000), in which detaining a student for suspicious behavior resulted in a pat-down that yielded. a knife; *In re* Josue T., 128 N.M. 56, 989 P.2d 431 (N.M. Ct. App. 1999), in which the student was suspected of having used marijuana, but after he was isolated, an unusually large bulge in his pants pocket led to an apprehension that he might have a weapon, and a school resource officer's search at the direction of school officials was justified by a reasonable suspicion; and J.A.R. v. State, 689 So. 2d 1242 (Fla. Dist. Ct. App. 1997), in which reasonable suspicion based on a student informer's testimony that another student had a gun permitted either the school resource officer or the administrator to isolate the student and conduct a pat-down search.

[39] *In re* Kevin P., 186 A.D.2d 199, 587 N.Y.S.2d 730 (N.Y. App. Div.1992).

[40] *In re* Angelia D.B., 211 Wis. 2d 140, 564 N.W.2d 682 (Wis. 1997). *See also* People v. Butler, 725 N.Y.S.2d 534 (N.Y. Sup. 2001), in which reasonable suspicion existed to support a pat-down given a school safety officer's concern that the defendant was wearing gang colors and could not produce student identification.

That same year, in an Indiana appellate court ruling, a school security officer's decision to search a student who was late in arriving at a school-sponsored academic program was regarded as an "improvisational" search not justified by the evidence of misconduct. The search was undertaken because the school had a policy of searching program participants with a handheld wand in order to check for weapons. At the time the student arrived at school, the metal detector had been locked in the principal's office, so the officer elected to conduct a pat-down search of the student, which included placing his hands in her pants pockets. Two partially smoked marijuana cigarettes, a wooden pipe, and a package of rolling papers were discovered in the student's pockets. Reasoning that notice of a metal detector search would not automatically imply consent to a more intrusive physical search, the reviewing state court found that the search could not be justified based solely on the student's tardiness.[41]

In balancing student privacy with the immediate need for a suspicionless search, a New York appeals court affirmed the permissibility of a pat-down search of all middle school students. School officials instituted the search in order to prevent the repetition of a Halloween tradition involving an egg-throwing melee. The egg throwing, in a previous year, had led both to damage of school property and injury to students. The school principal directed staff to pat down the outer garments of students as they entered the building. In the course of the pat-down, one student was discovered in possession of a handgun in his waistband. In a criminal adjudication, the student sought to suppress the evidence on the basis that the pat-down was an illegal search. The state appeals court ruled that the pat-down of outer clothing by school personnel was the least intrusive, most practical means of locating the concealed eggs, and represented a reasonable balance between the privacy expectation of students and the interests of school officials in maintaining order, as well as student safety.[42]

Student Strip-searches

Unquestionably, student strip-searches constitute the most intrusive form of searches and create the greatest risk of legal liability for school districts and their employees.[43] Almost all of the existing cases related to student strip-searches involve alleged drugs or stolen items. Judges occasionally have upheld such searches, but only in rare circumstances in which a strong evidentiary

---

[41] D.I.R. v. State, 683 N.E.2d 251 (Ind. Ct. App. 1997).
[42] Matter of Haseen N., 251 A.D.2d 505, 674 N.Y.S.2d 700 (N.Y. App. Div. 1998).
[43] In addition to a risk of liability for a constitutional tort under 42 U.S.C § 1983, at least one federal district court has indicated employee liability may be predicated on negligent infliction of emotional distress. Higginbottom *ex rel.* Davis v. Keithly, 103 F. Supp. 2d 1075 (S.D. Ind. 1999). *But see* Beard v. Whitmore Lake Sch. Dist., 2007 U.S. App. LEXIS 14749 (6th Cir. 2007), in which a federal appeals court rejected school district liability for "failure to train" in a case in which the school district acknowledged that teachers had improperly strip-searched students in a gym class to locate money missing from a student's purse. The appeals court reasoned that the district had a clear policy prohibiting such searches, and the plaintiffs failed to show the district was deliberately indifferent to the students' interests in being free from unreasonable searches and seizures.

basis supported individualized suspicion and the items sought were either drugs or weapons.[44] In an unusual and controversial decision involving a missing pair of gym shorts, a court upheld the alleged strip-searches of twenty-five high school students without individualized suspicion.[45] In this case, the court debated the level of intensity related to the search. The students claimed that they were required to pull their gym shorts below their knees. School officials disputed this claim and said that the students were also asked to turn down the waistbands of their gym shorts.[46] After discussing what constitutes a strip-search, the court concluded that the strip-search of students in this particular instance was reasonable.

In 2009, the United States Supreme Court delivered its most recent decision involving student strip-searches, *Safford Unified School District #1 v. Redding*, ruling that school officials acted unconstitutionally when they conducted a strip-search of a 13-year-old middle school student accused of hiding ibuprofen.[47] The eighth-grade female student was called into the assistant principal's office based on information provided by another student accusing the student of distributing prescription drugs to fellow students at the middle school. After an initial search of the student's backpack and outer clothing resulted in no evidence of prescription drugs, the assistant principal instructed the student to go to the school nurse's office, where she was instructed to remove all her clothes, except her underwear, exposing her breasts and partially her pelvic area to several teachers. Similar to the initial search of the student's backpack and outer clothing, the strip-search of the student did not reveal any evidence of concealed prescription drugs. The Supreme Court determined that the strip-search of a middle school student for prescription-strength ibuprofen was unconstitutional, but the Court did not explicitly rule on the legality of the student's strip-search. In its ruling, the Court reversed a federal appellate court's decision that the search was justified at its inception. The Justices believed that a strip-search must be reserved for only the most extenuating of circumstances, and determined the assistant principal did not have reason to believe the common painkillers were available in large quantities, were a particular threat to student welfare, or were in the student's underwear.

Only one month after the Supreme Court's *Redding* decision, a federal district court in Georgia ruled on the alleged strip-search of a high school student based on a student's missing iPod.[48] A student temporarily left the classroom to go to the restroom. Upon returning, he noticed that his iPod was missing from

---

[44] See Beard v. Whitmore Lake Sch. Dist., 402 F.3d 598, 605 (6th Cir. 2005), in which the federal appeals court invalidated a strip-search on the basis that the governmental interest in finding missing money is less weighty "than a search undertaken for items that pose a threat to the health or safety of students, such as drugs or weapons" and State *ex rel.* Galford v. Mark Anthony B., 189 W. Va. 538, 433 S.E.2d 41 (W.Va. 1993), in which a strip-search of a student to locate money missing from a teacher's purse was unreasonable in scope and excessively intrusive.

[45] Lamb v. Holmes, 162 S.W. 3d 902 (Ky. 2005).

[46] *Id.*

[47] 57 U.S. 364, 129 S. Ct. 2633, 174 L.Ed. 2d 354 (2009).

[48] Foster v. Raspberry, 652 F. Supp. 2d 1342 (M.D. Ga. 2009).

his desk drawer. Initially, the student asked his classmates to return the iPod, but none of the students admitted to taking the device. Shortly afterward, the student requested both the assistant principal and the school resource officer to locate the missing iPod. The school officials instructed all the students to open their backpacks, pull out their pockets, and untuck their shirts. After the initial search conducted by the assistant principal and the school resource officer, one of the students identified a female student as the person who stole the iPod. Following this allegation, the assistant principal instructed his secretary to take all the female students from the class to a storage closet. The secretary told the female student alleged to have stolen the iPod to remove her pants and underwear, where no iPod was found. The court held that the female student was subjected to a highly intrusive strip-search where there was no individualized suspicion, and the object of the search posed no immediate danger to anyone else at the school.

Three federal appellate court cases have provided guidance to school administrators regarding how and under what circumstances to conduct a student strip-search. First, in a 1993 Seventh Circuit case involving an Illinois high school student enrolled in a behavioral disorder program, school administrators acted on observations by teachers and administrators of an unusual bulge in the crotch area of the student's sweatpants. The student had been rumored to have smoked marijuana on the school bus and was known to have failed to complete an off-campus drug rehabilitation program. Teachers and students had previously reported that the student had been in possession of drugs at school. Believing that the student was hiding drugs in the crotch of his underwear, two male administrators accompanied the student to a locker room and observed the student after directing him to remove his street clothes and put on a gym uniform. In the course of the observation, no drugs were discovered.

The federal appeals court found that the administrators based their decision to conduct the search on a number of factors that justified the intrusive procedures. Given the reports by various teachers and aides, the student's history, and the administrator's observations, the totality of circumstances created a reasonable suspicion that the student was concealing drugs. The search was regarded as reasonable in scope because the search was conducted in the privacy of the locker area by persons of the same sex as the student, the student was allowed to change into gym clothes while his street clothing was physically examined, and the administrators stood a discreet distance from the student to undertake a visual inspection.[49]

Four years later, the Seventh Circuit upheld another student strip-search challenge. Here, a high school administrator who was supervising a student participating in an after-school smoking cessation program conducted a less-intrusive strip-search. The student had been caught smoking at school on two previous occasions and was required to attend the after-school program. During the program, he was noisy and distracting, his eyes were bloodshot and dilated,

---

[49] Cornfield v. Consol. High Sch. Dist. No. 130, 991 F.2d 1316 (7th Cir. 1993).

and his handwriting appeared erratic. The administrator suspected the student was using drugs and took him to the school nurse's office for evaluation. The nurse noted that the student's blood pressure and pulse were high and confirmed that the student's eyes appeared dilated. Although the nurse could not conclude that the student had been using drugs, the administrator took the student to a private room and required him to remove his shirt, hat, shoes, and socks. At all times, the student continued to wear his undershirt and pants. No drugs were discovered during the search.

In response to a civil suit against the administrator and the school district, the Seventh Circuit ruled that the search did not deny the protections of the Fourth Amendment. The court regarded the student's behavior and condition to be an appropriate basis on which to ground a suspicion of drug use, and held that the search was both justified at its inception and reasonably related to its objective. While recognizing that the more intrusive the search, the greater the standard of reasonable suspicion required, the court did not regard this search as unreasonably intrusive, particularly since the search was less intrusive than requiring the student to strip off all clothing.[50]

Nine years later, a Second Circuit court of appeals case reinforced the high standard necessary to conduct a legal strip-search. The case addressed a pre-announced search of all student bags prior to an off-campus trip, during which a lighter and cigarettes were found in a student's purse. Another student on the trip told a teacher that the student had expressed her intent to hide marijuana down her pants during the bag search. School personnel brought the student's mother to school and directed her to undertake a strip-search of the student under the supervision of the school nurse, predicating reasonable suspicion on what they viewed as a reliable informant, the student's past history of discipline problems, her denial of the allegation that she possessed marijuana, and possession of the lighter and cigarettes. The strip-search, which included having the student drop her skirt to the floor and pull her underpants away from her body to demonstrate nothing was hidden, did not reveal any marijuana. In rejecting an award of summary judgment for the school officials and the district, the Second Circuit insisted on a stringent standard of reasonable suspicion when strip-searches are involved, determining that the factors on which school officials relied were suspect because there was insufficient evidence establishing the reliability of the informant, the student's discipline problems were not related to drug use, school personnel did not explain why the student's denial was suspicious, and the contraband was not demonstrated to be related to illegal drug use.[51]

In a federal district court decision, four Michigan students reported to the assistant principal that a 14-year-old with attention deficit hyperactivity

---

[50] Bridgman v. New Trier High Sch. Dist. No.203, 128 F.3d 1146 (7th Cir. 1997).

[51] Phaneuf v. Fraikin, 448 F. 3d 591 (2d Cir. 2006). On remand, a federal district court granted qualified immunity to the school employees involved in the search on the grounds that the student's rights were not clearly established at the time the strip-search was conducted. Phaneuf v. Cipriano, 2007 U.S. Dist. LEXIS 5963 (D. Conn. 2007).

disorder had a dime roll of marijuana, which they had either seen or heard the student acknowledge. No marijuana was found in an initial search of the student's gym bag and pockets. Later that day, the four students reported to the assistant principal that the student had hidden the dime roll of marijuana between his buttocks. The assistant principal was aware that this student was regularly teased and bullied by the four students in class, that all four of the students were to be disciplined with a detention for damaging his property while at school, and that one of the students previously had been searched and found to be in possession of marijuana. The assistant principal and a school resource officer were present when the student was asked about the marijuana and repeatedly asserted that he had nothing to hide. The AP requested that the student "drop his drawers." Both the officer and the assistant principal testified that they advised the student he did not have to comply, and the search had to be entirely voluntary. They testified that the student seemed relaxed and eager to comply with the request. The student did lower his undershorts, and the officer pulled back the waistband to examine the space between the student's buttocks.

In rejecting the contention that the assistant principal and the school resource officer were protected by qualified immunity, the federal district court found the search highly intrusive and unaccompanied by the extensive investigation and careful accumulation of information that might justify a strip-search. The court ruled that the student's repeated statement that he had nothing to hide was not consent to a search and reasoned that consent is never to be presumed. Considering the "consent" in light of the totality of circumstances, the student's vulnerability, youth, and behavioral conditions affecting his impulse control and decision-making capacity mitigated against an informed and willing waiver of his privacy rights. As to the search, the court held it was neither justified at inception nor reasonable in scope. The court noted that the students who provided evidence all had a potential vendetta against the student, and that diminished their credibility.[52]

Typically, strip-search cases revolve around a particular student who school officials believe has weapons or drugs on their person. In the absence of individualized suspicion, school officials should be particularly wary of undertaking strip-searches. For instance, six seventh-grade girls from Indiana sued the school district and school employees for violating their rights under the Fourth Amendment in conducting a strip-search. The search was initiated when it was reported that $4.50 was missing from the girls' locker room at the end of a physical education class. The school principal directed that a search of the lockers and the students be undertaken. The search began with an inspection of lockers and bookbags, and then each of the girls was brought into the locker room to determine whether the missing money might be hidden in a bra. The federal district court ruled that strip-searching the seventh-grade girls was not reasonable, rejecting the claim of the principal and teachers that their actions

---

[52] Fewless *ex rel.* Fewless v. Bd. of Educ. of Wayland, 208 F. Supp. 2d 806 (W.D. Mich. 2002).

were protected under the doctrine of qualified immunity.[53] In the court's view, conducting a strip-search in an effort to recover the "grand sum" of $4.50 from young students was clearly a violation of the Fourth Amendment.[54] Similarly, in 2011, a North Carolina appellate court threw out drug-related evidence found while school administrators conducted general strip-searches of all students, seeking to find pills alleged to have been coming into the school. The court noted, "While certain aspects of the search here may have been reasonable based on the general suspicion that pills were coming into the school, the search of the student's bra without individualized grounds for suspecting that she had the pills on her person, was excessively intrusive."[55]

While some courts have granted immunity to public school employees who undertook strip-searches in the absence of individualized suspicion,[56] the Supreme Court of New Mexico confirmed the prevailing view of administrator liability for strip-searches. In that case, students who were strip-searched down to their undergarments to locate another student's missing ring were granted compensatory and punitive damages against school officials who violated their right to privacy. Students were subjected to highly intrusive searches when they exited the detention classroom to use toilet facilities. Two school employees would observe students through open stall doors while they urinated; then each student would be directed to leave their pants and underwear down for inspection after urinating. Following this inspection, students were told to lift their shirt or blouse, and female students were directed to lift their bras, exposing their breasts.

The Supreme Court of New Mexico refused to grant qualified immunity to the school employees for their conduct in initiating the highly intrusive searches.[57] The court quoted from a Seventh Circuit Court of Appeals decision that stated, "It does not require a constitutional scholar to conclude that a nude search of a thirteen-year-old child is an invasion of constitutional rights of some

---

[53] Under this doctrine, school officials would be immune from liability if their conduct did not violate clearly established rights of which a reasonable official would have been aware at the time of the conduct.

[54] Oliver by Hines v. McClung, 919 F. Supp. 1206 (N.D. Ind. 1995). See also Bell v. Marseilles Elementary Sch., 160 F. Supp. 2d 883 (N.D. Ill. 2001), in which a school resource officer's strip-search of 30 students in a gym class to find missing money violated privacy rights and the officer was not entitled to immunity.

[55] In re T.A.S., 713 S.E.2d 211, 216-17 (N.C. App. 2011).

[56] Jenkins v. Talladega City Bd. of Educ., 115 F.3d 821 (11th Cir. 1997). See also Thomas ex rel. Thomas v. Roberts, 323 F.3d 950 (11th Cir. 2003), in which strip-searches of male fifth-grade students to locate the sum of $26 missing from a student's desk was ruled unreasonably excessive, but the appeals court affirmed the district court's grant of qualified immunity. But see H.Y. v. Russell Cnty. Bd. of Educ., 490 F. Supp. 2d 1174 (E.D. Ala. 2007), in which school officials were not entitled to qualified immunity in a strip-search of middle school students to find $12 stolen from a teacher's purse. Konop v. Northwestern Sch. Dist., 26 F. Supp. 2d 1189 (D.S.D. 1998), in which the federal district court found a strip-search of female students participating in a gym class was unreasonable in light of the nature of the infraction, which involved locating the missing $200 allegedly taken from a student's locker.

[57] Kennedy v. Dexter Consol. Schs., 129 N.M. 436, 10 P.3d 115 (N.M. 2000).

magnitude."⁵⁸ The state supreme court first emphasized that no individualized suspicion accompanied the searches of students. Finding that the searches were not justified at inception, the court went on to note that such a highly intrusive search "was excessive in light of (the student's) youth, the significant possibility that the ring was simply lost and no infraction had occurred, and the non-dangerousness of the hypothesized infraction."⁵⁹

One exception to the general rule of avoiding a student strip-search may apply to investigations involving victims of sexual abuse. In one case involving the visual examination of a child's body, a federal appeals court ruled that school officials are entitled to qualified immunity when investigating whether a child has been abused, particularly when the investigation is initiated after the student has complained of pain in an area and is evasive about the circumstances that led to a suspected abuse injury.⁶⁰ In another case in which a sixth-grader alleged that a classmate had sexually assaulted her, a school resource officer who interviewed the student and a nurse who conducted a brief physical examination of the student to verify scratches on her back and arms were insulated from liability. The federal district court applied the two-pronged test of *T.L.O.* in determining that the search was justified at inception and reasonable in scope, reasoning that the school had a "great, even overwhelming" interest in the conduct of a sexual assault investigation involving a student.⁶¹ In response to the parent's contention that no investigation should have been conducted without parental presence and consent, the court acknowledged parental concerns for potential emotional trauma, but found the school's compelling need to promptly investigate incidents of student-on-student violence must prevail.⁶²

Searches Off of School Grounds

As judges have become increasingly supportive of school search policies involving the possession and/or use of drugs or weapons, there have been an increasing number of situations in which students supervised off school grounds during school-sponsored trips or programs have led judges to approve extraordinary measures involving student searches. Specifically, under a New Jersey junior high school's policy, students who participated in a voluntary field trip and picnic were subjected to a search of hand luggage before boarding the trip bus. School officials required parental approval, using a permission slip

---

⁵⁸ *Id.* at 441, 10 P.2d at 121, *citing* Doe v. Renfrow, 631 F.2d 91, 92-93 (7th Cir. 1980).

⁵⁹ *Id.* at 444, 10 P.2d at 123.

⁶⁰ Landstrom v. Ill. Dep't of Children and Family Servs., 892 F.2d 670 (7th Cir. 1990). *See also* Tenenbaum v. Williams, 193 F.3d 581 (2d Cir. 1999), in which qualified immunity applied to a child's removal from school and medical examination for signs of sexual abuse.

⁶¹ Wilson v. Cahokia Sch. Dist., 470 F. Supp. 2d 897, 911-912 (S.D. Ill. 2007).

⁶² *Id.* at 912. *See also* Villanueva v. San Marcos Consol. Indep. Sch. Dist., 2007 U.S. LEXIS 17208 (5th Cir. 2007), in which the federal appeals court affirmed a grant of summary judgment to a school nurse and school district after finding that a student's subjective belief that she was required to complete a pregnancy test at school and her unsubstantiated speculation that to refuse to take the test would have resulted in punishment did not constitute competent summary judgment evidence.

that included a statement that hand luggage would be searched. A state appeals court concluded that the interest of school officials in ensuring that students did not bring prohibited contraband on a field trip justified the policy. Although there was no evidence of individualized suspicion for the search, the court rationalized the general search policy by pointing to its deterrent potential in discouraging students from bringing prohibited items. The court also noted the special duty of supervision that was created in the context of a field trip, since supervising teachers would not have the level of control over students that was available in the school setting.[63]

Another interesting case involved a school principal/chaperone's decision to search student motel rooms during a class trip to Disney World. Prior to the trip, students were given a brochure that specifically warned they would be subjected to "room checks." Parents signed a form accepting responsibility for the costs of travel if their child were sent home early from the trip based on misconduct. The notice to parents also included a statement that possession or use of drugs or alcohol would result in early departure. The school administrator and his wife were returning to their room when they detected the strong odor of marijuana in the hallway adjacent to student rooms. The principal contacted the hotel representative, and they entered the rooms of students on the floor where the marijuana had been detected and also accessed the safes in those rooms. Marijuana and alcohol were found in the safe. The federal district court ruled that the search was reasonable under all the circumstances, noting that the students and parents were cautioned about the use of drugs or alcohol on the trip and students had been informed of the likelihood of room checks. This information reduced the students' expectation of privacy on the trip. More to the point, however, the court emphasized that school trips often present greater challenges to school personnel trying to maintain order and discipline than in-school settings. As a consequence, the school administrator's actions were regarded as reasonable; to hold otherwise would subject him to a greater risk of liability for injury to students, while at the same time denying him the authority necessary to lessen the risk of injury.[64]

Special Needs Doctrine

To be reasonable under the Fourth Amendment, a search should be based on individualized suspicion of wrongdoing. There are times, however, that exceptions to the individualized suspicion requirement in schools are justified based upon "special needs" beyond the control of local school officials; this is referred to as the Doctrine of Special Needs. Such special needs must be supported by the establishment of concerns for the health and well-being of

---

[63] Desilets v. Clearview Bd. of Educ., 265 N.J. Super. 370, 627 A.2d 667 (N.J. Super A.D. 1993). *But see* Kuehn v. Renton Sch. Dist., 694 P.2d 1078 (Wash. 1985), in which a blanket policy requiring the search of student luggage before a class trip was unreasonable because there was no individualized suspicion for a search.

[64] Rhodes v. Guarricino, 54 F. Supp. 2d 186 (S.D.N.Y. 1999).

students, while being balanced against the nature of the student's expectation of privacy interests and the degree of intrusion involved with that interest.[65] As such, the courts have recognized limited instances where the individualized suspicion of students is not always required in school environments. For example, the United States Supreme Court held in *Vernonia School District 47J v. Acton* that the random drug testing of student athletes does not require individualized suspicion.[66] As indicated by the courts, the Doctrine of Special Needs does not only apply to student athletes. In California, for example, a high school established a policy of randomly searching students' backpacks once a month as a means to maintain a drug- and weapon-free school.[67] During one random search of student backpacks, several school officials recognized that a particular student was acting nervously after he emptied the contents of his backpack. Upon closer examination of the inside of his backpack, the school officials found several bags of marijuana. The high school student subsequently was prosecuted as a juvenile and argued that the school lacked individualized suspicion to search his backpack. The court upheld the high school's randomized backpack search, stating that "the needs of schools to keep weapons off campuses is substantial" and that the Doctrine of Special Needs could be invoked in this case.[68] More recently, the United States Supreme Court expanded the Doctrine of Special Needs in *Board of Education of Independent School District No. 92 of Pottawatomie County v. Earls* to include the drug testing of all students participating in after-school activities.[69]

As a federal case from the Eighth Circuit Court of Appeals illustrates, a school district's practice of conducting random searches in secondary school classrooms is vulnerable to a Fourth Amendment challenge. Under the search protocol, students were directed to exit the classroom after removing all the contents from their pockets and placing all of their belongings, including backpacks and purses, on their desks. While waiting in the hall outside the classroom, a student's purse was searched, and marijuana was discovered in a container. The federal appeals court acknowledged that a student's legitimate expectation of privacy in personal belongings is limited in the school setting, but held that the school district's practice of subjecting students to full-scale, suspicionless searches effectively eliminated privacy in a student's personal belongings and was unaccompanied by any compelling justification.[70] In assessing the intrusiveness of the search against the student's expectation of privacy under the Fourth Amendment, the court emphasized:

> While the line separating reasonable and unreasonable school searches is sometimes indistinct, we think it plain enough that

---

[65] *See* Kennedy v. Dexter Consol. Schs., 129 N.M. 436, 10 P.3d 115 (N.M. 2000); Burnham v. West, 681 F. Supp. 1160 (E.D. Va. 1987); and Bellnier v. Lund, 438 F. Supp. 47 (N.D.N.Y. 1977).
[66] 515 U.S. 646 (1995).
[67] *In re* Daniel A., 2012 WL 2126539 (Cal. App. 2 Dist.).
[68] *Id.* at 5.
[69] Bd. of Educ. of Indep. Sch. Dist.t No. 92 of Pottawatomie Cnty. v. Earls, 536 U.S. 822 (2002).
[70] Doe v. Little Rock Sch. Dist., 380 F.3d 349 (8th Cir. 2004).

the (school district's) search practice crosses it. In light of the government's legitimate interest in maintaining discipline and safety in the public schools, the privacy that students in those schools are reasonably entitled to expect is limited. The (district's) search practice, however, effectively reduces these expectations to nothing, and the record contains no evidence of unique circumstances that would justify significant intrusions. The mere assertion that there are substantial problems associated with drugs and weapons in its schools does not give the (district) *carte blanche* to inflict highly intrusive, random searches upon its general student body.[71]

Even when searches do not involve the allegation of wrongdoing, the intrusive nature of a general search may implicate the Fourth Amendment. For example, the Tenth Circuit Court of Appeals reasoned that physical examinations required under provisions of a Head Start program could not be undertaken by school officials absent express parental consent. The examinations were performed on preschool students by registered nurses, who relocated the children to an empty classroom and used desks as examining tables. Children were required to remove their underclothes and submit to a genital examination and blood test. A federal appeals court concluded that the examinations were searches within the meaning of the Fourth Amendment and found that none of the forms the defendants provided gave explicit authorization to conduct the examination. Although the school district contended that a "special need" justified the search, the court held that school officials had acted out of carelessness and neglect rather than recognition that compliance with Fourth Amendment requirements would be impracticable.[72]

On the other hand, judges have also reasoned that both the magnitude and immediacy of a potential threat in the school setting may permit a school's use of a general search, including a pat-down search, when school officials have exhausted all other reasonable alternatives to such a search. For example, when a kitchen knife was reported missing following a middle school lunch period in which pizza had been served, school officials first searched the cafeteria area and then asked students in the cafeteria to come forward if they had information concerning the missing knife. When no student came forward, the school's vice principal obtained permission from the principal to conduct a pat-down of students. The students were divided into two groups, male and female, and were patted down by staff of the same sex. The knife was not found, and a 10-year-old student filed suit alleging a denial of Fourth Amendment rights to privacy. In rejecting the suit, a federal district court found the search was conducted in the least intrusive manner possible consistent with its purpose, and was justified by urgent and immediate concerns for the safety and welfare of students.[73]

---

[71] *Id.* at 357.
[72] Dubbs v. Head Start, 336 F.3d 1194 (10th Cir. 2003).
[73] Brousseau v. Town of Westerly, 11 F. Supp. 177 (D.R.I. 1998).

Detection Dogs Used in School Searches

In contrast to intrusive general searches, which receive heightened judicial scrutiny, judges have emphasized that using drug- and weapon-detection dogs,[74] as well as metal detectors,[75] is clearly permissible as part of a general search policy. School districts have characterized these approaches as screening devices rather than actual searches. When the screening procedures are minimally intrusive and there is no expectation of privacy in the object being searched, judges have affirmed the legitimacy of such practices. For example, when a Texas school district adopted a policy of random searches using detection dogs trained to look for drugs, alcohol, firearms, and other contraband in student automobiles parked on school property, a federal appeals court sustained the policy. The court emphasized that if it could be demonstrated that the dog had been proven reliable in detecting drugs, then the search of an automobile parked on school property is justified once the dog alerts.[76] Similarly, when a trained drug-detection dog alerted that a student's truck parked on school grounds might contain drugs, school officials had reasonable grounds to search the vehicle. The fact that a machete was found in the toolbox of the vehicle, instead of drugs, did not invalidate the search. The federal district court reasoned that the school official was legally in a position to view the contents of the toolbox when he discovered the machete, and taking possession of the machete constituted a valid plain-view seizure.[77]

While the use of drug-detection dogs to sniff areas that are not entitled to privacy—including lockers, automobiles, desks, and backpacks—does not constitute a search, federal courts appear divided on the issue of whether the use of a drug-detection dog to sniff a student would constitute a search requiring individualized suspicion. In 1981, the Seventh Circuit Court of Appeals took the position that the use of detection dogs to screen students was not a search that would require reasonable suspicion.[78] Given nearly identical factual circumstances, one year later the Fifth Circuit ruled otherwise, taking the view that using a dog to sniff a student was "indecent and demeaning," and held that

---

[74] *See, generally,* Bundick v. Bay City Indep. Sch. Dist., 140 F. Supp. 2d 735 (S.D. Tex. 2001) (drug-detection dog's alert to student's parked car justified search that led to discovery of machete in toolbox); Commonwealth v. Cass, 551 Pa. 25,709 A.2d 350 (Pa. 1998) (canine sniffing of student lockers justified by danger of drug use and limited expectation of privacy in school lockers); and State v. Barrett, 683 So. 2d 331 (La. Ct. App. 1996) (use of drug-detection dogs permissible to sniff selected classes consisting of "problem students" given concern for drug use and minimal intrusion on student privacy).

[75] *See, e.g., In re* Latasha W., 60 Cal. App. 4th 1524, 70 Cal. Rptr. 2d 886 (Cal. Ct. App. 1998) (metal detector used to discover knife); State v. J.A., 679 So. 2d 316 (Fla. Dist. Ct. App. 1996) (metal detector followed by pat-down and discovery of a handgun); *In re* S.S., 452 Pa. Super. 15, 680 A.2d 1172 (Pa. Sup. 1996) (boxcutter knife discovered during scan of students and pat-down of coat); and People v. Pruitt, 278 Ill. App. Ct. 3d 194, 662 N.E.2d 540 (Ill. App. Ct. 1996) (walk-through detector resulted in pat-down and discovery of handgun).

[76] Jennings v. Joshua Indep. Sch. Dist., 877 F.2d 313 (5th Cir. 1989). *See also* Horton v. Goose Creek Indep. Sch. Dist., 690 F.2d 470 (5th Cir. 1982).

[77] Bundick v. Bay City Indep. Sch. Dist., 140 F. Supp. 2d 735 (S.D. Tex. 2001).

[78] Doe v. Renfrow, 631 F.2d 91 (7th Cir. 1981).

the use would only be permissible if reasonable suspicion were established.[79] Finally, almost 20 years later, the Ninth Circuit Court of Appeals addressed this same question in the context of a high school search in which local law enforcement officials cooperated with school officials to arrange for the use of drug-detection dogs to inspect classrooms. As students exited the classroom, they walked by the dog, and in some instances, the dog alerted. The federal appeals court ruled that this protocol constituted a search of the students, concluding that the search was highly intrusive because it was involuntary and the use of dogs could engender fear. The court determined that the public school's interest in deterring student drug use would not have been placed in jeopardy by a requirement of individualized suspicion prior to the use of drug-detection dogs on students.[80]

Metal Detectors Used in School Searches

Public school district use of a metal detector has Fourth Amendment implications since "performing a search is the very purpose and function" of a metal detector.[81] However, whenever weapons are implicated, the degree of flexibility in the conduct of blanket student searches appears to increase. For example, a New York high school with an ongoing problem of violence and weapons possession among students set up metal detector scanning posts in the main lobby of the building. Students were told to remove all metal objects before passing through the posts; when crowding became a problem, a random procedure was used to select students who would pass through the metal detector. If a student activated the device, that student was told to remove all metal objects and cross through the posts a second time. If the student activated the detector a second time, a pat-down search was conducted. Using this procedure, a female student was discovered to have a switchblade knife. When she sought to suppress the weapon in a later criminal prosecution, the court ruled that the search was permissible, emphasizing that the use of a metal detector was a minimally intrusive search, and the more intrusive pat-down was only undertaken after the scanning device was twice activated.[82] In another case, a school board hired a private security firm to conduct searches

---

[79] Horton v. Goose Creek Indep. Sch. Dist., 690 F.2d 470, 479 (5th Cir. 1982).

[80] B.C. v. Plumas Unified Sch. Dist., 192 F.3d 1260, 1268 (9th Cir. 1999). In this case, the court granted qualified immunity to the defendants on the basis that it was not clearly established at the time of the searches that the use of dogs to sniff students in a school setting constituted a search.

[81] Pruitt, 278 Ill. App. Ct. 3d 194, 201, 662 N.E.2d 540, 545, *citing* United States v. Epperson, 454 F.2d 769, 770 (4th Cir. 1972). Here, a student passing through the metal detector set off the alarm and was subject to a pat-down by a police officer, who discovered a handgun. When the student sought to suppress this evidence in a criminal trial, a state appeals court held that the screening was minimally intrusive since no touching occurred unless the detector alerted, and, once the detector reacted, the facts were sufficient to justify a pat-down.

[82] People v. Duke, 183 A.D.2d 936, 583 N.Y.S.2d 850 (N.Y. App. Div. 1992).

in the district's schools with a hand-held metal detector.[83] School officials noticed a jacket being passed to the back of a high school classroom by students. School officials proceeded to retrieve the jacket, identify its owner, and scan it with a hand-held metal detector. During the scan, a gun was found in one of the jacket's pockets. Upholding the metal detector search, the court held that intrusive search was justified due to the more important purpose of keeping other students and staff safe.

An urban Pennsylvania high school enforced its policy forbidding drugs or weapons on school property by employing police officers to conduct metal detector scans and bag searches of students. Signs were posted warning of the search policy, and parents were notified of the policy periodically during the year. The procedure for conducting the searches involved bringing students into the gym, where they formed lines and stepped up to a table. At the table, students emptied their pockets, surrendered jackets or any bags in their possession, and were scanned by an officer using a metal detector. When a student surrendered a knife while emptying his pockets, he was arrested for possession of a weapon on school property. The Supreme Court of Pennsylvania held the search was justified given the high rate of violence in the district's public schools.[84]

Florida secondary school students were subjected to random, hand-held metal detector scans conducted in classrooms. Under the protocol, a classroom would be randomly selected, and students would be segregated by gender and directed to remove all metal objects from their clothing. If a detector sounded, the student would be asked to remove the metal object before a second scan. If the detector sounded a second time, the area would be patted down. During the search process, a student was observed taking off his jacket and moving it to the back of the room while the scanning procedure was taking place. The jacket was patted down, and a handgun was discovered. A state appeals court found that the search policy minimized the intrusion into students' privacy while meeting the school district's immediate concern to deter the presence of weapons in schools and promote a safe learning environment.[85]

Random Urinalysis Drug Testing

The United States Supreme Court has concluded that a school district's interest in deterring drug use and the desirability of reducing the risk of injury associated with drug use among students engaged in athletic programs and extracurricular activities justifies random urinalysis testing. In the first of two

---

[83] State v. J.A., 679 So.2d 316 (Fla. Dist. Ct. App. 1996), *review denied*, 689 So. 2d 1069 (Fla. 1997), *cert denied*, 522 U.S. 831 (1997).

[84] *In re* Interest of F.B., 555 Pa. 661, 726 A.2d 361 (Pa. 1999). *See* In Interest of S.S., 452 Pa. Super. 15, 680 A.2d 1172 (Pa. Super. 1996), in which a blanket search that included a pat-down of a student's coat was reasonable, though not based on individualized suspicion. On entering the school, students placed their coats on a table and were subject to a metal detector scan. In patting down the student's coat, a box cutter was discovered, and the student was subjected to juvenile court prosecution. The state court found that the search was reasonable given the uniformity of the search process and documentation of a high rate of violence in area schools.

[85] State v. J.A., 679 So. 2d 316 (Fla. Dist. Ct. App. 1996).

decisions, in 1995 the Court affirmed an Oregon high school's policy requiring random drug testing of student-athletes.[86] Granting that the drug testing of student-athletes was a search under the Fourth Amendment, the Court noted the results of the tests remained confidential and were neither released to law enforcement nor used for disciplinary purposes. The Court's majority balanced the intrusiveness of the search against the school district's legitimate interest in discouraging drug use, reasoned that the process of obtaining urine samples was not highly intrusive, and held that any compromise of the students' privacy interest was justified by the school district's substantial and important interest in fighting drug abuse among student-athletes.[87]

Seven years later, the United States Supreme Court extended the scope of permissible random urinalysis testing in public schools to all middle and high school students participating in "any" extracurricular activities[88] The Court majority once again balanced the student's interest in privacy against the school district's "custodial and tutelary responsibility," reasoning that students who participate in extracurricular activities voluntarily subject themselves to intrusions that lessen any expectation of privacy that might apply to the student body as a whole. The Court ruled that the government's interest outweighed the student's privacy rights. In reaching its decision, the Court's majority noted that urinalysis testing was an insubstantial interference with privacy, and the school district's interest was sufficient even if there was no evidence of a pervasive drug problem at the school or among students participating in extracurricular programs.[89]

Federal courts have also ruled on challenges to school districts' attempts to extend the use of mandatory drug testing beyond extracurricular activities. For example, the Seventh Circuit federal appeals court approved a school district policy requiring mandatory urinalysis testing, not only for students participating in extracurricular activities, but also for those students who drove an automobile on school grounds.[90] The appeals court emphasized that the school district had established sufficient evidence of a governmental need to test students using automobiles on campus for alcohol and marijuana use solely because the danger of even one student driving on school property while impaired was substantial.[91]

---

[86] Vernonia Sch. Dist. v. Acton, 515 U.S. 646, 115 S. Ct. 2386, 132 L. Ed. 2d 564 (1995).
[87] *Id.*
[88] Board of Educ. of Indep. Sch. Dist. No. 92 v. Earls, 536 U.S. 822, 122 S. Ct. 2559, 153 L. Ed. 2d 735 (2002).
[89] *But see*, York v. Wahkiakum Sch. Dist. No. 200, 178 P.3d 995 (2008 Wash.), in which the Supreme Court of Washington ruled that a school district's policy of conducting random drug testing violated student-athletes' rights under the state constitution.
[90] Joy v. Penn-Harris-Madison Sch. Corp., 212 F.3d 1052 (7th Cir. 2000).
[91] *Id.* at 1065. The policy could not be extended to testing for the use of nicotine, as the school district could not demonstrate a sufficient governmental need to justify this intrusion.

However, the application of random drug testing to students participating in the regular school curriculum remains suspect.[92] Again, out of the Seventh Circuit, the court rejected a school district policy requiring drug and alcohol testing for students suspended for fighting.[93] The appeals court ruled the policy violated the students' Fourth Amendment rights because the search could not be justified on the basis of either a reasonable suspicion or a special need that would permit suspicionless testing. In the appellate court's view, the student's violent behavior would not justify a reasonable suspicion of drug use, and a district's special need for drug testing could not be supported. The federal appeals court distinguished the case from other "special need" situations by noting that the voluntary participation of students in extracurricular activities involves a conscious decision to submit to policies that reduce the student's expectation of privacy, while a student's "unauthorized participation in disfavored activities"[94] (fighting) does not permit the same inference.[95]

Similarly, a federal district court in Texas struck down a school board policy in which a student's or parent's refusal to consent to drug testing was construed as the equivalent of a "positive" test. The student's first offense subjected him to suspension from participation in all extracurricular activities for 21 days and removal to in-school suspension for a minimum of three days. Continued refusal by a parent to consent to the child's being tested for drugs would, as with continued positive test results, result in escalation up to placing the child in an alternative school and disqualifying him from participating in any activity or receiving any honors for the year. Considering the students' increased expectation of privacy in the regular school setting and the dearth of evidence demonstrating a need to be met by the search, the federal court ruled that the district's drug testing program was unconstitutional under the Fourth Amendment.[96]

---

[92] See Trinidad v. Lopez, 963 P.2d 1095 (Colo. Sup. Ct. 1998), in which the state supreme court struck down random urinalysis drug testing as applied to the co-curricular marching band program. The court noted the marching band program was also an academic program, and there was no evidence to show a significant drug problem among the band participants or risk of physical injury.

[93] Willis by Willis v. Anderson Cmty. Sch. Corp., 158 F.3d 415 (7th Cir. 1998), cert. denied, 119 S. Ct. 1254, 143 L.Ed.2d 351 (1999). See also, Gruenke v. Seip, 225 F.3d 290 (3d Cir. 2000), in which a mandatory pregnancy test required by a high school swimming coach violated the student's right to privacy and her Fourth Amendment rights against unreasonable search and seizure.

[94] Id. at 422.

[95] The use of urinalysis testing in a case of reasonable individualized suspicion is illustrated in Hedges v. Musco, 204 F.3d 109 (3d Cir. 2000), in which a student who appeared to be under the influence of drugs was evaluated by a school nurse and, as a consequence, a school requirement that the student submit to a drug test before being readmitted to school was reasonable under all the circumstances.

[96] Tannahill ex rel. Tannahill v. Lockney Indep. Sch. Dist., 133 F. Supp. 2d 919 (N.D. Tex. 2001).

Searches of Student Cell Phones and Related Technological Devices

Over the past decade, searches of students' cell phones and related technological devices while on school premises have grown dramatically. Nearly 88% of the nation's teenagers owned or had access to a cell phone or smartphone in a 2015 study, and approximately 90% of those teenagers used these devices as their primary form of communication with their peers.[97] Generally, the search of student cell phones and related technological devices fall under the Fourth Amendment's legal standard of reasonableness set forth in the Supreme Court's seminal *New Jersey v. T.L.O.* ruling. Despite *T.L.O.'s* existing reasonable suspicion standard, there is considerable uncertainty, especially among the nation's lower courts, as to whether school officials can legally search students' cell phones without violating their Fourth Amendment privacy rights. In 2014, the United States Supreme Court held in *Riley v. California* that the search of a cell phone or related technological device incident to an arrest requires law enforcement officers to obtain a warrant.[98] In *Riley*, all nine Supreme Court justices unanimously acknowledged the pervasiveness of cell phone usage in society, as well as the unique privacy concerns posed by these modern technological devices.[99] While the impact of the *Riley* ruling on student cell phone searches is still uncertain, the decision clearly redefines the heightened expectation of privacy applied to an individual's digitally stored information on cell phones and related devices.

A related controversy facing today's school administrators is whether students' increased expectation of privacy related to their cellphones or related devices outweighs a school's interest in maintaining order and protecting student safety. Two lower court decisions illustrate the current confusion concerning how to properly apply the *T.L.O.* precedent and the reasonable suspicion standard to the search of student cell phones and related devices. In the first case, *Klump v. Nazareth Area School District*, a Pennsylvania teacher confiscated a high school student's cell phone because the student was violating the district's policy restricting the use of cell phones during official school hours.[100] Allegedly, the teacher and assistant principal called nine other students found on the student's cell phone number directory to determine if they also violated the district's restrictive cell phone policy, accessed the student's text messages, and had an instant messaging conversation with the student's younger

---

[97] See Mary Madden, et al., Pew Research Ctr., Teens, Social Media, and Technology Overview 2015, at 4 (2015), http://www.pewinternet.org/2015/04/09/teens-social-media-technology-2015/ (highlighting the fact that nearly 90% of teenagers own or have access to a cell phone or smartphone).

[98] Riley v. California, 134 S. Ct. 2473 (2014) (holding that law enforcement officers are now required to possess warrants to search the digital information found on cellphones and other personal electronic devices from arrested persons, unless an emergency circumstance exists).

[99] See Kevin P. Brady, *Student Cell Phone Searches Reasonable Suspicion in a Digital Age: The Future Implications of Riley v. California*, 309 Educ. L. Rep. 1 (2014).

[100] Klump v. Narareth Area Sch. Dist., 425 F. Supp. 2d 622 (E.D. Pa. 2006).

brother without identifying themselves as school officials. The assistant principal informed the student's parents that a text message on the student's cell phone made reference to marijuana. The court held that while the teacher was justified in confiscating the student's cell phone based on district policy prohibiting the possession or use of cell phones, the teacher and assistant principal unreasonably searched the student's cell phone. In the *Klump* case, the court held that school officials had no reasonable reason to suspect at the outset that a search of the student's cell phone would reveal that the student violated the district's policy against drug use. In a second lower court case, *J.W. v. Desoto County School District*, a Mississippi court reached a completely different decision and upheld a student's cell phone search by school officials.[101]

In *J.W.*, a middle school student brought a cell phone to school and opened the phone to retrieve a text message. When a school official witnessed the student using the cell phone, he asked the student for the cell phone and the student consented. Once in possession of the cell phone, the school official opened the student's cell phone and proceeded to review pictures on the phone, including a picture of a student holding a BB gun. The cell phone was then shown to the school principal and a police sergeant. Upon their review of the picture, the student was expelled from school. The court held that it was reasonable for school officials to suspect a student of communicating with another student based on the student's improper cell phone usage in direct violation of school policy.

Another legal case addresses the boundaries of reasonableness involving searches of students' electronic messages or digitally stored images on their cellphones or related technological devices. In the case of *In re Rafael C.*, several school administrators suspected that a student was involved in an incident involving a discarded firearm discovered in a trash can on school premises.[102] Shortly after finding the discarded firearm, the assistant principal brought the student into his office for questioning. During the questioning, the student became fidgety and reached into his pocket. The assistant principal asked nearby colleagues to restrain the student from reaching his hands into his pockets. While being restrained, the assistant principal reached into the student's pocket and removed his cell phone. After searching the cell phone's content, the assistant principal viewed a digital image on the student's cell phone, including a photo of the student holding what appeared to be the firearm found on school premises. Ultimately, the California Court of Appeals concluded that the search of the student's cell phone was reasonable, stating "considering all the circumstances, the search was justified at its inception and permissible in scope."[103]

---

[101] J.W. v. Desoto Cnty. Sch. Dist., No 09-00155 (N.D. Miss. Nov. 11, 2010).
[102] *In re* Rafael C., 245 Cal. App. 4th 1288 (Cal. Ct. App. 2016). (holding that school officials did not violate a student's Fourth Amendment search and seizure rights when a school administrator searched the student's cell phone in connection with an ongoing school investigation).
[103] *Id.* at 1291.

To date, the only federal-level court case addressing the constitutionality of student cell phone searches under the Fourth Amendment held that a Kentucky school administrator's search of text messages from a student's cell phone was unreasonable and violated the student's Fourth Amendment rights. In *G.C. v. Owensboro Public Schools*, the Sixth Circuit held that the search of a student's cell phone was unreasonable since it failed to satisfy reasonable suspicion.[104] A high school student voluntarily revealed to his assistant principal that he used drugs, suffered from depression, and had considered committing suicide. The assistant principal immediately notified the student's parents and he was taken to a mental health treatment facility the same day. The following school year, the student was seen texting on his cell phone in class, a violation of school rules. The teacher turned over the cell phone to another assistant principal, who read four of G.C.'s text messages on his cell phone. The assistant principal later testified that she was aware of the student's discipline issues and was looking "to see if there was an issue with which I could help him so that he would not do something harmful to himself or someone else." The Sixth Circuit's decision in *G.C.* sends a cautionary message to today's school administrators by narrowing the scope of circumstances under which school officials can legally conduct student cell phone searches under the current reasonable suspicion standard.

Another Fourth Amendment consideration for school administrators involving technology is searches involving video surveillance of school environments. In a leading case, *Brannum v. Overton County School Board*, a school district installed video camera surveillance equipment in a middle school's boys' and girls' locker rooms. The local school board approved the installation of video cameras as a constructive effort to improve school security. Video camera footage was transmitted to the assistant principal's computer terminal in his office. Additionally, the video was accessible through an internet connect to any person with the proper user name, password, and internet protocol address. Thirty-four students sued the district, claiming their constitutional rights to privacy were violated when school officials viewed and retained the captured images. The district court ruled that the video surveillance of middle school students while they changed their clothes in the locker room areas was an unreasonable search, and the students did have a legal expectation of privacy not to be unknowingly videotaped. The installation of surveillance cameras for security purposes was justified, but the camera's placement and subsequent operation was inconsistent with the intended purpose of enhanced security. The Sixth Circuit Court agreed. While granting qualified immunity to school board members and others less directly involved, this court denied qualified immunity to the middle school principal and assistant principal who were involved in the decision to install the cameras and who determined their location.

---

[104] G.C. v. Owensboro Pub. Schs., 711 F.3d 623 (6th Cir. 2013). (holding that a school official's search of the student's cell phone was an unreasonable search and seizure since, due to the school's knowledge of the student's prior behavioral problems, school officials had no specific reason at the time of the search to believe that he was engaging in an unlawful activity).

Another case, this one in Pennsylvania, resulted in the school district paying money damages related to the use of webcam information. In this instance, school officials in the Lower Merion School District monitored students at home through cameras in computers provided to students by the school.

School Searches Involving School Resource Officers (SROs) and Law Enforcement

Since the turn of the century, the presence of uniformed police officers in public schools has become commonplace.[105] Consequently, numerous court cases have been decided on the issue of whether the officers are held to a "probable cause" or "reasonable suspicion" standard of search. Typically, law enforcement officials are held to a reasonable suspicion standard when they are assisting school administrators conduct a search[106] or serving as a "school resource officer."[107] In making this determination, courts often consider "whether the officer was in uniform, whether the officer has an office on the school campus, how much time the officer is at the school each day, whether the officer is employed by the school system or an independent law enforcement agency, what the officer's duties are at the school, who initiated the investigation, who conducted the search, whether other school officials were involved, and the officer's purpose in conducting the search."[108]

In a case from Illinois, a school resource officer in an alternative school for students with discipline problems received reports from teachers that a student intended to sell drugs to students and planned to bring drugs to school that day. The student, who was suspected of drug possession, was standing at a locker with a student with a flashlight. Both students were talking and giggling, and this aroused the officer's suspicions because the two students seemed to think they were deceiving him. Considering it unusual for a student to have a flashlight at school, and knowing that both students were suspected of deal-

---

[105] Wilson v. Cahokia Sch. Dist., 470 F. Supp. 2d 897, 911-912 (S.D. Ill. 2007). The district court rejected the parent's contention that the school resource officer should be subject to the probable cause standard, determining that a sheriff's deputy serving as a school resource officer is a school employee under the direction of school authorities in the course of investigating a disciplinary infraction.

[106] Vassallo v. Lando, 591 F. Supp. 2d 172 (E.D.N.Y. 2008). *See also, In re* Angelia D.B., 211 Wis. 2d 140, 564 N.W.2d 682 (Wis. 1997), in which the court concluded that the reasonable suspicion standard should apply to trained law enforcement officers assisting administrators in the public school setting.

[107] *See,* M.D. v. State, 65 So.3d 563 (Fla. Dist. Ct. App. 2011), *reh'g denied* (2011), *review denied* (2011). *See also,* Shade v. City of Farmington, Minn., 309 F.3d 1054 (8th Cir. 2002), in which the Eighth Circuit emphasized that reasonable suspicion applies to SROs while in the scope of their duties in the school context. *But see,* State v. Meneese, 2012 Wash LEXIS 540 (Wash. 2012), in which the Supreme Court of Washington ruled that school resource officers were held to a probable cause standard when they are employed by the police department and have no ability to impose school discipline. *See also* State v. R.D.S., 2009 Tenn. App. LEXIS 440 (Tenn. App. Ct. 2009).

[108] State v. Alaniz, 815 N.W.2d 234, 238 (N.D. 2012).

ing drugs at school, the officer started a search and seized the second student's flashlight, discovering a quantity of crack cocaine in the handle. The student contended that the search was unconstitutional, but the state appeals court ruled that the reasonable suspicion standard applied to the officer when performing duties in the school setting.[109] Finding that the totality of circumstances would lead a reasonable person to suspect that the student was carrying drugs in the flashlight, the seizure and search of the flashlight were regarded as reasonable. The court emphasized that this was an alternative school for students with behavioral problems and this context, coupled with the suspicious conduct of the students and their history of suspected drug activity, heightened the urgency of maintaining a safe and secure learning environment.[110] The court was persuaded by the school official's intuitive judgment about the behavior of the students,[111] as well as his effort to develop the totality of circumstances implicating the student, including details of the context of the search, the age and history of the student, and the nature of that which was sought.

A relevant issue, especially for law enforcement officers, is the application of *Miranda* warnings against self-incrimination in school interrogation settings.[112] In 2011, the United States Supreme Court, in *J.D.B. v. North Carolina*, held that a minor student's age may be considered a relevant factor when determining whether juvenile suspects require a *Miranda* warning about their rights against self-incrimination. As a result of the Supreme Court's *J.D.B.* ruling, law enforcement officials must now take age into consideration when determining whether the juvenile suspect is in custody and entitled to the familiar warnings against self-incrimination based on the U.S. Supreme Court's 1966 *Miranda v. Arizona*

---

[109] People v. Dilworth, 169 Ill. 2d 195, 210, 661 N.E.2d 310, 319 (Ill. 1996). *See* State v. N.G.B., 806 So.2d 567 (Fla. Dist. Ct. App. 2002), in which a school resource officer's search of a student was justified on the basis of reasonable suspicion when the investigation was initiated by a school administrator, who then enlisted the officer's assistance; James v. Unified Sch. Dist., 959 F. Supp. 1407 (D. Kan. 1997), in which a police officer was granted qualified immunity for conducting a search of a vehicle on school grounds on the basis that it was not established that an officer must meet a probable cause standard when accompanying school officials in a search on school grounds; and S.A. v. State, 654 N.E.2d 791 (Ind. Ct. App. 1995), in which a search of a student's bookbag by a school liaison officer met the reasonable suspicion standard, and, when acting in his capacity as security officer for the school district, the officer's conduct was governed by the standard of reasonable suspicion. *See also* State v. D.S., 685 So. 2d 41 (Fla. Dist. Ct. App. 1996), in which the presence of a school resource officer in the conduct of a search on school grounds does not heighten the standard of reasonable suspicion for a search. *But see* State v. Tywayne H., 123 N.M. 42, 933 P.2d 251 (N.M. Ct. App. 1997), in which police acting as security for a school dance were held to a standard of probable cause for a search of a student.

[110] Dilworth, 169 Ill. 2d 195, 661 N.E.2d 310.

[111] *But see* A.S. v. State, 693 So. 2d 1095 (Fla. Dist. Ct. App. 1997), in which an assistant principal's observation that one student in a group was "fiddling" in his pockets while another was holding money in his hand would be insufficient to establish reasonable suspicion for a search of the student's wallet.

[112] Usually, when adult suspects are arrested on criminal charges, they are read their *Miranda* rights, which include the right to remain silent as well as the right to an attorney. However, *Miranda* warnings may also be required in situations that fall short of an arrest.

decision.[113] In North Carolina, J.D.B., a 13-year-old boy interrogated by a police detective in a school principal's office at the student's middle school, was suspected of being involved in a series of thefts of neighborhood homes. The police had evidence to suggest J.D.B. had stolen a digital camera and jewelry, and went to his school to interrogate him. The student was taken out of class and escorted to a conference room, where he was interrogated by the police in the presence of the school's assistant principal and an administrative intern. At one point, the assistant principal urged J.D.B. to "do the right thing" because "the truth always comes out in the end."[114] The student was subsequently charged in juvenile court with breaking and entering, and larceny. A trial court refused to suppress his confession, ruling that J.D.B. was not in police custody during the school interrogation, and thus no *Miranda* warning was required. As a result of the *J.D.B.* decision, in instances that involve interrogations of minor students conducted on school premises, courts must assess custody in one of four different scenarios: (1) when school officials question students independently and law enforcement is not present or involved; (2) when law enforcement is present during the questioning, but does not speak or otherwise participate; (3) when law enforcement is involved in the questioning, but makes a minimal contribution; or (4) when law enforcement actively participates in the questioning with the school official. Currently, most courts have a high custody threshold, finding that custody exists only when law enforcement actively participates in the student's interrogation.[115]

Student Seizures

Although most "seizures" involve the seizing of evidence obtained in a search, a relatively recent development in the area of Fourth Amendment jurisprudence applicable to public schools has to do with the seizure of a student. In the public school context, these seizures involve the removal of a student from the regular school setting in order to protect the health and safety of others,[116] or to investigate allegations of misconduct.[117] The student is regarded

---

[113] 384 U.S. 436 (1966) (ruling the U.S. Constitution's Fifth Amendment requires that law enforcement officials advise suspects of their legal right to both remain silent and obtain legal representation during formal interrogations while in police custody).

[114] *Id.* at 2395.

[115] *Id.* at 2396.

[116] *See* Johnson v. City of Lincoln Park, 434 F. Supp. 2d 467 (E.D. Mich. 2006) (student's violent conduct in struggling with police officers justified removal from school setting and charge of assaulting a police officer and resisting arrest) and Valentino v. Sch. Dist. of Phila., 2003 U.S. Dist. LEXIS 1081 (E.D. Pa. 2003) (student removed from classroom and held in police custody following threatening gesture toward an apprentice teacher).

[117] In one unique case, the school district implemented a policy of allowing police interviews with students during school hours and without parental consent. In the course of a police investigation, a student was subjected to four such interviews and a DNA sample was taken during one of the interviews. The federal appeals court granted a motion for summary judgment for the school principal, ruling that his peripheral participation in obtaining the DNA sample did not violate the student's Fourth Amendment rights. Burrelson v. Barnesville Sch. Dist., 434 F. Supp. 2d 588 (W.D. Wis. 2006).

as "seized" when a reasonable person under the same or similar circumstances would feel that they were not at liberty to leave.[118] While *T.L.O.* involved the search of a student and the seizure of materials found in her purse, the same two-pronged standard applied in that case appears appropriate to the seizure of a student. For example, in *Edwards v. Rees*,[119] a student removed from class for questioning related to a bomb threat challenged a "seizure" that involved twenty minutes of questioning by a vice principal. The federal appeals court concluded that the seizure was justified at inception because two students who had reported the threat implicated the student as the person responsible. The seizure was reasonable in scope because the questioning by the vice principal related directly to the bomb threat.

An increasing consideration when determining the legality of seizures in school environments is the length of time, or duration, of a particular seizure of a student. In Pennsylvania, for example, a high school student was alleged to have inappropriately touched a female student without her consent.[120] The alleged student victim reported the incident to the assistant principal. The accused student was brought into the assistant principal's office, where he denied all the allegations and held that the touching of the female student was consensual. The accused student was detained for several hours while an investigation was held, and was eventually suspended for four days for sexual harassment. After the suspension, he filed a complaint stating that his Fourth Amendment rights were violated based on the time he had spent in the assistant principal's office. The court upheld the student's seizure and opined that seizures in public schools should be reviewed based on the "reasonableness" legal standard.

Another consideration addressed by courts in seizures in school environments is whether excessive force has been used. While seizures involving removal from class and questioning seldom have led to liability,[121] concerns arise when the seizure involves excessive use of force. In a case addressed by the Eleventh Circuit Court of Appeals, a nine-year-old student in a gym class threatened to strike a teacher after being removed from an exercise activity. A school resource officer who witnessed the insubordinate conduct intervened, forced the student against a wall, and handcuffed her. The student wore the handcuffs for approximately five minutes, crying and complaining of the pain. Neither of the coaches present felt threatened by the child, and one testified that the conduct wasn't "major" and that he would have simply warned the child

---

[118] Gorthy v. Clovis Unified Sch. Dist., 2006 U.S. Dist. LEXIS 6271 at 3 (E.D. Cal. 2006).
[119] 883 F.2d 884 (10th Cir. 1989).
[120] Shuman v. Penn Manor Sch. Dist., 433 F.3d 141 (3d Cir. 2005).
[121] *But see* Howard v. Yakovac, 2006 U.S. LEXIS 27253 (D. Idaho 2006), in which a principal agreed to allow a parent, who was also a local magistrate, to question individual students about a flyer implicating his daughter in sexual activities. The district court found there were genuine issues of material fact regarding whether Fourth Amendment rights were violated by the interviews, since it was not clear that students knew they were free to leave if they did not want to answer questions, the evidence suggested that the parent threatened prosecution of at least one of the students, and some of the questions may have been beyond the scope of the school's interest or authority.

of the misconduct. The Eleventh Circuit affirmed a district court's summary judgment for the school district and the local law enforcement agency, but remanded the case after denying qualified immunity to the school resource officer. While the deputy may have acted reasonably in intervening and stopping the student, the court concluded that handcuffing was an unreasonable action because there was no indication that the student posed a threat to anyone's safety. The "seizure" was regarded as a punishment that clearly violated the student's rights under the Fourth Amendment.[122]

A growing number of seizure cases specifically involve students with special needs or disabilities. While the courts have acknowledged that the expectation of privacy afforded today's students with disabilities is below that of other students, existing court cases acknowledge that those with disabilities still retain some levels of expectations of privacy, especially against unreasonable restraint and seclusion by school officials. The majority of such legal claims in the past were filed based on federal special education legal considerations, but an increasing number of claims now are being filed based on Fourth Amendment considerations. In Ohio, for example, a student with disabilities was restrained by school officials who taped her to her chair, was forced to crawl on the floor of her classroom, and was secluded to the bathroom and "janitor's hallway" on multiple occasions.[123] The court reasoned that the allegations of an unreasonable seizure claim by the parents of the student were valid, based on criteria such as the student's multiple disabilities, the alleged length of the seizures, and the continued use of seclusion and isolation practices by school officials. However, there are instances where the court has found that a particular seizure of a student with disabilities was deemed reasonable. In New York, a police officer arrived at a school playground and witnessed other officers trying to restrain a middle school student with disabilities, who was flailing his arms, yelling, and kicking.[124] After several minutes of being unable to restrain the middle school student, a police officer informed the principal that he would have to handcuff the student. The student was handcuffed, and his mother was notified immediately. Once the student's mother arrived, the student's handcuffs were removed. The mother of the child subsequently sued the school district based on a claim of illegal seizure of her son. The court ruled that under the specific circumstances, the handcuffing of the student was reasonable, and the restraint was for only a relatively short duration of time. In an Alabama case that received national media attention, student resource officers (SROs) employed by the Birmingham Police Department and stationed at schools had the authority to use Freeze +P, an incapacitating chemical spray, on students under certain circumstances. A number of Birmingham high school students who were sprayed with or exposed to Freeze +P in 2009, 2010, and 2011. The students filed a civil rights laws lawsuit under Section 1983 against the

---

[122] Gray v. Bostic, 458 F.3d 1295 (11th Cir. 2006).
[123] H.M. v. Bd. of Educ. of the Kings Local Sch. Dist., 2015 WL 4624629 (S.D. Ohio 2015).
[124] E.C. v. Cnty. of Suffolk, 2012 WL 1078330 (E.D.N.Y).

Birmingham Board of Education. They alleged that the SROs used excessive force, in violation of the Fourth Amendment, by spraying them and by failing to adequately decontaminate them. The students also claimed that the constitutional violations were the result of a policy or custom of the Birmingham Police Department. The Eleventh Circuit Court of Appeals held that the six SROs who were held individually liable on the students' Fourth Amendment decontamination claims were entitled to qualified immunity, and reversed the judgments entered against them.

Conclusion

Litigation surrounding the legality of student searches in today's public schools continues to be active. More specifically, searches of student cell phones, vehicle searches, searches by school resource officers and law enforcement, student seizures, and the restraint and seclusion of students with disabilities continue to represent a significant number of Fourth Amendment cases involving student searches and seizures. Educators need to be aware of how the Fourth Amendment's reasonable suspicion legal standard is applied to different types of searches and seizures within the public school environment.

Case List

A.H. v. State
A.N.H. v. State
A.S. v. State
B.C. v. Plumas Unified Sch. Dist.
Beard v. Whitmore Lake Sch. Dist.
Bell v. Marseilles Elementary Sch.
Bellnier v. Lund
Bd. of Educ. of Indep. Sch. Dist. No. 92 v. Earls
Brannum v. Overton Cnty. Sch. Bd.
Bridgman v. New Trier High Sch. Dist.
Brousseau v. Town of Westerly
Bundick v. Bay City Indep. Sch. Dist.
Burnham v. West
Burrelson v. Barnesville Sch. Dist.
C.B. v. Driscoll
C.S. v. State
Chandler v. Miller
Commonwealth v. Cass
Commonwealth v. Williams
Cornfield v. Consol. High Sch. Dist. No. 130
Covington Cnty. v. G.W.
D.B. v. State
D.E.M., *In re*

D.I.R. v. State
Daniel A., *In re*
Desilets v. Clearview Bd. of Educ.
Doe v. Little Rock Sch. Dist.
Doe v. Renfrow
Dubbs v. Head Start
F.S.E. v. State
Fewless *ex rel.* Fewless v. Bd. of Educ. of Wayland
Foster v. Raspberry
G.C. v. Owensboro Public Schs.
Gorthy v. Clovis Unified Sch. Dist.
Gray v. Bostic
Greenleaf *ex rel.* Greenleaf v. Cote
Gruenke v. Seip
Gutin v. Washington Twp. Bd. of Educ.
H.M. v. Bd. of Educ. of the Kings Local Sch. Dist.
H.Y. v. Russell Cnty. Bd. of Educ.
Hedges v. Musco
Higginbottom *ex rel.* Davis v. Keithly
Horton v. Goose Creek Indep. Sch. Dist.
Howard v. Yakovac
In Interest of Angelia D.B.
In Interest of Doe
In Interest of S.S.
Ineirghe v. Bd. of Educ. of E. Islip
Interest of F.B., *In re*
J.A.R. v. State
J.N.Y., *In re*
J.W. v. Desoto Cnty. Sch. Dist.
James v. Unified Sch. Dist.
Jenkins v. Talladega City Bd. of Educ.
Jennings v. Joshua Indep. Sch. Dist.
Johnson v. City of Lincoln Park
Josue T., *In re*
Joy v. Penn-Harris-Madison Sch. Corp.
Kennedy v. Dexter Consol. Schs.
Kevin P., *In re*
Klump v. Nazareth Area Sch. Dist.
Konop v. Northwestern Sch. Dist.
Kuehn v. Renton Sch. Dist.
L.A., *In re*
Lamb v. Holmes
Landstrom v. Ill. Dep't of Children and Family Servs.
Latasha W., *In re*
M.D. v. State

Matter of Gregory M.
Matter of Haseen N.
Miranda v. Arizona
Murray, *In re*
Myers v. State of Indiana
New Jersey v. T.L.O.
Oliver by Hines v. McClung
Patrick Y., *In re*
People v. Alexander B.
People v. Butler
People v. Dilworth
People v. Duke
People v. Perreault
People v. Pruitt
People v. Williams
Phaneuf v. Cipriano
Phaneuf v. Fraikin
Rafael C., *In re*
Randy G., *In re*
Rhodes v. Guarricino
Riley v. California
Rinker v. Sipler
S.A. v. State
S.S., *In re*
Safford Unified Sch. Dist. #1 v. Redding
Shade v. City of Farmington, Minn.
Shamberg v. State
Shuman v. Penn Manor Sch. Dist.
Smith v. McGlothlin
State *ex rel.* Galford v. Mark Anthony B.
State of Iowa v. Jones
State v. Alaniz
State v. Barrett
State v. Best,
State v. D.S.
State v. Drake
State v. Gage R.
State v. J.A.
State v. Jonathon D.
State v. M.W.H.
State v. Meneese
State v. N.G.B.
State v. R.D.S.
State v. Tywayne H.
T.A.S., *In re*

Tannahill *ex rel.* Tannahill v. Lockney Indep. Sch. Dist.
Tenenbaum v. Williams
Thomas *ex rel.* Thomas v. Roberts
Trinidad v. Lopez
Valentino v. Sch. Dist. of Phila.
Vassallo v. Lando
Vernonia Sch. Dist. v. Acton
Villanueva v. San Marcos Consol. Indep. Sch. Dist.
Willis by Willis v. Anderson Comm. Sch. Corp.
Wilson v. Cahokia Sch. Dist.
York v. Wahkiakum Sch. Dist. No. 200

Key Words

alcohol
alternative school
anonymous tips
backpack
bomb threat
bookbag
cell phone search
cocaine
detection dogs
Doctrine of Special Needs
drug testing
excessive force
expectation of privacy
field trip
Fourth Amendment
gun
handcuffs
Head Start
illegal search
in loco parentis
individualized suspicion
informant
intrusive
justified at inception
justified in scope
knife
law enforcement officer
marijuana
metal detector
Miranda warning
misconduct

off school grounds
pat-down
police custody
privacy
purse
qualified immunity
reasonable suspicion
school locker
school resource officer
school safety
search
seizure
sexual abuse
smoking
state officers
strip-search
student athletes
students with disabilities
surveillance
suspension
suspicionless search
theft
threat
underwear
urinalysis
vehicle search
video
weapon

Takeaways

1. In cases involving student searches, the historic and continuing challenge for judges is how to strike the appropriate balance between the public school district's legitimate interest in maintaining a safe and appropriate learning environment and a student's reasonable expectation of privacy protected by the Fourth Amendment.

2. Although the legality of a search will depend on a standard of reasonable suspicion given the "totality of the circumstances" relating to the search, the gradual erosion of the student's privacy rights has been a trend in judicial opinions.

3. While students may contend that they have an expectation of privacy in the public school setting, the state's custodial and supervisory authority over the student, coupled with judicial perceptions of epidemic drug use

and unprecedented violence in public schools, continue to overwhelm whatever expectations of privacy students might once have assumed.
4. Courts continue to apply a standard of "reasonable suspicion" in the context of student searches, but that standard has weighed heavily in favor of school officials in recent decisions.
5. In this digital age, school officials need to be wary of Fourth Amendment considerations when conducting searches of student cell phones or other technological devices.

Practical Extension

Listed below are eight recommendations for public school administrators to minimize intrusion into students' Fourth Amendment rights.

1. It remains true that searches are more likely to be permissible when there is evidence implicating a particular student. School officials must continue to evaluate the totality of circumstances justifying a search, giving consideration to the weight and credibility of evidence implicating an individual student, the age and previous history of the student, and the nature of that which is sought. However, when searches for drugs or weapons are involved, judges have shown extraordinary deference in permitting student searches, even when that search may be highly intrusive.
2. In deciding how intrusive a student search to undertake, teachers must recognize that the more intrusive the search, the greater the degree of individualized suspicion required. A student's expectation of privacy in a locker, desk, automobile, bookbag, or purse has been significantly reduced in recent decisions, and is likely to become more attenuated in the future.
3. Highly intrusive searches, such as strip-searches, continue to require a substantial degree of individualized suspicion based on specific and reliable evidence and should never be undertaken unless serious infractions, such as possession of drugs or weapons, are suspected. In the limited cases in which strip-searches have been addressed, courts have required a high degree of individualized suspicion, often involving the corroboration of more than one reliable informant and other credible evidence tending to confirm drugs or weapons possession. Such a standard approximates the requirement of probable cause for a search, suggesting that any strip-search in the public school setting should best be left to the discretion of local law enforcement rather than school officials.
4. Generally, suspicionless searches continue to require that school officials document the nature and immediacy of the school district's "special need" to provide security and safety.
5. Blanket pat-down searches have been justified when concerns about weapons possession are paramount and evidence of a danger is particularized. Courts have authorized less-intrusive searches, involving drug-detection

dogs and metal detectors, on the basis that these activities are not true "searches" and involve little genuine intrusion on the student's expectation of privacy. However, federal courts are divided on the extent to which searches of this type require documentation of serious drug or violence problems in the particular school setting. Policies on the use of urinalysis testing have been validated in application to students involved in extracurricular activities, but students must be given adequate notice of the drug testing policies, and the procedures should be followed carefully to ensure that the initial search involves minimal intrusion on the student's privacy. These drug testing policies should emphasize the deterrent potential of the search as a means of discouraging drug use, and should be limited to students engaged in extracurricular activities.

6. When considering student cell phone searches, the emerging case law has distinguished the confiscation of a student's cell phone by a school official compared the intrusive searches of digitally stored information placed on a student's cell phone. While school district-level policies prohibiting the possession and use of student cell phones during official school hours are valid, school administrators need to be wary of going beyond the confiscation of cell phones and actively searching the varied digital content of a student's cell phone.

7. An emergent area of litigation involves student "seizures" in school settings, especially students with disabilities. When a student is removed from a classroom setting, school officials must be able to articulate a reasonable suspicion justifying the removal, and any interviews should be limited to an inquiry that is within the scope and authority of school officials.

8. Educators need to regularly monitor existing restraint and seclusion practices involving students with disabilities at their school, and to be aware of individual state laws involving established procedures for the implementation and monitoring of these practices. In recent years, an increasing number of legal cases involve the use of excessive physical force, especially school resource officers (SROs) when attempting to restrain students with disabilities in school environments.

Chapter 5

Student Records

Justin Bathon, John S. Gooden, and James A. Plenty

Introduction

The private information of students must be protected by schools. It is a simple proposition, and certainly a strong guiding principle for actions among school leaders in protecting students and families under their care. Unfortunately, what began as a simple proposition has, over the years, become rather complex legally; this chapter, for example, investigates and now involves multiple federal laws. Further, changes in technology within the past generation have strained the delicate balance of privacy constructed by those laws. As the recommendations for practice at the end of this chapter articulate, though, even amidst the complexity and constantly changing nature of student records, some common principles are still useful to school leaders today.

FERPA Overview

Prior to 1974, student records in the United States largely were not legally protected at the federal level. In an effort to protect the privacy and rights of students' educational records, Congress first enacted the Family Education Rights and Privacy Act (FERPA)[1] in 1974. Since then, the statute and accompanying regulations have been updated many times. The most recent statutory changes to the act took effect on January 3, 2012. FERPA, as a spending clause statute, only applies to public schools and those few private schools that receive federal funding. The law applies equally to both P-12 and higher education institutions.

The act essentially achieves four goals, with the primary focus on the two core access provisions.[2] First, FERPA mandates that parents or legal guardians must have access, the ability to amend, and disclosure rights to a student's educational records; second, that no one else can access, amend, or disclose without permission. This two-part privacy protection serves as the core of the law. Third, the law also provides that students or parents may request a hearing on any educational records that are inaccurate or are an invasion of privacy.

---

[1] The FERPA statute is 20 U.S.C. 1232g, and the subsequent regulations are 34 CRF Part 99.20.
[2] Lynn M. Daggett, *FERPA in the Twenty-First Century: Failure to Effectively Regulate Privacy for All Students*, 58 Cath. U. L. Rev. 59, 62 (2008).

Fourth, schools must provide annual notice to parents and adult students of their FERPA rights. Within this basic mandate, though, both regulatory guidance and litigation have produced nuanced understandings of the essential meanings of these core goals of the law.

The two primary components of FERPA are in response to the two competing interests underlying the law of student records, the need for sharing and the need for privacy. Different parties to the educational process fall on different sides of this tension on different questions. For instance, on issues of discipline, educators are frequently content to keep information private within the school, while parents frequently demand access to the records that led to a disciplinary decision. Alternatively, sharing educational information on technology platforms frequently makes the teaching job easier, while parents demand that their children's educational data remain private and off of the cloud-based data platforms. The essential tension between sharing and privacy underlies each school records request. It is important for principals to understand the different purposes and motivations at issue in each student record question.

To deal with the changing tensions, Congress drew a bright line essentially mandating sharing for parents and guardians and mandating privacy for requests coming from everyone else. This relatively bright-line rule provides a great deal of clarity in the treatment of student records, but can also cause issues, particularly as technology continues to redefine the nature of a record away from paper in a file cabinet and toward a file in the cloud.

FERPA Details

Various details within the FERPA statute and regulations are important to know when handling a student records issue; those details are provided under specific subheadings below, for clarity. The most recent amendments to the statute came in 2012 and, although more recent attempts to update the law have been proposed in Congress, nothing has passed as of this writing.

Remedies & Enforcement under FERPA

It is perhaps best to start at the end result to provide context as to the impact FERPA can have on a school. Congress was limited in the remedy that could be used against schools failing to comply with FERPA, since it is a spending clause statute. According to FERPA, the U.S. Department of Education has the authority to terminate federal financial assistance to those who fail to comply with the act.[3] Technically, then, the only substantial stick available against a school for failing to comply with FERPA is the withholding of federal funds. The U.S. Department of Education has additionally used the courts on occasion to force schools, mostly universities, to comply through an injunction with FERPA, such as in a case against Miami University and Ohio State University.[4]

---

[3] 34 C.F.R. §§ 99.67.
[4] U.S. v. Miami Univ., 294 F.3d 797 (6th Cir. 2002).

A similar case concerning student records has emerged in Kentucky, but with the university using FERPA to seek protection against open records requests.[5]

While the U.S. Department of Education has been successful in suits against schools under FERPA, parents have not experienced the same success over the last 20 years. The U.S. Supreme Court, in *Gonzaga University v. Doe*, found that parents had no private right of action against a school for a FERPA violation.[6] Thus, the major threat of a lawsuit by parents is not present on FERPA questions.

Parents may not directly sue schools; however, the law does give the parent or eligible student the right to file complaints against an educational entity for disclosing education records in violation of FERPA with the Family Policy Compliance Office of the U.S. Department of Education.[7] The office provides assistance on FERPA to education agencies and institutions, state and local officials, parents, and eligible students. The office also investigates alleged violations of the law. A written complaint alleging specific violations of the act must be filed within 180 days of the date of the alleged violation.[8] If the written complaint is sufficient, an investigation may be initiated.

After such an investigation of the complaint, the office will provide the educational agency and the complainant written notice of its findings, which will include the basis for reaching its conclusion. If the educational agency has not complied with FERPA, the office will include a statement of the specific steps that must be taken for the institution to comply, and must allow a reasonable time for compliance. If the institution or educational agency does not comply, either voluntarily or within a reasonable time, the secretary may withhold further payments, issue a cease and desist order, or terminate eligibility to receive funding under any applicable program.[9] More information about the Family Policy Compliance Office is available at its website, http://familypolicy.ed.gov/. The website contains an especially useful and detailed Frequently Asked Questions option for school officials.[10]

Definition of Educational Records

Perhaps the topic most contested and difficult to determine under FERPA is the exact definition of an educational record for purposes of the statute, especially in novel situations. FERPA defines educational records as any records, files, documents, and other materials which (i) contain information directly related to a student and (ii) are maintained by an educational agency or institution or by a person acting for such agency or institution.

---

[5] Ellie Kaufman, *University of Kentucky sues student newspaper over sexual assault case*, CNN, http://www.cnn.com/2016/09/01/us/university-of-kentucky-sues-student-newspaper-sexual-assault/.
[6] 536 U.S. 273 (2002).
[7] 34 C.F.R. §§ 99.63.
[8] 34 C.F.R. §§ 99.60-99.67.
[9] *Id.*
[10] FERPA Frequently Asked Questions, Family Policy Compliance Office, http://familypolicy.ed.gov/ferpa-school-officials.

The implementing regulations go on to further define a "record" as any information recorded in any way, including, but not limited to, handwriting, print, computer media, video or audio tape, film, microfilm, and microfiche.

Thus, the definition of an educational record is defined rather broadly, particularly in terms of the type of media used to construct the record. Many common documents in schools thus are educational records, and subsequently protected by FERPA. Placement documents, progress reports, financial aid information, and cumulative academic records are just some examples of records normally maintained by schools that include information considered confidential. If released, a violation of a student's privacy would occur. Transcripts and other records obtained from schools in which the student was enrolled are also covered under FERPA. To release any of these records specifically covered under FERPA, the school must have written permission from the parents or eligible student.[11]

Of particular interest for school officials are the voluminous materials generated by students within the classroom and commonly shared in the class. This question, in fact, was considered by the U.S. Supreme Court in the case of *Owasso Independent School District v. Falvo* which found that peer grading of student papers did not violate FERPA.[12] In the case, a parent challenged the school's practice of having students grade the papers of their known peers, thus being aware of each other's grades on the work. Further, the school in question was asking students to call out the grades and the student names for the teacher to record in the gradebook. Thus, the entire class was aware of each grade that was given to each student. The Supreme Court, though, found that the process of grading the papers can actually be an instructive activity, and that temporary possession of the assignment was not "maintaining" for the purposes of FERPA. Only when the final assignment was turned into the teacher for storage, and a final grade assigned, was FERPA triggered. This case opened the door to much within the classroom, including such group work, falling outside the bounds of FERPA. Thus, as long as shared student work within the classroom has an instructional purpose and is not the final record maintained by the teacher, there is flexibility to share student work within the class itself.

Further, FERPA specifically articulates additional records that are not covered under the law. For instance, an education record does not cover notes made by school officials or teachers that are in the exclusive possession of the individual and will not be shared with others. The notes that teachers maintain for their own use are not educational records. FERPA also excludes records created and maintained by a law enforcement unit of a school or district for law enforcement purposes. Additionally, the law does not cover medical records that are created, maintained, or used in the treatment of "an eligible student who is eighteen years old by a physician, psychiatrist, psychologist, or other

---

[11] *Id.*
[12] 534 U.S. 426 (2002).

recognized professional or paraprofessional acting in his or her professional capacity."[13] Finally, student employment records are an exception in FERPA.[14]

Directory Information

A major exception to the coverage of the definition of educational records is student directory information. Directory information is not considered harmful or an invasion of privacy and may be disclosed without the permission of the parent or eligible student. It includes the student's name, address, telephone number, email address, photograph, date and place of birth, major field of study, participation in officially recognized activities and sports, weight and height of members of athletic teams, dates of attendance, grade level, enrollment status, and honors and awards received.[15] The institution may provide the dates of attendance and the overall time the student attended the school (i.e., academic years or semesters); however, it should not include the student's daily attendance records.

To release directory information, the school district must provide notice and an opportunity for the community to respond to the categories covered. If an institution does not define the scope of the directory information, give public notice, or seek parental consent as required by FERPA, it is not permitted to release the information. Further, school districts must give parents or eligible students the opportunity to prevent the release of directory information.[16] An Ohio Supreme Court case considered the issue when a private school choice organization questioned a school district's limited definitions of directory information. The choice organization wanted access to parental contact information for students, including email addresses and phone numbers. The school district had not previously included these in their definition; thus, they did not release those records in response to the request. The Ohio Supreme Court affirmed the district's decision, finding that a district could not be compelled to change its definition of directory information based on the charter school request.[17]

Some information cannot be included in directory information, however. Under no circumstance may an institution release the following information about a student: nationality, race, ethnicity, gender, transcripts, grade point average, or grade reports. This information must not be released to anyone without prior written consent of the parents or eligible student. School officials, faculty, and staff can access this information only if they have a legitimate need to do their jobs. The 2012 legislative amendments made changes to the usage of student PIN numbers, permitting usage when the number could not be used to identify students. This provision was challenged by the Electronic Privacy

---

[13] *Id.*
[14] *Id.*
[15] 34 C.F.R. §§ 99.3.
[16] 34 C.F.R. §§ 99.37(c)(2).
[17] State *ex rel.* Sch. Choice Ohio, Inc. v. Cincinnati Pub. Sch. Dist., 2016 WL 3922996 (Ohio 2016).

Information Center, but the District of Columbia Federal Court found they did not have standing to challenge the law.[18]

Finally, federal laws require the local education agency (LEA) receiving assistance under the Elementary and Secondary Education Act of 1965 (ESEA) to provide directory information upon request to military recruiters in the following three categories: names, addresses, and telephone listings. An eligible student or parent may request that the information not be disseminated unless with prior written permission, and the school or agency must comply with the request. These statutes also indicate that schools provide military recruiters the same access to secondary students that is generally given to postsecondary institutions and prospective employers.[19]

Personally Identifiable Information (PII)

FERPA expressly prohibits the release of educational records that contain personally identifiable information outside of directory information. Thus, determining whether a record has personally identifiable information can be a matter of dispute. The FERPA statute itself provides little guidance on these questions, but the supporting regulations to FERPA provide a non-exclusive list. PII includes, but is not limited to: directory information, the name of the student's parents or other family members, a social security number or student number, or a list of personal characteristics that would make the student's identity easily traceable.[20] Further, if an education record of a student contains information on more than one student, the parent or eligible student may inspect and review or be informed of only the specific information about their child.

One technique permitted and used by school districts is to scramble or redact the personally identifiable information contained in an education record before disclosure. Understanding who is requesting the information and their likely existing knowledge, though, is important in making the access decision.[21] First, if the requesting party likely knows the student for whom the information was requested, the school may not release the data even if redacted. Further, even when a party is unlikely to know a specific student, if the redacted data would be linkable by a reasonable person in the community, it also may not be released. Thus, even in redaction, schools should be cautious in disclosing educational records.

Other Educators & Law Enforcement

Under FERPA, prior written consent is not required to release information to other school officials who have "legitimate educational interests," or to officials of another school or school system in which the student seeks or intends to enroll. However, notification of the transfer to parents is required,

---

[18] Electronic Privacy Info. Ctr. v. U.S. Dept. of Educ., 48 F. Supp. 3d 1 (D.C. 2014).
[19] Elementary and Secondary Education Act of 1965 (ESEA). 34 C.F.R. §§ 9528.
[20] 34 C.F.R. §§ 99.3.
[21] Id.

and they must receive a copy of the record, if desired, and have an opportunity to challenge the records' contents. Written consent is not necessary when providing educational records to federal, state, and local education authorities for the purpose of an educational program audit, evaluation, or compliance. Officials processing student financial aid, institutions involved in organizing and conducting studies and improving instruction, and accrediting organizations are not required to have written consent as long as PII is not disclosed. Those officials requiring access to educational records for law enforcement purposes and in school-initiated judicial proceedings do not need written consent. This is true even if the school has been ordered not to disclose the existence of the records. Finally, written consent is not necessary when appropriate individuals are dealing with an emergency situation.

Additionally, FERPA specifically exempts from the definition of "education records" those records that a law enforcement unit of a school or school district creates and maintains for a law enforcement purpose. FERPA defines a law enforcement unit as "an individual, office, department, [or] component" of a school or school district that is officially authorized or designated by the school district to enforce federal, state, or local law, or that maintains the physical safety and security of the school district. Nothing in FERPA prohibits an educational agency or institution from contacting its law enforcement unit, orally or in writing, to investigate a possible violation or enforce state, local, or federal laws.[22]

Access by Custodial and Noncustodial Parents

Because FERPA does not distinguish between custodial and noncustodial parents, an educational agency or institution must give full rights to either parent. However, if the agency or institution has been provided with evidence that there is a court order, state statute, or legally binding document relating to a divorce, separation, or custody that specifically revokes these rights, information cannot be disclosed to the noncustodial parent. A signed statement alone by one parent will not serve to bar the other parent from access to student records.

Access to information by noncustodial or joint-custody parents with whom a child is not living during the school year often presents a challenge for schools, particularly if that information must be mailed to each parent. FERPA permits a school to "charge a fee for a copy of an education record that is made for the parent or eligible student," unless the imposition of the fee effectively prevents a parent or eligible "student from inspecting the record." A noncustodial parent may be placed on a school's mailing list and receive the same information that is mailed to the custodial parent. The custodial and/or noncustodial parent may be charged a fee for actual expenses incurred by the school for providing such records.[23]

---

[22] 34 C.F.R. §§ 99.31.
[23] 34 C.F.R. §§ 99.11.

Student Reaching Age of Majority and Higher Education

Once a student turns 18 years old, or enrolls in college at any age, the right to decide access is transferred from the parents to the student. The school may still disclose the student's educational records if the student is claimed as a dependent for income tax purposes, however. If the student is enrolled in both a high school and postsecondary school, the two schools may exchange information about the student. If a student is under 18 years old, the high school may share any information received from the postsecondary institution with parents because they retain their FERPA rights at the high school. However, the parents do not have the same rights at the postsecondary institution unless the eligible student is dependent for tax purposes, or the student gives parents permission to access his or her educational records.[24]

Records of Records

Each institution must maintain a record that indicates all individuals who have requested and/or obtained access to students' education records and the specific legitimate interest for requesting the information.[25] This record of access is available only to parents or eligible students, school officials, records custodians, and those authorized by law. The record of disclosures and requests must be kept as long as the institution retains the record. FERPA requires that educational agencies or institutions not destroy any educational records if there is an outstanding request to inspect the records.[26]

Press Access & FERPA

A growing issue relative to student records is access by the press, particularly utilizing state open records requests as an attempt to gain access to student records.[27] While the majority of this litigation has occurred at the higher education level, the implications of these decisions also apply to P-12 contexts should requests by the press arise. On one hand, higher education cases have found that FERPA preempts the press's First Amendment right to access of information,[28] as well as that FERPA serves as a viable exemption under certain state open records laws, such as in Iowa.[29] On the other hand, in Illinois, the Seventh Circuit found that admission records to the University of Illinois were covered under state open records laws and not FERPA, thus permitting press access to specific preferential admission records that later led to the resignation of many top officials at the university.[30] Scholars have argued that FERPA serves as a viable exception to state open records laws, or may preempt

---

[24] 34 C.F.R. §§ 99.3.
[25] 34 C.F.R. §§ 99.32.
[26] 34 C.F.R. §§ 99.10(e).
[27] Erin Escoffery, *FERPA and the Press: A Right to Access of Information?*, 40 J.C. & U.L 543 (2014).
[28] U.S. v. Miami Univ., 294 F.3d 797 (6th Cir. 2001).
[29] Press-Citizen Co., Inc. v. Univ. of Iowa, 817 N.W.2d 480 (Iowa 2012).
[30] Chicago Tribune Co. v. Bd. of Trs. of Univ. of Ill., 781 F. Supp. 2d 672 (No. Dist. Ill. 2011).

state laws on federal constitutional grounds,[31] but for now the issue remains unsettled. Many state open records statutes specifically include FERPA as an exception, so school leaders facing inquiries by the press should read the state open records law to determine if such an exception exists.

Technology Issues

As technology has continued to evolve, the existing FERPA framework has had to contend with new challenges and questions. The law was conceived and written for a pre-digital era, so that several provisions now struggle to keep up with the rapidly changing nature of student records. For instance, Lynn Daggett, a Gonzaga University law professor and frequent author on this topic, has faulted congressional inaction for FERPA's lack of attention to twenty-first century realities.[32] Daggett specifically cites the vastly more powerful digital tools that permit electronic discovery within massive databases of information instead of drawers in a file cabinet. Student records have been subpoenaed for activities ranging from illegal downloads of music to property owners in lead paint lawsuits by defending property owners trying to prove student inability in school.[33] Further, Daggett identified concerns among both research and commercial requests for student records where information about the children could advance scholarly knowledge, but simultaneously advance corporate profits.[34] Additionally, state laws play a larger role in the technology issues, with some states passing specific records limitations.[35]

Such concerns caused the U.S. Department of Education's Privacy Technical Assistance Center to release new guidance for students using online education services.[36] The site takes the form of a student privacy toolkit that addresses data security, data governance, data breaches, data destruction, third-party service contracts, and special education digital tool specifics. The toolkit includes technical guides, as well as specific case studies, as examples for best practice. It can be found online at http://ptac.ed.gov/toolkit.

But, even as the U.S. Department of Education races to provide guidance, new technologies continue to emerge, and legal scholars are articulating new questions never before contemplated by the law. For instance, Sarah Pierce West raised the issue of whether body camera videos among law enforcement officers, which personally identify students, meet the definition of an educational record.[37] Jules Polonetsky and Omer Tene investigated how FERPA functions

---

[31] Mathilda McGee-Tubb, *Deciphering the Supremacy of Federal Funding Conditions: Why State Open Records Laws Must Yield to FERPA*, 53 B.C. L. Rev. 1045 (2012).

[32] *See* Daggett, *supra* note 2, at 84.

[33] *Id.* at 97.

[34] *Id.* at 99-101.

[35] Dylan Peterson, *EdTech and Student Privacy: California Law as a Model*, 31 Berkeley Tech. L. J. 961 (2016).

[36] Privacy Technical Assistance Center Toolkit, U.S. Department of Education, http://ptac.ed.gov/toolkit.

[37] Sarah Pierce West, *They Got Eyes in the Sky: How the Family Educational Rights and Privacy Act Governs Body Camera Use in Public Schools*, 65 Am. U. L. Rev. 1533 (2016).

within the emerging online learning platforms, including the popular Massive Open Online Courses (MOOCs).[38] Elise Young[39] and Elana Zeide[40] approached the question through the lenses of "big data" in education, as essentially all information in schools is digitized and preserved in massive, cloud-based databases. As student information continues to digitize in various formats, FERPA will unquestionably be challenged to maintain relevance. For schools facing this technological revolution every day in their classrooms, they are best served by remembering the essential tensions behind FERPA and consulting legal counsel for guidance. As Louis Schulze articulates, digital tools can support progressive pedagogies and ultimately additional student learning, thus FERPA's lack of guidance cannot stand as a barrier to cutting-edge academic instruction and student learning opportunities.[41]

Special Education Students

State education agencies and institutions must afford special education students the same privacy rights as other students. Defining "education records" of special education students is subject to both the FERPA and IDEA regulations.[42] In most instances, FERPA is the dominant statute on the issue of education records; in fact, IDEA regulations for both Part B and Part C (early childhood) specifically reference and incorporate FERPA,[43] and IDEA specifically relies upon the FERPA definition of education records.[44] In large part, the voluminous records generated in the execution of the individualized education plan create education records under the FERPA definition. But, records that are also subject to IDEA, such as health records, also become subject to FERPA thereafter.[45]

Minor differences are notable, however. For instance, FERPA has a 45-day window for granting access to the education records, whereas IDEA regulations require an agency to comply with a request to inspect and review any educational records without unnecessary delay and before any IEP meeting, due process hearing, discipline procedure, or resolution session.[46] The definition of "parent" under IDEA is broader than FERPA, including adoptive, foster, and

---

[38] Jules Polonetsky & Omer Tene, *Who is Reading Whom Now: Privacy in Education from Books to MOOCs*, 17 Vand. J. Ent. & Tech. L. 927 (2015).

[39] Elise Young, *Educational Privacy in the Online Classroom: FERPA, MOOCs, and the Big Data Conundrum*, 28 Harv. J. L. & Tech. 549 (2015).

[40] Elana Zeide, *Student Privacy Principals for the Age of Big Data: Moving Beyond FERPA and FIPPS*, 8 Drexel L. Rev. 339 (2016).

[41] Louis N. Schulze, Jr., *Balancing Law Student Privacy Interests and Progressive Pedagogy: Dispelling the Myth that FERPA Prohibits Cutting Edge Academic Support Methodologies*, 19 Widener L. J. 215 (2009).

[42] Individuals with Disabilities Education Act (IDEA), 34 CFR §§ 300.613.

[43] 34 C.F.R. §§ 300.611.

[44] *Id.*

[45] 34 C.F.R. §§ 300.612.

[46] 34 C.F.R. §§ 613.

surrogate parents, thus broadening who has access to records.⁴⁷ The notifications required under IDEA also demand notification of rights under IDEA.

Significant differences can emerge in issues of longer-term records retention and destruction.⁴⁸ The Department of Education has published a valuable cross-walk comparison tool⁴⁹ that addresses all of the different components of student records under IDEA Part B, IDEA Part C, and FERPA, that is highly recommended for school officials challenged to function under both laws in a records dispute.

Protection of Pupil Rights Amendment

The Protection of Pupil Rights Amendment (PPRA), in contrast to FERPA, is primarily concerned with the initial collection of student records rather than the later sharing thereof. The law provides parents and guardians consent and opt-out rights as to this information. Like FERPA, the PPRA applies to programs that receive funding from the U.S. Department of Education. The law protects specific categories of information from surveys, analysis, or evaluation without parental consent. The specific categories are summarized as: (1) political affiliations; (2) mental or psychological problems; (3) sex behavior or attitudes;⁵⁰ (4) illegal, anti-social, self-incriminating or demeaning behavior; (5) critical appraisals of individuals with family relationships; (6) relationships covered by privilege; (7) religious practices; and (8) income beyond lunch status.⁵¹ The categories protect both students and information about their family. Further, any materials concerning these categories that are used for commercial purposes are subject to the same requirements.

As with FERPA, the PPRA has been interpreted to this point as containing no private right of action for parents against schools that commit PPRA violations.⁵² Lynn Daggett's in-depth review of the PPRA is still the most detailed look and is recommended for principals wanting to more deeply understand the law and its origins.⁵³ A more recent look at the issues of student information privacy, from a broader perspective, is provided by Emily Waldman.⁵⁴

---

⁴⁷ 34 C.F.R. §§ 300.30.

⁴⁸ 34 C.F.R. §§ 624.

⁴⁹ Kala Surprenant, Frank Miller & Sarone Pasternak, *IDEA and FERPA Confidentiality Provisions*, U.S. Department of Education (2014), https://www2.ed.gov/policy/gen/guid/ptac/pdf/idea-ferpa.pdf.

⁵⁰ *See* Kathleen Conn, *Sex Surveys in K-12 Public Schools: Parents vs. School Districts*, 242 Educ. L. Rep. 505 (2009).

⁵¹ 20 U.S.C. § 1232h.

⁵² C.N. v. Ridgewood Bd. of Educ., 430 F.3d 159 (3d Cir. 2005).

⁵³ Lynn M. Daggett, *Student Privacy and the Protection of Pupil Rights Act as Amended by No Child Left Behind*, 12 U.C. Davis J. Juv. L. & Pol'y 51 (2008).

⁵⁴ Emily G. Waldman, *Show and Tell? Students' Personal Lives, Schools, and Parents*, 47 Conn. L. Rev. 699 (2015).

Recommendations for Practice

1. FERPA is the primary law regarding student records and likely supersedes state law where federal and state law conflict. It is important to look at the state's open records and freedom of information laws for additional guidance, as such laws may articulate specific components such as the specific parameters of directory information. In particular, new state laws impacting digital information have added records requirements beyond FERPA.

2. Without a private right of action on behalf of parents, the only remedy available to school violations is the withholding of federal funding. The U.S. Department of Education has been extremely reluctant to utilize that option. However, upon an investigation initiated by the Department, schools should work diligently to comply with any legal violations that might have occurred, or any lack of policy or procedure to guide the school's actions.

3. School districts should maintain policies and procedures for student records. These should include relevant provisions to FERPA, but also general storage, maintenance, and destruction policies.

4. Educational institutions are required to advise parents of their rights to inspect student records. Eligible students and parents must be notified annually of the categories of personally identifiable information that the institution has designated as directory information and will release without written consent. The notice must also inform parents and students of their right to refuse to permit the disclosure of directory information from their files, as well as the time period for submitting a written statement refusing to allow the release of directory information.

5. Schools should be clear about which other school officials will have access to students' educational records. Once access decisions for those personnel have been made, the school should notify parents of those personnel with access and limit access to any other school officials for the remainder of the year until the next notification cycle.

6. Administrators are required to transmit annual FERPA and PPRA notices to individuals with disabilities and parents who have a primary or home language other than English in an "effective way." This may mean the use of alternate formats for the annual notice, such as audiotape, Braille, computer diskette, large-print documents, or information written in their native language.

7. In light of the technology revolution, the use of computerized recordkeeping is ever increasing. These data will replace most paper documents. It is important to keep in mind, however, that the same principle of confidentiality must be applied to digital data as to paper documents.

8. In the event of a data breach, either paper or digital, school officials should have either an adopted policy, or a viable procedure, ready and available to guide actions of the school or district in response to the breach.

9. In response to a request for records from the press, school officials should seek legal guidance from school board counsel. The presently conflicting nature of cases on the primacy of state or federal law requires additional care within each jurisdiction to determine the appropriate response.
10. Redaction of records can be a useful tool to alleviate concerns of personally identifiable records. However, school officials should be wary of instances where even redaction of the data is insufficient to fully protect the privacy of the student from reasonable estimations of student identity. This is particularly the case in the event of personal identification of multiple students within a single record.
11. The school system's records custodian must be aware that custodial and noncustodial parents have equal rights of access to their child's records, absent a court order limiting those rights. A parent who asserts a desire to limit records access to the other parent should be informed that the school district is unable to do so unless the parent produces a valid court order so specifying. Further, a policy is crucial in grandparent or other nonparent care situations where legal custody has not been established. To assure compliance, a school should have a fixed procedure that both school officials and requesting parties should follow to determine the relevant rights.
12. There must be a written agreement with contractors doing audits, evaluations, or maintaining digital, cloud-based data. The agreement must specify points of contact, state that the data is owned by the institution, and identify the penalties for violating the terms of agreement.
13. On matters of the classroom, the Supreme Court has provided some instructional flexibility, as much student work product in classrooms does not become an educational record until the final dispensation by the teacher. Thus, while keeping FERPA in mind, it should not serve as a substantial bar to instruction or innovation in the classroom.
14. FERPA and other student privacy laws balance the essential tension between privacy and sharing. Understanding and contextualizing the tension, as well as the laws, will better position the school officials to manage records disputes, particularly as new media technology continues to challenge our notions of student records.

Case List

C.N. v. Ridgewood Bd. of Educ.
Chicago Tribune Co. v. Bd. of Trs. of Univ. of Ill.
Gonzaga Univ. v. Doe
Owasso Indep. Sch. Dist. v. Falvo
Press-Citizen Co., Inc. v. Univ. of Iowa
State *ex rel.* Sch. Choice Ohio, Inc. v. Cincinnati Pub. Sch. Dist.
U.S. v. Miami Univ.

Key Words

access to records
age of majority
computerized recordkeeping
digital data
directory information
educational records
educator access
Elementary and Secondary Education Act of 1965 (ESEA)
Family Educational Rights and Privacy Act (FERPA)
Family Policy Compliance Office
federal funds
First Amendment
grades
IDEA
law enforcement
local education agency (LEA)
noncustodial parents
online education
online records
open records law
personally identifiable information
press access
privacy
Protection of Pupil Rights Amendment (PPRA)
records retention
redaction of records
sharing records
special education students
student records

Takeaways

1. Student records are legally protected at the federal level under the FERPA law of 1974.
2. School officials often are faced with the conundrum of needing to share student information while also needing to maintain student privacy.
3. It is important that school teachers understand that student records and information cannot be shared with anyone other than the student's parent or guardian.
4. Schools have an obligation to protect a student's personally identifiable information (PII).
5. School teachers should consider FERPA and PII when requiring students

to sign up for a new educational tool or application. Teachers should consult with school administrators prior to requiring students to register for an online tool that requires them to share personally identifiable information.
6. School teachers should not share a class directory without parental consent to disclose the information.
7. Teachers can share student educational information with other teachers within a school system for the purpose of education.

Practical Extension

1. A parent is upset about the grade their child receives on an essay. The parent contacts the teacher to ask how other essays were graded, and requests to see copies of other students' essays to compare how they were graded. How should the teacher proceed?
2. The local military recruitment office reaches out to a guidance counselor, asking the school to share student directory information of all juniors with their office for recruitment purposes. How should the guidance counselor proceed?

Chapter 6

Students' Speech Rights in an Online Era

Mark Anthony Gooden and Bradley W. Davis

Introduction

Prior to 1969, the courts applied a reasonableness test to judge school policies. Judges upheld a school rule if they determined a reasonable relationship existed between the rule and some educational purpose. Even if judges believed a rule was unwise, unnecessary, or unfairly restrictive of the rights of students and/or teachers, they followed this custom.[1] Because judges regarded school officials as the experts on education, they surmised that educators should be provided broad discretion in the creation and implementation of school policies. Accordingly, the courts were reluctant to substitute their judgment for that of school officials.[2]

However, this hands-off inclination of the courts changed with the decision handed down in the *Tinker v. Des Moines Independent School District*[3] case. For over five decades, *Tinker* has been the standard established by the Supreme Court for how school officials should address student free speech issues in schools. Although advancements in technology have somewhat changed the way courts consider student speech relative to the online context and Internet cases, clearly the landmark case that establishes the foundation of such decisions remains *Tinker*.

This chapter addresses *Tinker* and related cases that offer guidance for school administrators on how best to approach school-related speech and student behaviors that are expressed via electronic means. The chapter begins with a brief recap of what is and what is not protected student speech. It then transitions to a presentation of cases involving the Internet and electronic speech. Following that are discussions of cyberbullying and searches of electronic devices. Finally, the chapter closes with relevant recommendations for educational leaders.

---

[1] Raul R. Calvoz, Bradley W. Davis & Mark A. Gooden, *Cyber Bullying and Free Speech: Striking an Age-Appropriate Balance*, 61 Clev. St. L. Rev. 357 (2013).

[2] David Schimmel, Leslie R. Stellman, Cynthia K. Conlon, & Louis Fischer, Teachers and the Law (9th ed. 2015).

[3] Tinker v. Des Moines Independent School District, 393 U.S.503 (1969).

Legal Issues

Student Speech

While *Tinker, Bethel v. Fraser*,[4] *Hazelwood v. Kuhlmeier*,[5] and *Morse v. Frederick*[6] (henceforth *Tinker* and progeny) are covered in greater detail elsewhere, a brief recap of their collective definition of constitutionally protected student speech is warranted here. In *Tinker*, the U.S. Supreme Court described the wearing of armbands in protest of the Vietnam War as "pure speech" because it was "a silent, passive, expression of opinion, unaccompanied by any disorder or disturbance."[7] In this landmark case, the Supreme Court moved beyond the previously established reasonableness test by ruling that students do not lose their constitutional rights to freedom of expression when they enter the schoolhouse gate.[8] The *Tinker* decision did not provide students with unbridled freedom to say or write anything they wish, but it did dramatically expand the boundaries of student expression. Later cases more clearly defined and restricted said boundaries.

Decided in 1986, *Bethel* represented the U.S. Supreme Court's move to more clearly distinguish impermissible student expression as it ruled that school officials have the authority to regulate vulgar, indecent, or obscene speech.[9] Two years later, the Court's decision in *Hazelwood* held that where a school sponsors an activity in such a way that the speech bears the imprimatur of the school, the official has the right to restrict student speech "so long as their actions are reasonably related to legitimate pedagogical concerns."[10] In addition to *Bethel* and *Hazelwood*, the protection of fellow students from speech that could reasonably be considered to encourage drug use or other illegal activity, as exemplified in *Morse*, has since been established as a satisfactory exception to *Tinker*.[11]

Tinker and progeny clearly illustrate that school administrators are agents of the state and, as a result, are required to grant students their First Amendment rights to freedom of speech. Conversely, administrators are also responsible for maintaining order in schools. Conflict between these, at times, competing responsibilities has become more pronounced in recent years, thus increasing the need for clear school policies.

Tinker and progeny establish a starting point and a framework for analyzing First Amendment free speech cases involving the rights of students. Any new cases involving electronic speech will likely invoke an analysis that involves at least one of these important cases, though the first three are the most common

---

[4] Bethel v. Fraser, 478 U.S. 675 (1986).
[5] Hazelwood v. Kuhlmeier, 484 U.S. 260 (1988).
[6] Morse v. Frederick, 551 U.S. 393 (2007).
[7] Tinker v. Des Moines Indep. Sch. Dist., 393 U.S. 503, 508 (1969).
[8] *Id.* at 506.
[9] Bethel Sch. Dist. No. 403 v. Fraser, 478 U.S. 675 (1986).
[10] Hazelwood Sch. Dist. v. Kuhlmeier, 484 U.S. 260, 273 (1988).
[11] Morse v. Frederick, 551 U.S. 393 (2007).

in First Amendment, student speech jurisprudence. In the growing number of Internet free speech cases that have been decided over the last two decades, it appears that administrators can still benefit significantly from studying the framework established by *Tinker* and progeny.

Free Speech and the Internet

Although the *Tinker* speech took place on campus, the ruling provided guidance for cases relating to school-related speech expressed off campus. A district court employed the same type of *Tinker* analysis in the case of *Beussink v. Woodland R-IV School District*,[12] in which Brandon Beussink, a high school student, was suspended for 10 days because of a webpage he created at home. On the webpage, Brandon used vulgar language to criticize his high school, its web presence, and school officials. The suspension caused Beussink, who had already missed eight days of school, to be "dropped" a letter grade in each class pursuant the school's absenteeism policy. Consequently, he failed the semester. Beussink and his family filed suit.

Citing *Tinker*, the court found that Beussink's page did not materially and substantially interfere with the operation of the school.[13] The page was neither created at school, nor was it created using school resources. In fact, Beussink did not intend for his website to be viewed at school and he did not access it there until asked to do so by school officials. *Tinker* offers guidance here in the sense that Beussink's Internet speech was silent and passive, prior to being accessed by another student.

Applying an already-established First Amendment framework, school personnel may determine whether a webpage is visited an inordinate amount of times, thereby causing a disruption. If the webpage was created on campus and contains obscene material, such as a *Bethel*-type speech situation, then the student can be punished. If the page was not created on campus, but causes a material and substantial disruption in school, then the student may also be punished. Relatedly, in 1998, when *Beussink* was decided, the federal district court seemed to be driving home the point that school personnel must not punish students simply because of the "inappropriateness" of the content of their Internet speech or expression on the webpage.

In another Internet case, Nick Emmett created an unofficial homepage about his high school. He posted two mock obituaries of friends and allowed visitors to vote on who would go up next in this mock obituary list. Emmett was suspended for five days as a result of the content on his website; the principal claimed he was placed on emergency suspension for intimidation, harassment, and disruption to the educational process. The student brought suit to prevent the school district from enforcing the suspension.[14] Siding with Emmett, the court found that the school presented no evidence "that the mock obituaries or

---

[12] Beussink v. Woodland R-IV Sch. Dist., 30 F. Supp. 2d 1175 (E.D. Mo. 1998).
[13] *Id.*
[14] Emmett v. Kent Sch. Dist. No. 415, 92 F. Supp. 2d. 1088 (W.D. Wash. 2000).

voting on his website were intended to threaten anyone, did actually threaten anyone, or manifested any violent tendencies whatsoever."[15] Consequently, the school district was blocked from enforcing the short-term suspension.

In *Mahaffey v. Aldrich*,[16] Joshua Mahaffey was initially suspended for contributing to the creation of a webpage constructed off campus with another student in the district. The site was entitled "Satan's Web Page," and Mahaffey claimed it was meant to be humorous. On the page, students posted a list of people they wished would die as well as people they thought were "cool." The site also contained Satan's mission instructing viewers to kill someone; however, it discouraged viewers from actually committing this crime. A fellow student reported the site to the police; they then contacted the school officials, who ultimately suspended Mahaffey for the remainder of the semester. A federal district court held that Mahaffey's suspension violated his First Amendment rights because there was no proof of disruption to the school caused by the website. Also missing was a clear determination that the website was created on school property. Citing *Tinker*, the court determined that even if the page had not been created on campus, the school district could punish Mahaffey for his speech on the website, if that speech "substantially interfere[d] with the work of the school or impinge[d] upon the rights of other students."[17] However, no evidence was offered that suggested such interference occurred. Furthermore, Mahaffey's statements on the website did not constitute threats as the school officials had originally charged in his suspension. Thus, the speech was protected by the First Amendment.

In *Layshock v. Hermitage School District*,[18] a high school senior named Justin Layshock created a parody profile of his principal on MySpace. The profile included crude and vulgar language, allusions to excessive alcohol use, and a photo of the principal which was copied from the school's website. Layshock told a few close friends at school about the profile, and eventually word of it reached most of the student body. In addition, a few other parodies (which were described as even more crude and vulgar) of unknown origin appeared on the Internet and word of their cyber-presence was spread throughout the school community.

Layshock, while in a meeting with his mother, the district superintendent, and the co-principal, admitted to creating the parody. Although no disciplinary action was taken at that time, nearly three weeks later Layshock and his parents received a letter notifying them that an informal hearing would be held to consider disciplinary action against him. At the hearing, in addition to other consequences, Layshock received a 10-day, out-of-school suspension and was to be placed in an exclusionary instructional setting for the remainder of the school year. In cases involving off-campus speech, such as this one, the duty falls

---

[15] *Id.* at 1090.
[16] Mahaffey v. Aldrich, 236 F. Supp. 2d 779, 781 (E.D. Mich. 2002).
[17] *Id.* at 784.
[18] Layshock v. Hermitage Sch. Dist., 650 F. 3d 205 (3d Cir. 2011), *cert. denied sub nom.* U.S. LEXIS 726 (U.S. Jan. 17, 2012).

upon the school to demonstrate a sufficient nexus between student behavior and any alleged on-campus disruption. The school argued that Layshock's website parody, along with the others of unknown origin, were constantly accessed by students, causing the school to shut down its computer system to student use for five days.[19] According to the school, the lack of computer access resulted in the cancellation of several classes and interfered with the students' ability to use the computers for their school-intended purposes. Consequently, the school district's technology coordinator devoted nearly 25% of his time dealing with the disruption caused by the profiles on MySpace, and the school principal testified at the temporary restraining order (TRO) hearing that he had to spend at least 25-30% of his time dealing with the disruptions, including the investigation into the source of the website parodies.[20]

Though the school district officials were focused on making a convincing case, they failed to make a causal link between Layshock's off-campus conduct and any material and substantial disruption of campus operations. Most notably, the school district was unable to connect the alleged disruption specifically to Layshock's conduct, insofar as there were three other mock profiles of the principal of unknown origin that were accessible during the same timeframe. Moreover, the school did not demonstrate distinctly that the disruptive discussions and resultant reactions of administrators were caused by Layshock's parody profile. Indeed, according to the court, Layshock and his parents evinced instances in which students objected to the investigation, rather than the profile. Thus, the school district was unable to demonstrate that a material disruption emanated from Layshock's irreverent profile.

In *J.S. v. Blue Mountain School District*,[21] a case with a similar fact pattern, a student named J.S. and a classmate created a mock profile of their principal on MySpace. Consequently, the school officials swiftly delivered 10 days of suspension, a term which encompassed the date of a school dance. Because the school district provided no evidence for their assertion that the MySpace profile had the potential to create substantial disruption of school activities, the court ruled they had interfered with J.S.'s First Amendment free speech rights.

Not since the *Morse v. Frederick* decision in 2007 had a student speech case made its way to the United States Supreme Court, until 2021. Given the rapid rise and expansion of social media outlets and the growing number of electronic cases previously mentioned in this chapter, it is not an overstatement to suggest the Supreme Court's ruling in *B. L. v. Mahanoy Area School District*[22] may very well have sweeping implications for the future of student electronic speech. In 2017, Brandi Levy was a high school sophomore trying out for the varsity cheerleading squad. After learning that she failed to make the cut, thus forcing her to remain on the junior varsity squad, Brandi used

---

[19] *Id.*
[20] *Id.*
[21] J.S. v. Blue Mt. Sch. Dist., 650 F.3d 915 (3d Cir. 2011), *cert. denied*, 2012 U.S. LEXIS 726, (U.S. 2012).
[22] Mahanoy Area Sch. Dist. v. B.L., 594 U. S. ____ (2021).

vulgar language to express her frustration to at least 250 of her Snapchat friends by posting a picture of herself and a friend with their middle fingers extended, accompanied by the "puerile" caption "Fuck school fuck softball fuck cheer fuck everything"[23]. Upon learning of the Snapchat post that was created off-campus and outside of school hours, school officials suspended Brandi from the junior varsity squad for a year. The District Court and the Third Circuit Court of Appeals both held that the school's decision violated Brandi's First Amendment rights, but for different reasons. Interpreting *Tinker*, the District Court found that Brandi's Snapchats failed to cause a substantial disruption at the school, and therefore the punishment violated her First Amendment rights. The Third Circuit affirmed, but interpreted *Tinker* as providing "an additional freedom" to school officials if "student protest speech," regardless of time and place created, "materially disrupts classwork or involves substantial disorder or invasion of the rights of others." However, they found that this additional freedom did not apply to Brandi's off-campus speech because it was "speech that is outside school-owned, -operated, or -supervised channels and that is not reasonably interpreted as bearing the school's imprimatur."

The Supreme Court accepted the case to decide whether *Tinker*, which permits public school officials to regulate speech that would materially and substantially disrupt the school environment, applies to student speech that occurs off campus. In finding *Tinker* applicable, the Supreme Court noted three important points in the decision. First, relative to off-campus speech, schools will rarely take the place of parents, thus circumscribing the reach of the *in loco parentis* construct. Stated differently, school officials protect, guide, and discipline students when the parents are not there (at school). But at home, controlling such speech is a parental responsibility. Second, regulating speech at school and at home would encompass all student speech uttered during a day. Allowing the school such broad control would call into question other types of protected expression, like religious and political speech. Consequently, schools would gain the increased burden to justify such broad intervention at the point of application. Finally, the High Court asserted that the school has an interest in protecting unpopular student expression, especially off campus, because doing so supports the nurturing of our democracy. The Court makes another important point about the school's legitimate interest in regulating off-campus conduct such as severe bullying, harassment, or threatening behaviors that target particular individuals, such as teachers or fellow students. The Court also notes that protection may not extend to students who fail to follow rules, or who engage in security breaches.

Interestingly, the recent Supreme Court ruling aligns with these Internet cases, including two Pennsylvania decisions found below. *Beussink, Kent, Mahaffey, Layshock, Blue Mountain*, and now *Mahanoy*, all have some commonalities in addition to being free speech cases involving student rights, the Internet, and a perceived intention by students to disrespect and/or criticize

---

[23] *Id* at 175.

school officials. All six cases involved situations where the students participated in off-campus conduct that in the end was found to be protected speech. In each case, the schools defended their actions by relying upon poorly conceived or underdeveloped nexuses between the punished behavior and alleged campus disruption. This lack of explicit connection contributed to courts finding violations of students' First Amendment rights. The Supreme Court's much anticipated ruling can offer some clarity.

Other cases relating to online speech provide further guidance as to best practices for school personnel. In *Doninger v. Niehoff*,[24] Avery Doninger, a high school senior in Burlington, Connecticut, became frustrated at school officials over developments regarding a music festival she had been planning. Doninger posted a public message to her fellow students on the social networking site LiveJournal. Though the site allowed for the author to make the text private, Doninger decided to make it public and invited others to respond to her criticisms of the superintendent and her principal. She expressed her frustration using offensive and inappropriate language; for example, referring to school officials as "douchebags in central office."[25] Additionally, her message contained misleading and false information regarding the planning of the music festival and the actions of school officials. Specifically, she alleged that school officials had cancelled the festival, when in fact they had given her the option to change the venue and/or date. Doninger's blog called on students and their parents to write to the school superintendent in order to "piss her off more."[26] The following day, as a result of this blog post, school officials were faced with "a deluge of phone calls and emails, several disrupted schedules, and many upset students."[27]

When school officials—who, prior to her blog posting, had advised Doninger as to the proper way for student leaders to address issues of concern with the administration about—discovered the message, they disqualified her from running for class secretary for her senior year. They thought her conduct in posting the blog message failed to reflect the qualities of civility and citizenship which the school expected of class officers and leaders. Doninger's mother disagreed, arguing the punishment was too harsh, and asked for an alternative, but the officials refused. Her disqualification from class secretary candidacy was Doninger's only punishment, as she was not suspended from school nor did she receive any other written discipline in her permanent school file. Moreover, she continued as a member of student council and as a leader of her music class. The court found that Avery did not have a First Amendment right to run for a voluntary extracurricular position as a student leader while engaging in offensive communications regarding school administrators. Importantly, the punishment was not excessive and was not necessarily meted out based on school officials being upset with the student.

---

[24] Doninger v. Niehoff, 642 F. 3d 334 (2007), *cert. denied*, 132 S. Ct. 499 (2011).
[25] *Id.*
[26] *Id.*
[27] *Doninger*, 642 F.3d 334, *348; 2011 U.S. App. LEXIS 8441, **35 page 13.

In *Wisniewski v. Board of Education of the Weedsport Central School District*,[28] Aaron Wisniewski, a middle school student, created an instant messaging (IM) icon that suggested a named teacher at the school should be shot and killed. Wisniewski shared his IM icon with fifteen of his friends and fellow classmates over three weeks. The school district's hearing officer found that Wisniewski's icon posed a threat to his teacher and a disruption of the educational environment. Although he created the icon on his home computer, the court stated that "[t]he fact that Wisniewski's creation and transmission of the IM icon occurred away from school property does not necessarily insulate him from school discipline."[29] He was suspended, and his parents brought a suit against the school board and superintendent, alleging that Wisniewski's suspension violated the First Amendment. A United States District Court granted summary judgment in favor of the school district, and his parents appealed. However, the Second Circuit Court of Appeals affirmed the district court's holding that Wisniewski's actions posed a reasonably foreseeable risk that the drawing would come to attention of school authorities and would materially and substantially disrupt the work and discipline of school. School officials had clear policies against threatening teachers, no matter the medium.

The *Doninger* and *Wisniewski* cases are different from the previous five cases in that they demonstrate reasonable rules, and especially reasonable sanctions, and thus do much to strengthen educators' arguments in online speech cases wherein students target school officials. A growing number of incidents where students target other students have occurred over the past few years. Often, this Internet-based behavior, which has been made easier to promote by the creation and rapid improvement of handheld technologies and wireless networks, is also harder to regulate.

Cyberbullying

Bullying is perhaps an all-too-common part of the school experience. In an effort to discourage bullying, school officials often create and enforce rules that encourage students to be respectful of one another and also urge them to be good citizens. Naturally, merely establishing rules is not a panacea to a problem that has likely been in existence as long as there have been schools. Moreover, advancements in technology have given rise to a relatively new category of bullying that is facilitated through its use. The new type of bully may not use physical size to intimidate others, but instead may spread disparaging or intimidating content via social media, text messaging, and the like. Ninety-five percent of American teenagers have access to a smartphone;[30] thus, modern technology has made it easier for bullies to harass others day and night with the dexterity of their fingers, rather than the power of their fists.

---

[28] Wisniewski v. Bd. of Educ. of the Weedsport Cent. Sch. Dist., 494 F.3d 34 (2d Cir. 2007).
[29] *Id.*
[30] MONICA ANDERSON AND JINJING JIANG, PEW RESEARCH CENTER, TEENS, SOCIAL MEDIA & TECHNOLOGY 2018 (2018).

Cyberbullying is defined on the U.S. Department of Health and Human Service's stopbullying.gov website as "bullying that takes place using electronic technology," where such technology can include "devices and equipment such as cell phones, computers, and tablets as well as communication tools including social media apps like Instagram, Snapchat, and TikTok, as well as text messages, audio/video chat, and websites."[31] In addition to lobbing insults and encouraging others to pile on, cyberbullies commit offenses such as stealing other students' passwords and sending false messages to others from the victim's account, or sending hateful, anonymous messages. Cyberbullying can take on a variety of different forms and is limited only by the bandwidth and imagination of the bully.[32]

Cyberbullying increases the number of students willing to become bullies because perpetrators feel comfortable or even safe in participating; doing so does not require them to be face-to-face with the potential victims, and can even be done anonymously.[33] Accordingly, some students fail to truly consider the consequences or the detrimental effect of spreading malicious or threatening messages on the Internet about schoolmates. Moreover, such behavior can, and often does, lead rather easily to sending such threats directly to peers and/or school personnel. Cyberbullying is difficult for parents and educators to regulate, because often students are more technologically proficient and social media savvy than adults. Forty-eight states have laws in place forbidding cyberbullying or electronic harassment,[34] although these laws vary in scope, particularly in regard to whether or not there can be criminal sanctions for cyberbullying.

Because cyberbullying remains a relatively recent phenomenon, the relevant caselaw is rather slim, but has grown rapidly in recent years with the decline in Facebook's popularity and the rapid increase in usage of other social media apps, namely Snapchat. However, studies on the correlate of traditional bullying provide assistance in comprehending the reality and growth of cyberbullying, which can similarly cripple the self-esteem of a child or adolescent.[35] Thus, cyberbullying can become just as problematic as traditional bullying, particularly with society's increasing reliance on technology. The following sections address recent cases on the matter.

In *J.C. v. Beverly Hills Unified School District*,[36] plaintiff J.C., a high school student, posted a video to YouTube capturing a conversation held between friends about another classmate, C.C. J.C.'s friends refer to the other classmate

---

[31] U.S. Dep't of Health and Human Services, *What is Cyberbulling*, https://www.stopbullying.gov/cyberbullying/what-is-it/.

[32] *Id.*

[33] For a discussion of cyberbullying, *see, e.g., Cyber bullying Stalks Students*, at http://www.detnews.com/2003/editorial/0311/09/a13-319592.htm.

[34] Sameer Hinduja & Justin Patchin, *State Cyberbullying Laws: A Brief Review of State Cyberbullying Laws and Policies*. http://cyberbullying.org/Bullying-and-Cyberbullying-Laws.pdf.

[35] Justin W. Patchin & Sameer Hinduja, *Bullies Move Beyond the Schoolyard: Preliminary Look at Cyberbullying*, YOUTH VIOLENCE AND JUVENILE JUSTICE, Apr. 2006, at 149.

[36] J.C. v. Beverly Hills Unified Sch. Dist., 711 F. Supp. 2d 1094 (2010).

as "spoiled," a "slut," and "the ugliest piece of shit [they've] ever seen in [their] life."[37] At one point during the four-minute-and-thirty-six-second video, J.C. herself is heard off camera encouraging one of the friends to continue with her rant about the classmate. Upon learning of the video from the target of the insult, C.C., who had arrived on campus with her mother the morning following the video's initial posting to YouTube, school administrators decided to suspend J.C. for two days. Incidentally, J.C. previously had been suspended for secretly videotaping her teachers at school.

Following the suspension, J.C. filed suit claiming that her First Amendment rights had been violated when she was disciplined for off-campus behavior. Despite the lewd and vulgar nature of the language in J.C.'s video, the court determined that *Fraser* was not applicable, as that decision pertained to speech that occurred on campus. Instead, they moved forward with *Tinker* in their analysis and were therefore charged with the task of determining if the video created, or was likely to create, a substantial disruption of school activities. Regarding a potential disruption, the court reviewed a wide variety of non-electronic speech cases, which, when analyzed in concert, allow schools to censor or discipline off-campus speech when the school "can point to a well-founded expectation of disruption ... based on past incidents arising out of similar speech."[38] With regard to an *actual* disruption, the court found that C.C. and her mother being upset, along with five students temporarily being taken out of class for questioning regarding the video, did not constitute a substantial disruption. The school district offered no evidence that campus instruction was negatively affected, or that the usual order of business for any district personnel had been greatly disturbed (as was the case for the principal and superintendent in *Doninger*). The court held that "[f]or the *Tinker* test to have any reasonable limits, the word 'substantial' must equate to something more than the ordinary personality conflicts among middle school students that may leave one student feeling hurt or insecure."[39] The court deemed the district's punishment of J.C. an unallowable transgression of her First Amendment right to free speech.

A more recent and similar case regarding Snapchat-based group bullying of a single target went the opposite direction of *J.C.* In *Doe v Hopkinton Public Schools*,[40] the court upheld the school's decision to punish members of the hockey team for participating in the Snapchat bash session of one of their teammates, arguing that bullying is harmful speech that can invade the rights of others. A key difference in *Doe* was that unlike *J.S.'s* YouTube recording, which occurred off campus and after school, the Snapchat video recordings took place on school property during school activities.

---

[37] *Id.* at 1098.
[38] *Id.* at 1116.
[39] *Id.* at 1119.
[40] Doe v. Hopkinton Pub. Schs, 2020 U.S. Dist. LEXIS 173127.

While the case seems rather dated because the social media platform involved was MySpace, *Kowalski v. Berkeley County Schools*[41] remains highly instructive. Per the facts of the case, Kara Kowalski, a high school senior, was suspended for five days in response to her creation of a MySpace page constructed for ridiculing a fellow student. On the page, Kowalski and fellow classmates alleged that the target of the page, S.N., had herpes. In fact, the page was titled S.A.S.H., which was purported to stand for either Students Against Shay's Herpes or Students Against Sluts' Herpes. Shortly after the page's creation, several other students started to add material to the website, including insulting language and software-altered images of S.N. depicted with herpes symptoms on her face. Kowalski and crew apparently completed some of these additions using school computers, and a district-supplied Internet connection, during an after-hours class.

S.N. and her parents visited the vice principal's office the next morning with a printout of the S.A.S.H. webpage. Dreading spending an entire school day among peers who had contributed to the MySpace page, S.N. left school with her parents and went home for the day. Upon reviewing the webpage's content and deeming it a violation of the school's bullying policy, the head principal decided to suspend Kowalski for 10 days, imposed a 90-day "social suspension" barring her from school events in which she was not directly involved, precluding her from crowning the school's new "Queen of Charm" (a position in which Kowalski was the incumbent), and disallowed her participation in cheerleading for the remainder of the year. In response to an appeal from Kowalski's father to reduce the punishment, the school principal reduced the suspension to five days, but kept all other consequences in place.

Kowalski brought suit against the school claiming violations of her First Amendment right to free speech. Her argument rested mainly on the fact that her speech occurred off campus, and therefore was entitled to the protection an ordinary citizen would be afforded for online speech. The court disagreed, citing the almost immediate and widespread participation in the S.A.S.H. webpage—some of which even occurred via school property—as a substantial disruption of school practices. The court went on to explain that the S.A.S.H. webpage held the potential to interrupt S.N.'s ability to "have a suitable learning experience," and that students who participated in the page were "indisputably harassing and bullying" and were "in violation of Musselman High School's regulations prohibiting such conduct."[42] Additionally, the court rejected Kowalski's notion that her behavior was not school-related, stating that "every aspect of the webpage's design and implementation was school related,"[43] as its title indicated it was made for students. Moreover, she invited students to join the page; one of those students even participated from a school computer the same day the page was created. Consequently, the court ruled in the school district's favor and affirmed the disciplinary decision.

---

[41] Kowalski v. Berkeley Cnty. Schs., 652 F.3d 565 (2011).
[42] *Id.*
[43] *Id.* at 569.

Several cases have since been decided using *Kowalski* as precedent for upholding schools' decisions to punish students' off-campus, online speech. A notable example is *A.S. v. Lincoln Cty. R-III School District*,[44] in which a student, C.S., was cyberbullied via private Snapchat memes by fellow student A.S. The school district's decision to enforce A.S.'s suspension was upheld because, as creator of the memes, he encouraged his followers to share the meme depicting C.S. in a casket with funeral visitation with "crying" and "praying hands" emojis. As a direct result of A.S.'s encouragement, the memes quickly spread outside of the private Snapchat group and across the high school community, having a number of impacts during and after homecoming weekend.

School administrators can consider several points from these and other cases to formulate proactive solutions for dealing with cyberbullying. For example, does the school's code of conduct include a definition of cyberbullying along with specific consequences for violations? Such policies have played key roles in recent court decisions to affirm school-based punishment for off-campus speech on social media. Has the school taken steps to block controversial websites or sites that do not promote the academic goals of the school? Do students and parents clearly understand the computer-use policies, including what is acceptable and not acceptable when online? Taking preventive steps built around careful consideration of these questions can help school personnel avoid potential legal action.

Threats

Regarding the aforementioned *Mahaffey v. Aldrich*[45] case involving the meant-to-be-humorous "Satan's Web Page," school district officials, in addition to their allegation of substantial disruption, argued that Mahaffey's webpage constituted a threat, but ultimately were unable to convince the court of this assertion.[46] In crafting their arguments, school officials cited two student-centered, traditional speech cases: *Lovell v. Poway*[47] and *Doe v. Pulaski*,[48] from the Ninth and Eighth Circuits, respectively. In each of these cases, the courts reached the same conclusion: "true threats" are not protected.[49] The following paragraphs trace cases relating to student-borne electronic speech and potential of a true threat.[50]

In *J.S. v. Bethlehem*,[51] a middle school student and his parents sought review of a school district's decision to permanently expel him based on his off-campus creation of an Internet website containing threatening and derogatory comments about a teacher and the principal. The decision was affirmed, and J.S. and

---

[44] A.S. v. Lincoln Cnty. R-III Sch. Dist., 429 F. Supp. 3d 659.
[45] Mahaffey v. Aldrich, *supra* note 16.
[46] *Id.*
[47] Lovell v. Poway, 90 F.3d (9th Cir. 1996).
[48] Doe v. Pulaski, 306 F.3d. 616 (8th Cir. 2002).
[49] Watts v. United States, 394 U.S. 705.
[50] *Id.* at 847.
[51] *Id.*

his parents appealed. Eventually, the state's highest court held that the student's website did not constitute a "true threat," even though he asked there why a teacher should die, displayed a picture of her head severed from her body, and solicited funds to hire a hit man to kill the teacher. The court found that the website was a crude and highly offensive attempt at humor or parody, but did not reflect a serious expression of intent to inflict harm—despite the teacher having taken a leave of absence due to the fear she experienced after viewing website. The suspension ultimately was upheld, but for reasons separate from the true threat claim.

Bell v. Itawamba County School Board[52] is another case involving electronic speech construed by school officials as a threat. Taylor Bell, a Black student, recorded a rap song disparaging two basketball coaches from his high school, intimating they had engaged in inappropriate conduct with female students. Bell posted the song recording to his personal Facebook profile and also made it publicly available via YouTube. Two lyrical segments of the song found particularly threatening by the school were as follows: 1) "looking down girls' shirts / drool running down your mouth / messing with wrong one / going to get a pistol down your mouth"; and 2) "middle fingers up if you can't stand that nigga / middle fingers up if you want to cap that nigga."[53] Upon reviewing the song, which contained a multitude of vulgar insults and allegations pointed at the coaches, the school suspended Bell for seven days and ordered him transferred to an alternative, disciplinary campus. Bell and his mother contested the punishment, which was eventually affirmed by the school board. Subsequently, Bell and his mother brought suit alleging a violation of his First Amendment right to free speech.

A federal district court was charged with determining whether Bell's speech was indeed a threat, and if not, whether it was protected under *Tinker*. Prior to legal action, the school board argued Bell's song equated to "harassment and intimidation of teachers and possible threats against teachers"[54]—an assertion with which the court agreed, stopping short of labeling it a "true threat." Bell appealed to the Fifth Circuit Court of Appeals, where a divided three-judge panel reversed the district court and ruled in his favor, finding that the rap song was not a true threat or substantially disruptive under *Tinker*. However, the school district successfully sought to have the entire Fifth Circuit panel hear the case. The majority found it unnecessary to decide whether Bell's speech constituted a legally defined "true threat," instead finding that the school board reasonably could have forecasted a substantial disruption at school based on the threatening, intimidating, and harassing language in Bell's rap recording. Hence, Bell's punishment was upheld, and the U.S. Supreme Court has since denied his petition for appeal.[55]

---

[52] Bell v. Itawamba Cnty. Sch. Bd., 799 F.3d 379 (2015).
[53] *Id.* at 384.
[54] *Id.* at 388.
[55] Bell v. Itawamba Cnty. Sch. Bd., S. Ct. 1166 (2016).

A second case involving threats originating from electronic speech is *D.J.M. v. Hannibal*.⁵⁶ A tenth-grader in the Hannibal School District, D.J.M., sent from his home computer a series of instant messages to a fellow classmate suggesting he might procure a gun, take it to school, and shoot individuals mentioned by name. Due to growing concerns about D.J.M.'s intentions, the classmate forwarded some of the messages to an adult friend, as well as the school principal. The school notified local authorities, who took a statement from D.J.M. and placed him into custody. A week later, while D.J.M. was still in juvenile detention, the district superintendent imposed a 10-day suspension, which was eventually extended for the remainder of the school year. In her decision to suspend D.J.M., the superintendent cited a violation of the student code of conduct which resulted in significant disruption and fear in the school. D.J.M.'s parents appealed the suspension to the school board, but were unsuccessful. Later, they appealed the suspension to the district court, arguing for a First Amendment rights to free speech violation for actions that took place off campus. The court disagreed with D.J.M., finding his speech to be unprotected, true threats, and affirmed the school district's disciplinary decision.

A subsequent appeal to the Eighth Circuit again was unsuccessful for D.J.M. and his parents, despite their assertions that D.J.M.'s speech was made in jest out of teenage frustration in response to goading by the classmate.⁵⁷ It is worth noting that the appeals court opinion suggested that even if D.J.M.'s speech was *not* considered a true threat, his free speech claims would not pass the substantial disruption portion of *Tinker*. School officials reportedly dedicated considerable time to responding to concerned parents wishing to know if their children were on a rumored "hit list" and what safety measures the school was taking to prevent gun violence on campus. The Eighth Circuit determined it was "reasonably foreseeable that D.J.M.'s threats about shooting specific students in school would be brought to the attention of school authorities and would create a risk of substantial disruption within the school environment,"⁵⁸ and thus affirmed the district court's ruling.

Lovell and *Pulaski* confirm the fact that true threats, be they conveyed traditionally or electronically, are outside the protection of the First Amendment. In *J.S. v. Bethlehem*, *Bell v. Itawamba*, and *D.J.M. v. Hannibal*, we see courts considering engaging in an analysis of true threats, yet ultimately reverting to the *Tinker* test when threats are not present. *Tinker* circumscribes the speech in these threatless cases, for in each instance speech was found to be disruptive to the school environment, even though it was also created off-campus. To be clear, this is off-campus speech that is considered by the court to have a viable connection to on-campus activity because it materially and substantially disrupted the school environment, thus making the school's case compelling enough for the court to uphold the disciplinary decisions of the defendant districts. The *Mahanoy* case makes it interesting to think about the above cases

---

⁵⁶ D.J.M. v. Hannibal Pub. Sch. Dist. #60, 647 F.3d 754 (2011).
⁵⁷ *Id.* at 762.
⁵⁸ *Id.* at 765.

because it involved off-campus speech for which Brandi was wrongly punished, in violation of her First Amendment rights.

Internet Use Policies

A common theme in the preceding cases has been a lack of clear Internet use policies for guidance. In December 2000, the Children's Internet Protection Act (CIPA) was signed into law.[59] CIPA requires that schools and libraries receiving E-rate federal funding adopt and implement "technology protection" measures on all computers with Internet access as a condition of receiving those funds. Specifically, each school or library must verify that it has adopted and implemented an Internet safety policy, and also that it has installed filters used to ensure student safety and to block Internet access to obscenity, child pornography, and material harmful to minors.[60] The purpose of the E-rate is to assist schools and libraries in obtaining telecommunications and Internet access at discounted rates. CIPA provides that a school having computers with Internet access may not receive services at discount rates unless the school, school board, local educational agency, or other authority running the school submits certifications that officially verify an Internet safety policy has been adopted and implemented. The policy should pertain to minors and adults and be in accordance with the certifications.[61]

An additional requirement for certification with respect to minors, purposed toward the prevention of cyberbullying, was established in 2011. In order to maintain E-rate funding, schools and libraries must update their policies and educate youth about "appropriate online behavior, including interacting with other individuals on social networking websites and in chat rooms, and cyberbullying awareness and response".[62]

Similarly, a school or library will receive certification with respect to adults when it verifies 1) that it is enforcing an Internet safety policy using blocking software that prevents access to visual depictions that are obscene or depicting child pornography, and 2) that it is enforcing the operation of such technology as a protection measure during any use of such computers. If a school or library does not receive E-rate funds, it still may be required to comply if it receives funds under some other federal statute, which typically entices schools districts to comply through the "threat of a lawsuit, the lure of federal money, or a threat of a cutoff of federal funds."[63] For instance, libraries that receive funds under Section 224 of the Museum and Library Services Act must comply.[64] In 2003, the American Libraries Association challenged the constitutionality of CIPA requirements, charging that if they installed filters on their computers, it would

---

[59] Pub. L. 106-554, codified at 20 U.S.C. § 9134 and 47 U.S.C. § 254 (h).
[60] 47 U.S.C. § 254(h).
[61] 47 U.S.C. § 254(h)(5)(A)(i).
[62] Federal Communications Commission, Consumer Guide: Children's Internet Protection Act 1 (2012).
[63] MICHAEL W. LAMORTE, SCHOOL LAW: CASES AND CONCEPTS 10 (2005).
[64] 20 U.S.C. § 9134(b).

force them to abridge the First Amendment rights of their patrons. The Supreme Court disagreed, holding that CIPA did not impose an unconstitutional condition by requiring filters on public library computers, and it did not violate First Amendment free speech rights of patrons. In addition, the Court held that the requirement was not an abuse of Congress's spending power.[65]

Because of CIPA, many school districts have implemented some form of an Internet safety policy, or what is sometimes referred to as an Acceptable Use Policy. However, such policies vary in adequacy and ability to address issues associated with student use of the Internet. Although typically such policies cover the basics of rules and regulations of Internet use in schools, a common problem is that authors offer no guidance relative to students who have attained the age of 17, i.e., those individuals who are considered adults for the purpose of the statute.[66] Many administrators fail to disable filters during adult use, or to inform these students that this is within their rights to request access under the statute. CIPA provides that an administrator, supervisor, or other person authorized by the certifying authority may disable the technology protection measure during use by an adult to enable access for bona fide research or other lawful purpose.[67] For this reason, it is a good idea for schools to include this in their Internet safety policy.

School districts should consciously avoid creating policies that are vague and overbroad. Writing well-crafted Internet safety policies also is connected to granting students due process, because effective ones give notice to students and staff of the types of behaviors that are acceptable when accessing the Internet using the school's computers.

Conclusion

The cases above outline court action regarding issues involving student expression and the Internet. *Beussink v. Woodland R-IV School District*, originally decided in 1998, emphasized the role of *Tinker* and progeny in the ruling of Internet/electronic student speech cases. The enduring quality of the First Amendment principles is confirmed by cases that followed *Beussink*. The principles clearly point to the fact that personal student expression, generated on or off campus, will be protected unless it causes or is meant to cause a substantial and material disruption. Moreover, expression that is found to be a threat, causes a material and substantial disruption, and/or interferes with the rights of others, will not be protected for the purposes of the First Amendment.

Speech that is created in school on district computers can be restricted more easily by school personnel, especially if the purpose of the machines relates to the curriculum in some fashion, which is a common use of school computers. An Internet safety policy can offer leaders additional support in

---

[65] United States v. Am. Libraries Ass'n, 123 S. Ct. 2297 (2003).
[66] 47 U.S.C. § 254(l)). A minor is defined by the statute as "someone who has not attained the age of 17."
[67] 47 U.S.C. § 254(h)(5)(D).

regulating activity and educating students, as it helps to define approved and prohibited activity for students using computers in schools. Filters can facilitate this responsibility of school officials and allow for flexibility in application; this will help to avoid violating the rights of older students who are "adults," who need to have filters disabled to do legitimate research. The recommendations provided below are consistent with the content reported in this chapter.

Recommendations for Practice

1. First Amendment speech expressed on the Internet via social media or other medium, like *Tinker* speech, cannot be punished unless it significantly interferes with a school function, causes, or is likely to cause a disruption, or interferes with the rights of others. Students cannot be punished for such expression merely because it is disrespectful or unpopular. *Mahanoy* confirms that this will be true regardless of where the speech is created.

2. Speech expressed in the form of cyberbullying does not belong to a special class. Administrators should approach instances of cyberbullying with the understanding that it is ultimately subject to the parameters set forth by *Tinker* and its progeny. Schools have significant interest in regulating off-campus conduct, especially when said behavior involves serious or severe bullying or harassment of particular individuals or threats aimed at teachers or fellow students

3. CIPA mandates, among other things, creating an Internet safety policy and adding filters to school computers. It is likely that your school has some form of Internet use policy. If not, check with your district. Some districts may not have filtering software in place because of cost or other reasons. Whether they have filters or not, districts should have some form of an Internet use policy. This may include non-CIPA school districts.

4. Administrators employing such filters should be aware that this blocking software is not infallible and that it likely will over- or under-block. Make this fact known to students and parents. Compensate for the shortfall of the software with the Internet safety policy. Remember these policies have the secondary purpose of educating students about proper behavior on the Internet.

5. When creating Internet safety policies, be sure to avoid vague language in the actual rules of use. It is important to spell out in clear, unambiguous language the purpose of your Internet safety policy and what actions are permitted and prohibited when students are using the schools' computers. This includes using email, instant messages, and material posted on webpages or blogs. Be sure to define all terms. Include language in Internet safety policies about social networking sites and cell phones.

6. Administrators should include in the Internet safety policy when blocking software may be disabled. Even schools with policies usually fail to address when and why filtering software may be disabled. There are cases when

"adults" or older minors need to do bona fide or legitimate research, and this is permitted by CIPA. A minor is defined as anyone who has not attained the age of 17, and an older minor is 17 or older.[68]

7. Have students and parents sign the Internet safety policy. Such signed agreements should be kept on file. Students without signed policies should not be permitted to use the Internet at school. If you decide to do an opt-out policy, make sure parents understand the terms.

8. Make sure students receive due process. Discipline for inappropriate Internet use should be fair and fit the infraction. The other side of the coin of having specific, well-defined policies is having clear and fair punishment for breaking rules. Examples of first-time infractions may include suspension of privileges for a reasonable period of time. Define threats and cyberbullying for students and encourage students to be good citizens when using the Internet, refraining from engaging in prohibited activities. Students should be warned that serious infractions bring about serious penalties that may result in punishment beyond the school's discipline decision.

9. Make sure students understand that computers belong to the school and are to be used primarily for curricular purposes only. School officials often use computers for other purposes that may further the mission of the school.

10. Inform students that computers are school property and can be searched at any time. Therefore, there is a diminished expectation of privacy; computers are analogous to hall lockers that can be searched. This is important in light of the fact that recent virus creators have been high school-age students who use school computers and networks.[69] Requiring students to store data on a server is a possible solution to this problem.

11. Promote positive computer experiences by teaching students to be good citizens when using the Internet.

Case List

A.S. v. Lincoln Cty. R-III Sch. Dist.
Bell v. Itawamba Cnty. Sch. Bd.
Bethel Sch. Dist. No. 403 v. Fraser
Beussink v. Woodland R-IV Sch. Dist.
B.L. v. Mahanoy Area Sch. Dist.
D.J.M. v. Hannibal Pub. Sch. Dist. #60
Doe v. Hopkinton Pub. Schs.
Doe v. Pulaski
Doninger v. Niehoff
Emmett v. Kent Sch. Dist. No. 415

---

[68] 7 U.S.C. § 254(h)(7)(D); 47 U.S.C. § 254(h)(6)(D).
[69] *PC viruses: Never Open Your Door to Strangers*, http://www.usatoday.com/tech/news/2002/05/02/virus-ordeal.htm.

Hazelwood Sch. Dist. v. Kuhlmeier
J.C. v. Beverly Hills Unified Sch. Dist.
J.S. v. Blue Mt. Sch. Dist.
Kowalski v. Berkeley Cnty. Schs.
Layshock v. Hermitage Sch. Dist.
Lovell v. Poway
Mahaffey v. Aldrich
Mahanoy Area Sch. Dist. v. B.L.
Morse v. Frederick
Tinker v. Des Moines Indep. Sch. Dist.
United States v. Am. Libraries Ass'n
Watts v. United States
Wisniewski v. Bd. of Educ. of the Weedsport Cent. Sch. Dist.

Key Words

bullying
Children's Internet Protection Act
curricular
cyberbullying
website
electronic speech
E-rate
Facebook
filters
First Amendment
free speech
harassing
Instagram
insults
Internet
Internet safety policy
legitimate pedagogical concerns
library
Museum and Library Services Act
off-campus conduct
older minor
opt-out policy
protected speech
reasonableness test
reasonably foreseeable
school property
searches
smartphone
Snapchat

social suspension
student expression
substantial disruption
suspension
temporary restraining order
threat
vulgar/indecent/obscene speech
webpage
YouTube

Takeaways

1. The expansive digital age has led to an increasingly complex balance of rights and interests with respect to speech for students and educators. In this heightened cyber environment, school teachers and leaders have greater access to student speech, yet they do not necessarily have greater control over all student speech.

2. While teachers may have greater authority and control over speech in their classrooms, school administrators are limited in their disciplinary options for students' online speech that occurs outside of the school setting. Before intervening to limit or punish students for off-campus speech, school administrators should consider whether or not the speech occurred using a school-issued device or on a school's electronic platform.

3. When considering whether or not to discipline students for off-campus, online speech, school leaders should review the *Tinker* standard to determine whether the speech (1) substantially interferes with the operation of the school, (2) substantially interferes with the rights of others, and/or (3) if the speech could foreseeably interfere substantially with the orderly operation of the school or the rights of others.

4. Student access to school-issued devices, online learning management systems, and digital tools for educational purposes adds another level of complexity with respect to student speech rights. Namely, the educational purpose of these devices, systems, and tools extends the school environment into off-campus settings. As such, school leaders may have both the authority and responsibility to protect education rights of others by enforcing safe learning environments in off-campus cyber settings.

5. School leaders should work closely with teachers, parents, and students to establish acceptable technology use policies. These policies should then be incorporated into student codes of conduct in order to maximize awareness and understanding of the policies for parents and students.

Practical Extension

1. A student shows a teacher a screenshot of a classmate who made disparaging remarks about the teacher publicly on SnapChat. The student used inappropriate language, mocked the teacher, and called the teacher an "idiot." How should the teacher proceed? Based on your knowledge of *Tinker* and off-campus speech, does the school have the authority to discipline the student for inappropriate online behavior?

2. A student posts disparaging remarks about a teacher in a message board. The message board is part of a teacher's classroom page on Google Classroom, the school's learning management system. The teacher and all students in the Google Classroom can see the inappropriate comments that the student posted. Does the school have the authority to discipline the student?

3. A student reports feeling uncomfortable coming to school because of being "bullied" on TikTok by another student. Does the school district have the authority to discipline the student allegedly doing the bullying for off-campus online behavior? Why or why not?

Chapter 7

Fundamentals of Federal Disability Law

Julie F. Mead[1]

Introduction

All teachers, regardless of assignment, play a central role in ensuring that schools provide equitable opportunities for all students. For children with disabilities, achieving equal educational opportunity requires that their teachers have a strong understanding of the fundamentals of federal disability law, including the part teachers play in implementing those requirements. Accordingly, it is important for all teachers to have a working knowledge of three federal laws: Section 504 of the Rehabilitation Act of 1973,[2] the Americans with Disabilities Act,[3] and the Individuals with Disabilities Education Act (IDEA).[4] These laws affect the relationships teachers build with their students both in the classroom and in all school activities. As will be explained more fully, all teachers have a role in each of four central processes: (1) evaluation of children suspected of having a disability; (2) determining whether a child meets the definition of a "child with a disability" under each law; (3) the development of an individualized plan for those students found to be eligible; and (4) determining the appropriate goals, services, and placement for a child with a disability. Understanding the purposes these laws serve and the requirements for practice they delineate empowers the teacher to support the diverse needs of learners in the classroom, and to advocate for the rights and needs of all students. This chapter is designed to explore the major tenets of these important laws and to serve as an introduction to the principles they define.

---

[1] Judith I. Risch contributed to earlier versions of this chapter.
[2] 29 U.S.C. § 794 (2008): 34 C.F.R. § 104.1 *et seq.* (2009).
[3] 42 U.S.C. § 12101 *et seq.* (2008).
[4] 20 U.S.C. § 1400 *et seq.* (2004); 34 C.F.R. § 300 *et seq.* (2006).

Section 504 of the Rehabilitation Act of 1973

Of the three laws discussed in this chapter,[5] Section 504 of the Rehabilitation Act of 1973 (Section 504) is the oldest and, in some ways, the simplest. As a civil rights statute, its purpose is straightforward: it bars discrimination on the basis of disability by any recipient of federal funds.[6] As such, it applies to all public schools in the United States and any private schools that also receive federal monies. Accordingly, schools and school districts must ensure that all the programs offered are accessible to persons with disabilities. As an antidiscrimination statute, its coverage extends from birth to death. Therefore, it has implications for students, employees, parents, and members of the general public who wish to access the benefits created by a school.

Teachers are probably most familiar with Section 504's application to students. Those students who have a "physical or mental impairment which substantially limits one or more major life activities"[7] must receive an education comparable to that of their nondisabled peers.[8] Major life activities "include, but are not limited to, caring for oneself, performing manual tasks, seeing, hearing, eating, sleeping, walking, standing, lifting, bending, speaking, breathing, learning, reading, concentrating, thinking, communicating, and working."[9] The disability may be permanent (e.g., a visual impairment, cerebral palsy, or attention deficit disorder) or temporary.[10] In the case of temporary disabilities, the issue is whether the disability substantially affects the person for a sufficient period of time. As the Office for Civil Rights (OCR) explained: "[t]he issue of whether a temporary impairment is substantial enough to be a disability must be resolved on a case-by-case basis, taking into consideration both the duration (or expected duration) of the impairment and the extent to which it actually limits a major life activity of the affected individual."[11] It should be noted, however, that Congress amended the definition of "disability" in 2008,

---

[5] Please be aware that states may have adopted laws and regulations that go beyond the federal requirements. It is also important to understand those provisions as they may dictate additional requirements and practices for teachers.
[6] 29 U.S.C. § 794 (2012).
[7] 34 C.F.R. § 104.3(j)(1)(i).
[8] 34 C.F.R. § 104.3(k)(2).
[9] 42 U.S.C. §12102 (2012).
[10] *See, e.g., In re* Castillo v. Schriro, 15 N.Y.S.3d 645 (N.Y. Sup. Ct. 2015); Antone v. Nobel Learning Communities, Inc., No. 11-3717 2012 WL 174540 (D.N.J. Jan. 19, 2012); Davis (CA) Joint Unified Sch. Dist. 31 IDELR 186 (OCR 1999).
[11] *Protecting Students with Disabilities: Frequently Asked Questions about Section 504 and the Education of Children with Disabilities,* U.S. Dep't. of Educ., http://www2.ed.gov/about/offices/list/ocr/504faq.html.

clarifying that "transitory" disabilities with an actual or expected duration of less than six months are excluded from the definition of a person with a disability.[12]

The determination of whether a child has a mental or physical impairment that substantially limits one or more major life activities must be based on an evaluation, though unlike the procedures that are required under the IDEA, Section 504 regulations are much less specified.[13] For some students, schools may elect to follow IDEA procedures for evaluation to consider eligibility under both Section 504 and the IDEA simultaneously, because the more stringent IDEA procedures likewise satisfy the requirements of Section 504.[14] For other students, schools may conduct a Section 504 consideration only. It is likely, for example, that IDEA procedures would be used to examine a child struggling in classes and suspected of having a specific learning disability with the goal of determining whether the student meets the eligibility requirements under both the IDEA and Section 504, just under Section 504, or under neither statute. In contrast, a child with a peanut allergy who is doing well in all classes will likely be evaluated using Section 504 only. In both cases, teachers may contribute to the evaluation by providing their observations of the child's functioning both in the classroom and in other school activities (e.g., recess or the lunchroom). Some teachers may also be asked to administer more formal interventions or assessments, depending on the nature of the suspected disability and the concerns raised about the child's performance.

Once a child with a disability is identified through the school's evaluation, Section 504 requires that the child receives meaningful access to the educational program provided by a school. Providing an education comparable to that of nondisabled peers means that school personnel may be required to make reasonable modifications or accommodations[15] in order that the student's disability does not serve as a barrier to how the child can access information or demonstrate learning.[16] Reasonable accommodations may be physical (e.g., Braille, preferential seating, a note-taker, assistance with carrying supplies) or instructional (e.g., a sign-language interpreter, extended time on a test, vo-

---

[12] 42 U.S.C. § 12102(3)(B) (2012). The revisions were made as part of the 2008 Amendments Act to the ADA, which included a conforming provision that likewise revises the meaning of "disability" under Section 504. See Pub. L. No. 110-325, § 7, 122 Stat. 3553 (2008).

[13] 34 C.F.R. §104.35.

[14] UNITED STATES DEPARTMENT OF EDUCATION, OFFICE FOR CIVIL RIGHTS, PROTECTING STUDENTS WITH DISABILITIES: FREQUENTLY ASKED QUESTIONS ABOUT SECTION 504 AND THE EDUCATION OF CHILDREN WITH DISABILITIES question 19, https://www2.ed.gov/about/offices/list/ocr/504faq.html.

[15] Although it is common for school personnel to use the terms modifications and accommodations interchangeably, the Office for Civil Rights cautions that "accommodations" actually refers to the employment context and the term "modifications" is the proper term for the actions taken outside that context. UNITED STATES DEPARTMENT OF EDUCATION, OFFICE FOR CIVIL RIGHTS, PROTECTING STUDENTS WITH DISABILITIES: FREQUENTLY ASKED QUESTIONS ABOUT SECTION 504 AND THE EDUCATION OF CHILDREN WITH DISABILITIES, https://www2.ed.gov/about/offices/list/ocr/504faq.html.

[16] 34 C.F.R. § 104.34(a) (2016).

cabulary assistance) and may include special education and related services.[17] Consideration must also be given to any modifications the child may need to participate in extracurricular or co-curricular activities in order to have equal access to all school programs and activities.[18] For example, a child who is deaf may require a sign-language interpreter in order to participate on the school's soccer and debate teams. Modifications are determined by staff members in consultation with the parents[19] and are outlined in an accommodation plan. Although technically the regulations do not require it,[20] most schools prudently use written accommodation plans.[21]

Ensuring nondiscriminatory access to children with disabilities also requires attention to issues of harassment and bullying.[22] As such, schools must investigate any complaint of disability harassment in a timely fashion and then take appropriate action. As OCR explained in 2014 guidance:

> If a school's investigation reveals that bullying based on disability created a hostile environment—i.e., the conduct was sufficiently serious to interfere with or limit a student's ability to participate in or benefit from the services, activities, or opportunities offered by a school—the school must take prompt and effective steps reasonably calculated to end the bullying, eliminate the hostile environment, prevent it from recurring, and, as appropriate, remedy its effects. Therefore, OCR would find a disability-based harassment violation under Section 504 and Title II [of the ADA] when: (1) a student is bullied based on a disability; (2) the bullying is sufficiently serious to create a hostile environment; (3) school officials know or should know about the bullying; and (4) the school does not respond appropriately.[23]

In order to ensure that all discriminatory treatment based on the status characteristic of disability be addressed and eradicated, Section 504 also protects individuals in two other circumstances: any person who "has a history" of a disability[24] (e.g., someone with a history of cancer) and any person who "is regarded as having" a disability[25] (e.g., someone who is HIV positive, but does not have AIDS). Note that in both cases, the person does not have a disability that impairs function. In other words, a disability does not actually exist.[26]

---

[17] 34 C.F.R. § 104.33(b) (2016).
[18] 34 C.F.R. §104.37 (2017).
[19] 34 C.F.R. § 104.35(c) (2016).
[20] 34 C.F.R. §§104.31 – 104.39 (2016).
[21] *See, e.g., A Parent and Teacher Guide to Section 504: Frequently Asked Questions*, FLA. DEP'T. OF EDUC., http://www.fldoe.org/core/fileparse.php/7690/urlt/0070055-504bro.pdf.
[22] Catherine Lhamon, Dear Colleague Letter, U.S. DEP'T. OF EDUC., (Oct., 21, 2014), https://www2.ed.gov/about/offices/list/ocr/letters/colleague-bullying-201410.pdf.
[23] *Id.* at 4.
[24] 34 C.F.R. § 104.3(j)(1)(ii).
[25] 34 C.F.R. § 104.3(j)(1)(iii) (2016).
[26] 34 C.F.R. § 104.3(j)(2) (2016).

These categories are included in the law and necessary to ensure that no one suffers the effects of discrimination because someone assumed a disability existed. Importantly, these provisions recognize that discrimination is no less abhorrent simply because the person or persons discriminating jumped to an erroneous conclusion. Persons protected by the law in these two categories do not need accommodations or modifications.[27] Rather, they simply need the discriminator to stop their improper behavior.

Section 504 also has implications for staff who have disabilities. Again, the Act protects those individuals who have mental or physical impairments that substantially limit them, or have a history of such impairments, or are regarded as having such.[28] Just as students must be reasonably accommodated in order to access educational opportunities, employees' disabilities must be reasonably accommodated in order to access employment opportunities.[29] Reasonableness has its bounds, however, and employers are not required to substantially alter the qualifications or essential requirements of a job in order to accommodate a worker's disability.[30] In addition, the employer is not expected to bear undue administrative or financial burdens when considering accommodations.[31] Teachers with disabilities should engage in conversations with their employer to determine the reasonable accommodations needed to do their jobs,

Parents with disabilities also enjoy protection under Section 504. Schools must ensure that parents with disabilities, through reasonable accommodations, when necessary, have access to parent-teacher conferences and any meetings concerning the child's progress and behavior in school.[32] For example, a teacher planning to meet with a parent who utilizes a wheelchair for mobility would have to be sure the meeting place was accessible to the parent. Schools would also need to provide a sign-language interpreter for parents who are deaf.[33]

Americans with Disabilities Act

Using its constitutional power to regulate interstate commerce,[34] Congress enacted the Americans with Disabilities Act (ADA) in 1990.[35] The ADA extends the nondiscrimination protections of Section 504 beyond recipients of federal

---

[27] UNITED STATES DEPARTMENT OF EDUCATION, OFFICE FOR CIVIL RIGHTS, PROTECTING STUDENTS WITH DISABILITIES: FREQUENTLY ASKED QUESTIONS ABOUT SECTION 504 AND THE EDUCATION OF CHILDREN WITH DISABILITIES question 36, https://www2.ed.gov/about/offices/list/ocr/504faq.html.
[28] 34 C.F.R. § 104.3 (2016).
[29] 34 C.F.R. § 104.11(a)(1) (2016).
[30] 34 C.F.R. § 104.12(a) (2016).
[31] Southeastern Cmty. Coll. v. Davis, 442 U.S.397 (1979).
[32] Rothschild v. Grottenthaler, 907 F.2d. 286 (2d Cir. 1990).
[33] Id.
[34] United States Constitution, Article 1, Section 8, Clause 3 ("Congress shall have Power... to regulate Commerce with foreign Nations, and among the several States...").
[35] Pub. L. No. 101-336, 104 Stat. 327 (1990).

financial support to private employers and commercial establishments.[36] The law is divided into five titles, as follows:

Title I – prohibits employment discrimination.[37]

Title II – applies to all subdivisions of state and local government, regardless of whether they receive federal financial assistance.[38] Students in public schools are protected under this title.[39]

Title III – prohibits discrimination by businesses that serve the public (e.g., stores, restaurants, hotels and motels, etc.).[40] Title III's provisions also apply to nonsectarian private schools, although private schools are not held to the same programmatic accessibility standards as are public schools. Private schools need only accommodate those children with disabilities that can be served with minor adjustments to the academic program.[41]

Title IV – applies to telecommunications services such as telephone and television companies.[42]

Title V – contains several miscellaneous but important provisions, including a statement that the ADA should not be read to require lesser standards than those of Section 504;[43] that a state's immunity from suit under the Eleventh Amendment is abrogated by the ADA;[44] that ADA's provisions apply to Congress and all agencies of the legislative branch;[45] that the term "individual with a disability" does not include active drug users[46] or transvestites;[47] that homosexuality and bisexuality are not "impairments" under the ADA, and that various other "conditions" are not included under the term "disability."[48]

Congress amended the ADA in 2008[49] in order to correct what legislators considered inappropriate interpretations of the act by the U.S. Supreme Court.[50]

---

[36] 42 U.S.C. § 12101 (2012).

[37] 42 U.S.C. §§ 12111-12117 (2012).

[38] 42 U.S.C. §§ 12131-12165 (2012).

[39] *Questions and Answers on the ADA Amendments of 2008 for Students with Disabilities Attending Public Elementary and Secondary Schools*, U.S. DEP'T. OF EDUC., http://www2.ed.gov/about/offices/list/ocr/docs/dcl-504faq-201109.html.

[40] 42 U.S.C §§ 12181-12189 (2012).

[41] *See, e.g.*, U.S. Department of Justice, Civil Rights Division, *Justice Department Settles with Private Montessori School to Prevent Disability Discrimination* (Sept. 29, 2014), https://www.justice.gov/opa/pr/justice-department-settles-private-montessori-school-prevent-disability-discrimination.

[42] 47 U.S.C. § 225 (2012).

[43] 42 U.S.C. §§ 12201-12213 (2012).

[44] 42 U.S.C. § 12202 (2012).

[45] 42 U.S.C. § 12209 (2012).

[46] 42 U.S.C. § 12210 (2012).

[47] 42 U.S.C. § 12208 (2012).

[48] 42 U.S.C. § 12211(a) and b) (2012) (conditions enumerated include, among others, pedophilia, exhibitionism, voyeurism, compulsive gambling, kleptomania, and pyromania).

[49] *See* Pub. L. No. 110-325, 122 Stat. 3553 (2008).

[50] *Id.* at § 2, citing Sutton v. United Air Lines, Inc., 527 U.S. 471 (1999) and Toyota Motor Mfg., Ky., Inc. v. Williams, 534 U.S. 184 (2002).

The revisions clarify the definition of "major life activities"[51] and direct that "[a]n impairment that substantially limits one major life activity need not limit other major life activities in order to be considered a disability."[52] Moreover, the consideration of whether a disability substantially limits a person "shall be made without regard to the ameliorative effects of mitigating measures."[53] Finally, the revisions direct that reviewing courts should construe the definition of a disability "in favor of broad coverage of individuals under this Act."[54]

Even with these clarifications, Title II of the ADA largely mirrors the requirements of Section 504 with respect to the protections for students in the public school classroom and, accordingly, the requirements of both acts are often jointly referred to as "Section 504/ADA."[55] For public schools, then, additional ADA requirements often relate to construction and renovation requirements associated with physical accessibility. The ADA also has far more extensive regulations with respect to employment, so teachers with disabilities should familiarize themselves with their rights under the ADA.[56]

Individuals with Disabilities Education Act

The Individuals with Disabilities Education Act (IDEA) is without doubt the most prescriptive of the three acts with regard to the educational experience of children with disabilities. The theory of action undergirding the law can be simply stated: If states and local school personnel follow a prescribed set of procedures requiring the consideration of the unique needs of each individual child with a disability and design an individualized program to meet those needs, equitable and appropriate education will result and children with disabilities will no longer be excluded or inappropriately served. First enacted in 1975 as the Education for All Handicapped Children's Act (EAHCA),[57] Congress renamed the statute the Individuals with Disabilities Education Act (IDEA) in 1990, at the same time it enacted the ADA. Unlike Section 504 and

---

[51] 42 U.S.C. § 12102(2)(A) (2012) ("major life activities include, but are not limited to, caring for oneself, performing manual tasks, seeing, hearing, eating, sleeping, walking, standing, lifting, bending, speaking, breathing, learning, reading, concentrating, thinking, communicating, and working.").

[52] 42 U.S.C. § 12102(4)(C) (2012).

[53] 42 U.S.C. § 12102(4)(E)(i) (2012). Mitigating measures include "medication, medical supplies, equipment, or appliances, low-vision devices (which do not include ordinary eyeglasses or contact lenses), prosthetics including limbs and devices, hearing aids and cochlear implants or other implantable hearing devices, mobility devices, or oxygen therapy equipment and supplies." 42 U.S.C. § 12102(4)(E)(i)(I) (2012).

[54] 42 U.S.C. § 12102(4)(A) (2012).

[55] *See, e.g.*, Perry A. Zirkel, *A National Update of Case Law 1998 to the Present under the IDEA and Section 504/A.D.A.*, NAT'L. ASS'N. OF STATE DIRECTORS OF SPECIAL EDUC., http://www.nasdse.org/LinkClick.aspx?fileticket=gDUBs9sKzRw%3d&tabid=578.

[56] U.S. EQUAL EMP'T OPPORTUNITY COMM'N, *Your Employment Rights as an Individual with a Disability*. https://www.eeoc.gov/laws/guidance/your-employment-rights-individual-disability.

[57] Pub. L. No. 94-142, 89 Stat. 773 (1975).

the ADA, the IDEA is a funding statute, rather than a civil rights statute.[58] It provides funds to assist states to meet the needs of students whose disabilities "adversely affect a child's educational performance"[59] such that special education and related services are needed.[60] This piece of child welfare legislation serves as a complement to Section 504. You might say that Section 504 is the "stick" (punishing those who violate it by termination of federal funds), while the IDEA is the "carrot" (providing federal financial incentives for the appropriate delivery of special education[61] and related services[62]).

Note, too, that eligibility under the IDEA requires three separate considerations: (1) a mental or physical impairment[63] (2) that adversely affects educational performance[64] and (3) requires special education and related services to address the needs identified.[65] Therefore, a student with disabilities who is protected against discrimination under Section 504/ADA may not meet the more narrow definitions of disability to be able to qualify for services under the IDEA. To be eligible under IDEA, the student's profile of needs and abilities must match the definition of one or more disability categories specified by the IDEA.[66] These disability categories are "intellectual disabilities, hearing impairments (including deafness), speech or language impairments, visual impairments (including blindness), serious emotional disturbance . . ., orthopedic impairments, autism, traumatic brain injury, other health impairments, and specific learning disabilities."[67] Thus, those served under the IDEA are a subset of those protected under Section 504/ADA. For example, a child with a life-threatening food allergy would be protected from discrimination under Section 504 and the ADA, but may not qualify as a "child with a disability" under the IDEA. In addition, a child could have an impairment (e.g., a visual impairment or health-related issue) that is not severe enough to "adversely af-

---

[58] 20 U.S.C. § 1400(d)(1) (2012).
[59] 34 C.F.R. § 300.8 (2016).
[60] 20 U.S.C. § 1401(3)(A)(ii) (2012).
[61] 20 U.S.C. § 1401(29) (2012), ("The term 'special education' means specially designed instruction, at no cost to parents, to meet the unique needs of a child with a disability, including—(A) instruction conducted in the classroom, in the home, in hospitals and institutions, and in other settings; and (B) instruction in physical education.").
[62] 20 U.S.C. § 1401(26) (2012) ("The term 'related services' means transportation, and such developmental, corrective, and other supportive services (including speech-language pathology and audiology services, interpreting services, psychological services, physical and occupational therapy, recreation, including therapeutic recreation, social work services, school nurse services designed to enable a child with a disability to receive a free appropriate public education as described in the individualized education program of the child, counseling services, including rehabilitation counseling, orientation and mobility services, and medical services, except that such medical services shall be for diagnostic and evaluation purposes only) as may be required to assist a child with a disability to benefit from special education, and includes the early identification and assessment of disabling conditions in children.").
[63] 20 U.S.C. § 1401 (3) (2012); 34 C.F.R. § 300.8 (2016).
[64] 34 C.F.R. § 300.8 (2016).
[65] 20 U.S.C. § 1401(3)(A)(ii) (2012).
[66] 20 U.S.C. § 1401(3) (2012); 34 C.F.R. § 300.8 (2016).
[67] 20 U.S.C. § 1401(3) (2012).

fect[] ...educational performance" as required by the regulations to qualify for services under the IDEA.⁶⁸ However, that child may still be entitled to accommodations under Section 504/ADA in order to receive an education comparable to students who are not disabled. Similarly, a child may have a disability that adversely affects educational performance, but the child's needs can be met in the regular classroom without special education services. That child, too, while eligible for accommodations under Section 504/ADA, would not be eligible under the IDEA because special education is not needed.⁶⁹

Figure 7.1 depicts the relationships of these eligibility standards. As shown, those people who are protected by Section 504 and the ADA are a subset of "all people." School-aged children, too, are subset of "all people." The intersection of those two groups depicts those children eligible under Section 504 and the ADA. A subset of the intersection represents those children who have a disability who meet the definition of a children with a disability under the IDEA. As is shown, a child who is found to be a "child with a disability" under the IDEA would likewise be protected under both Section 504 and the ADA. To keep this relationship clear, it may be helpful to remember this statement: All children eligible under the IDEA are also eligible under Section 504 and the ADA, but not all children eligible under Section 504 and the ADA are eligible under the IDEA.

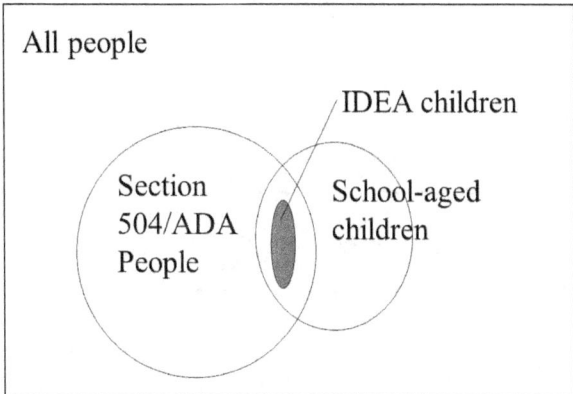

Figure 7.1: Relationship of Eligibility Standards⁷⁰

The IDEA is an extremely detailed law that requires school districts to document and justify the services provided to eligible children with disabilities. The IDEA creates a federal statutory right, or an entitlement, for each student with a disability. That entitlement is known as the right to a free appropriate public education (FAPE), which consists of special education and related ser-

---

⁶⁸ 34 C.F.R. § 300.8 (2016).
⁶⁹ See, e.g., Marshall Joint Sch. Dist. v. C. D. *ex rel* Brian D., 616 F. 3d 632 (7th Cir. 2010).
⁷⁰ Figure 1 is adapted from JULIE K. UNDERWOOD & JULIE F. MEAD, LEGAL ASPECTS OF SPECIAL EDUCATION AND PUPIL SERVICES 42 (1995).

vices designed to address the unique needs of the individual child.[71] The law creates an affirmative obligation on the part of the state and its local school districts to identify and serve all eligible students with disabilities within their geographic boundaries,[72] sometimes referred to as the "child find" obligation.[73] This obligation to identify, locate, and serve children with disabilities also extends to those children whose parents have chosen to enroll them in private schools.[74] Students may be referred for evaluation by any school personnel or by parents. Once referred, school officials must review the child's records and design a series of assessments in order to determine whether the suspicions of a disability are founded.[75] Parents must be provided notice of their rights under the law, and must consent in writing to an evaluation before any testing may commence.[76] Once the evaluation is complete, the school personnel meet with the parents as an "IEP team" to determine eligibility together.[77] As mentioned before, the mere presence of a disability does not qualify a child for services under the IDEA.[78] Rather, eligibility is dependent on whether the disability adversely affects educational performance such that special education is needed, the degree to which may be further specified in the state's plan of service.[79] The IDEA also requires that students be reevaluated at least once every three years.[80]

Teachers have a very important role in evaluation of a child suspected of having a disability. A teacher may be the first to notice that a child is struggling

---

[71] 20 U.S.C. § 1401(9) (2012).

[72] 20 U.S.C. § 1412(a)(3). IDEA uses the terms "state education agency" (SEA), 20 U.S.C. § 1401(32) (2012), and "local education agency" (LEA). 20 U.S.C. § 1401(19) (2012). It should be noted that some charter schools may be LEAs for the purposes of IDEA. 20 U.S.C. § 1413(e)(1)(B) (2012).

[73] DIXIE SNOW HUEFNER & CYNTHIA M. HERR, NAVIGATING SPECIAL EDUCATION LAW AND POLICY 106 (2012).

[74] 20 U.S.C. § 1412 (a)(3)(A) (2012); 34 C.F.R. § 300.111 (2016). The rights afforded children enrolled by their parents in private settings are not coextensive with those of children in the public setting. These students enjoy only a group entitlement as opposed to an individual one, and must be served "consistent with [their] number and location." 20 U.S.C. § 1412 (a)(10)(A) (2012); 34 C.F.R. § 300.132 (2016). In addition, IDEA only requires LEAs to expend federal dollars on those children in private schools and makes no requirements for the expenditure of state or local funds, 20 U.S.C. § 1412 (a)(10)(A)(i)(I) (2012); 34 C.F.R. § 300.133(c) (2016). Of course, states may impose additional requirements through state statutes.

[75] 20 U.S.C. § 1414 (b)(2) (2012).

[76] 20 U.S.C. § 1414 (a)(1)(D) (2012).

[77] IEP refers to the individualized education program. 20 U.S.C. § 1401(14) (2012).

[78] Although the mere presence of a disability does qualify a child for *protection from discrimination* and an education comparable to that of nondisabled peers under Section 504/ADA.

[79] 34 C.F.R. § 300.100 (2016).

[80] 20 U.S.C. §1414(a)(2)(B)(ii).

and may be the first to suspect a disability is the cause of the child's struggles.[81] If so, the teacher is obligated to refer the child for evaluation under the IDEA.[82] Once a referral is made, all of the child's teachers will be asked to provide input into how the child currently functions, identifying both strengths and concerns. As noted earlier with regard to Section 504, teachers may also be assigned the task of implementing interventions or administering more formal assessments as part of the evaluation. It is also important to note that IDEA requires that every IEP team include "not less than 1 regular education teacher of such child (if the child is, or may be, participating in the regular education environment)" and "not less than 1 special education teacher, or where appropriate, not less than 1 special education provider of such child."[83] While it may be obvious why the law requires a special educator to be part of the team, it must be emphasized that the "regular" educator has an equally important role and obligation to share their expertise. The "regular education teacher" contributes by helping the team understand the "general curriculum" and by providing insight into the measures necessary for "the child to be involved in and make progress in the general education curriculum."[84] In fact, in one significant case, a court invalidated an IEP because the team did not include a regular educator when there was a possibility the child could be placed in a regular classroom.[85] The court considered that omission a "significant violation of the structural requirements of the IDEA's procedures."[86]

---

[81] IDEA also requires that the team consider other causes for any child's learning difficulties. As the relevant provision requires: "In making a determination of eligibility ..., a child shall not be determined to be a child with a disability if the determinant factor for such determination is— (A) lack of appropriate instruction in reading, including in the essential components of reading instruction ...; (B) lack of instruction in math; or (C) limited English proficiency." 20 U.S.C. §1414(b)(5).

[82] 20 U.S.C. § 1412(a)(3).

[83] 20 U.S.C. §1414(d)(1)(B) (2012). The full composition of the IEP team is specified as follows: The term "individualized education program team" or "IEP Team" means a group of individuals composed of—
  (i) the parents of a child with a disability;
  (ii) not less than 1 regular education teacher of such child (if the child is, or may be, participating in the regular education environment);
  (iii) not less than 1 special education teacher, or where appropriate, not less than 1 special education provider of such child;
  (iv) a representative of the local educational agency who--
    (I) is qualified to provide, or supervise the provision of, specially designed instruction to meet the unique needs of children with disabilities;
    (II) is knowledgeable about the general education curriculum; and
    (III) is knowledgeable about the availability of resources of the local educational agency;
  (v) an individual who can interpret the instructional implications of evaluation results, who may be a member of the team described in clauses (ii) through (vi);
  (vi) at the discretion of the parent or the agency, other individuals who have knowledge or special expertise regarding the child, including related services personnel as appropriate;
  (vii) whenever appropriate, the child with a disability. Id.

[84] 20 U.S.C. §1414(d)(1)(A)(i)(II)(aa) (2012).

[85] M.L. v. Federal Way Sch. Dist., 394 F.3d 634 (9th Cir. 2005).

[86] Id., at 651.

Once eligibility is determined, the IEP team, which includes the parents, collaborates to produce an individualized education program (IEP).[87] The IEP is a document that delineates measurable annual goals for the child and specifies the kind and nature of services to be provided to or on behalf of the child.[88] As such, the IEP is the document by which FAPE is defined for an individual child—an individualized equity plan, if you will. Note that FAPE does not have a unitary definition under the law;[89] that is, what constitutes FAPE for one child may not provide FAPE for another. A child's unique needs dictate the goals and services defined by the IEP. This fact reveals a foundational characteristic of the IDEA. All decisions must be based on individualized determinations of need, as opposed to considerations of group instruction or programmatic design. You might say the "I" looms large in the IDEA.

The IDEA requires that an IEP include the following elements in order to achieve FAPE for a child:[90]

- Present levels of academic achievement & functional performance
- Measurable annual goals
- How the child's progress will be measured & reported
- Special education and related services
- Supplementary aids and services
- Program modifications or supports
- An explanation for the extent, if any, the child will not participate in the regular class
- How the child will participate in statewide and district-wide assessments including needed accommodations OR alternative assessments
- Projected date, frequency, location, and duration of services
- Transition service needs for children aged 16 or older

In general, there are three overriding principles for IEP construction. The IEP must be based on child's unique needs. It must be designed to allow the child to progress in the general curriculum and it must be aligned to state content standards. IEPs must be updated at least once per year.[91] It is also important to understand that once an IEP is adopted, all teachers who interact with the child have an obligation to implement the IEP. As detailed as the law is, the IDEA does not assign roles and responsibilities to various teachers. Rather, it presumes that school personnel act as a team to provide FAPE to a child.

In 1982, the Supreme Court provided further explanation of FAPE and what it requires, with particular focus on the meaning of the word "appropriate." The Court explained that FAPE does not require that a child's potential be maximized, but rather that the IEP be "reasonably calculated to enable the

---

[87] 20 U.S.C. § 1414(d) (2012).
[88] The IEP should also specify any curricular adaptations, supports, supplementary aids, and services. 20 U.S.C. § 1414 (d)(1)(A)(i)(IV) (2012); 34 C.F.R. § 300.320(a)(3) (2016).
[89] Board of Educ. of Hendrick Hudson Cent. Sch. Dist. v. Rowley, 458 U.S. 176, 202 (1982) (declining to establish a single test to determine whether FAPE has been provided).
[90] 20 U.S.C. §1414(d)(1)(A).
[91] 20 U.S.C. §1414(d)(4)(A)(i).

child to receive educational benefits."[92] FAPE is a "basic floor of opportunity,"[93] a minimum level of service below which a district may not go.[94] Recently, the Supreme Court clarified the standard for FAPE, declaring that "[t]he adequacy of a given IEP turns on the unique circumstances of the child for whom it was created"[95] and "[t]o meet its substantive obligation under the IDEA, a school must offer an IEP reasonably calculated to enable a child to make progress appropriate in light of the child's circumstances."[96]

Once the IEP team determines the child's IEP goals, the team must determine the issue of placement.[97] The IDEA requires that children with disabilities be educated in the least restrictive environment (LRE), another central principle of the IDEA. LRE requires that children be educated with their nondisabled peers to the "maximum extent appropriate."[98] The LRE principle was codified in the original EAHCA, and amendments made to the IDEA in 1997 and 2004 strengthened this principle by creating a strong presumption in favor of educating children with disabilities in traditional classroom settings.[99] The IEP team must first consider how the child's needs can be met in the regular class environment. This consideration must include a discussion of the curricular adaptations and supports, supplemental aids, and services that may make it possible to deliver the child's IEP in the general classroom.[100] However, even given that strong presumption of regular class placement with support, the LRE for some students may require placement in other than the regular classroom for part or all of the school day.[101] It is incumbent upon school personnel to show why—given the "nature and severity of the [child's] disability,"[102] and even with the addition of supplementary aids and services, as well as curricular adaptations and supportive services—FAPE cannot be achieved in the regular class setting for part or all of the child's school day. To that end, the law requires that school districts make available a "continuum of alternative placements" (e.g., resource rooms, special classes, special schools),[103] but that these other placements only be used when equity demands such a difference.

---

[92] *Id.* at 207. However, state law may place requirements for a higher level of service on its LEAs.
[93] *Id.* at 201.
[94] *Id.* at 200.
[95] Endrew F. v. Douglas Cnty. Sch. Dist., 137 S.Ct. 988, at 1001 (2017).
[96] *Id.* at 999.
[97] 20 U.S.C. § 1414(e) (2012); 34 C.F.R. § 300.327 (2016). Note that placement is based on the IEP, not the other way around.
[98] 20 U.S.C. § 1412(a)(5) (2012).
[99] S. REP. NO. 105-17, (1997), *available at* 1997 WL 244967; *see also* Julie F. Mead, *Expressions of Congressional Intent: Examining the 1997 Amendments to the IDEA*, 127 WEST ED. LAW REP. 511(1998).
[100] 20 U.S.C. § 1414(d)(1)(A)(i)(V) (2012); 34 C.F.R. § 320(a)(5) (2016).
[101] *See, e.g.*, Baquerizo v. Garden Grove Unified Sch. Dist., 826 F.3d 1179 (9th Cir. 2016); T.M. v. Cornwall Cent. Sch. Dist., 752 F.3d 145 (2nd Cir. 2014); Houston Indep. Sch. Dist. v. V.P. *ex rel.* Juan P., 582 F.3d 576 (5th Cir. 2009).
[102] 20 U.S.C. § 1412(a)(5) (2012).
[103] 34 C.F.R. § 300.115 (2016).

If a child's poor performance in the regular class motivates the IEP team to reexamine the appropriateness of a placement, it is helpful to note that the provisions of the IDEA essentially offer two explanations for such a problem: either the child is inadequately supported in the traditional classroom, or the child is inappropriately placed in that setting. The law requires that the IEP team carefully examine the first question before considering the second.

It is also important for all teachers to comprehend that LRE is related to, but is not synonymous with, "inclusion." Inclusion is an educational philosophy defined as "providing all students within the mainstream appropriate educational programs which are challenging and yet geared to their capabilities and needs as well as any support and assistance they and/or their teachers may need to be successful in the mainstream."[104] Some even argue that all students with disabilities should be included at all times, regardless of the nature and severity of their disabilities. This stance, often referred to as "full inclusion," is inconsistent with the IDEA. The IDEA does not require that students with disabilities be included as much as *possible*—it requires that students with disabilities be included as much as *appropriate*.[105] The IDEA is predicated on the principle that sometimes appropriateness (that is, equity) requires something other than what is traditional to meet the unique needs of an individual child. However, it is certainly true that for the vast majority of students with disabilities, an individualized examination of the needs of the child and the appropriate settings to address those needs will result in an "included" placement for all or part of the school day.

The final core component of the IDEA is the explicit articulation of procedural protections.[106] In order to protect the child's entitlement and to ensure that all decision making occurs in the proper context, the IDEA mandates detailed procedural requirements and safeguards. If parents believe that the school is not providing an appropriate education for their child, they can challenge the district through a "due process" hearing.[107] This hearing is presided over by an impartial hearing officer supplied by the state. The hearing officer makes findings of fact, and then applies the law to the facts of the situation.[108] Parents may challenge any decision relative to the process (e.g., evaluation, eligibility, appropriateness, placement). Likewise, if the district believes that parents are obstructing the school's ability to meet its obligation of FAPE for the child by refusing to consent to an evaluation, the district may request a due process hearing to settle the dispute.[109] Hearing decisions may be appealed in state or federal court.[110] Provisions also require school districts to make mediation

---

[104] WILLIAM STAINBACK, SUPPORT NETWORKS FOR INCLUSIVE SCHOOLING: INTERDEPENDENT INTEGRATED EDUCATION, 3 (1990).
[105] 20 U.S.C. § 1412(a)(5) (2012).
[106] 20 U.S.C. § 1415 *et.seq.* (2012).
[107] 20 U.S.C. § 1415(f) (2012).
[108] 20 U.S.C. § 1415(h) (2012).
[109] 20 U.S.C. § 1414(a)(1)(D)(ii)(I) (2012).
[110] 20 U.S.C. § 1415(i)(2) (2012).

available as a mechanism for resolving any dispute with parents and avoiding the more adversarial hearing process.[111] Another major addition to the law in 1997, and revised in 2004, includes the creation of provisions detailing procedural safeguards for children with disabilities facing disciplinary sanctions.[112] These provisions essentially codify earlier case law and require disciplinarians, including teachers, to ensure that children with disabilities are treated equitably by the process.[113]

Finally, case law has established that parents who prevail at the hearing or in court may be entitled to remedies under the court's broad authority to fashion "such relief as the court determines is appropriate."[114] These remedies include recovery of attorney fees;[115] reimbursement of costs, including tuition costs borne by the parent;[116] and compensatory education.[117]

Figure 7.2 provides an illustration of the core components of IDEA. Central to the IDEA is the child's entitlement—a *free appropriate public education* as defined by an *Individualized Education Program* delivered in the *least restrictive environment*. The context for determining the child's entitlement has three characteristics: *individualized determinations, parental involvement,* and *group decision making*. All of which is guaranteed by *procedural protections,* which can be invoked by two guardians of the child's entitlement, parents and the school. As noted earlier, teachers play an important and role in implementing this law, which is designed to engineer equity for each child with a disability. All teachers have obligations with respect to evaluation, eligibility determinations, program development, and placement. The more teachers understand these processes and how they relate to equity, the better able schools will be able to meet the needs of the diverse learners in their care.

---

[111] 20 U.S.C. § 1415(e) (2012).

[112] 20 U.S.C. § 1415(k) (2012).

[113] Essentially these provisions, like the judicial interpretations from which they stem, demonstrate that when school officials consider the discipline of students with disabilities, they must ask three critical questions to ensure that the disciplinary sanction does not result in discrimination on the basis of disability and to ensure equity: (1) Is the behavior a manifestation of the disability?; (2) Does the disciplinary consequence result in a change of placement, thereby invoking the procedures of IDEA?; and (3) Was the child receiving appropriate programming at the time the misbehavior occurred?

[114] 20 U.S.C. § 1415(i)(2)(C) (2012).

[115] 20 U.S.C. § 1415(i)(3) (2012).

[116] Sch. Comm. of Town of Burlington v. Dep't of Educ. of Mass., 471 U.S. 359 (1985); Florence Cty. Sch. Dist. Four v. Carter, 510 U.S. 7 (1993).

[117] *See, e.g.,* B.D. v. District of Columbia, 817 F.3d 792 (D.C. Cir. 2016); Doe v. East Lyme Bd. of Educ., 790 F.3d 440 (2d Cir. 2015); Ferren C. v. Sch. Dist. of Phila., 612 F.3d 712 (3d Cir. 2010). For a general discussion of remedies under the IDEA, *see* DIXIE SNOW HUEFNER AND CYNTHIA M. HERR, NAVIGATING SPECIAL EDUCATION LAW AND POLICY, 61-274 (2012).

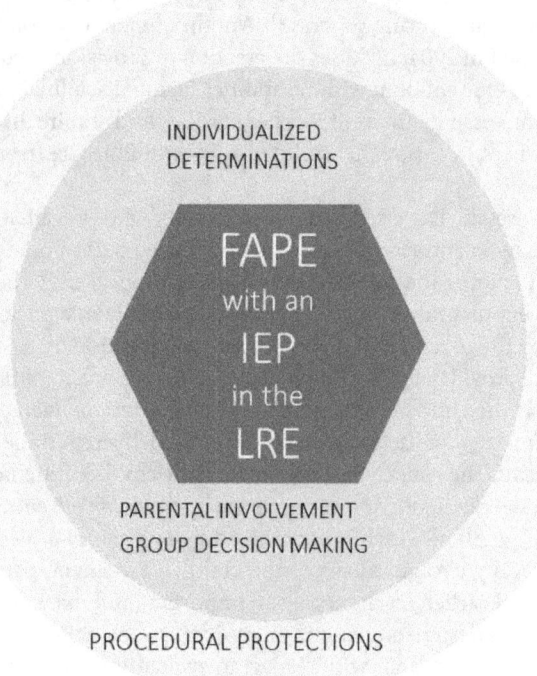

Figure 7.2: IDEA's core concepts

Recommendations for Practice

Considering the issues related to this topic, savvy teachers would do well to consider the following recommendations for practice:
1. Seek staff development opportunities to better understand their responsibilities to accommodate students with disabilities in the classroom.
2. Develop an understanding of the accommodations and protections offered to students through Section 504, the ADA, and the IDEA.
3. Explore how state laws and local school and school district policies interpret these federal guidelines and how they may outline additional processes and protections to students and their parents.
4. Understand their role when serving on an IEP team and be prepared to share their expertise.
5. Carefully examine the Section 504/ADA plans and IEPs of each student assigned to them to ensure they understand how the child functions, what the child needs, what goals have been set for the child, and how they should contribute as part of the team implementing the IEP to ensure equity for each child.

Case List

Antone v. Nobel Learning Communities, Inc.
B.D. v. District of Columbia
Baquerizo v. Garden Grove Unified Sch. Dist.
Board of Educ. of Hendrick Hudson Cent. Sch. Dist. v. Rowley
Castillo v. Schriro
Doe v. East Lyme Bd. of Educ.
Endrew F. v. Douglas Cnty. Sch. Dist.
Ferren C. v. Sch. Dist. of Phila.
Florence Cnty. Sch. Dist. Four v. Carter
Houston Indep. Sch. Dist. v. V.P. *ex rel.* Juan P.
Marshall Joint Sch. Dist. v. C. D. *ex rel* Brian D.
M.L. v. Federal Way Sch. Dist.
Rothschild v. Grottenthaler
School Comm. of Town of Burlington v. Dep't of Educ. of Mass.
Southeastern Cmty. Coll. v. Davis
Sutton v. United Air Lines, Inc.
T.M. v. Cornwall Cent. Sch. Dist.
Toyota Motor Mfg., Ky., Inc. v. Williams

Key Words

accommodations
Americans with Disabilities Act: Titles I, II, III, IV, V
bullying
child with a disability
disability
discrimination
due process protections
Education for All Handicapped Children's Act
evaluation
federal funds
free appropriate public education (FAPE)
harassment
hearings
impairment
inclusion
individualized education program (IEP)
Individuals with Disabilities Education Act
least restrictive environment (LRE)
major life activity
meaningful access
private schools

procedural due process
related services
remedies
Section 504 of the Rehabilitation Act of 1973

Takeaways

1. Section 504 of the Rehabilitation Act of 1973 requires schools that receive federal funds to provide modifications and accommodations to students who have a mental or physical limitation that substantially limits their ability to perform major life activities (which include, but are not limited to, caring for oneself, performing manual tasks, seeing, hearing, eating, sleeping, walking, standing, lifting, bending, speaking, breathing, learning, reading, concentrating, thinking, communicating, and working). Students with 504 plans may receive accommodations in school to level the playing field; 504 plans remove the barriers created by a disability to ensure that the student is able to succeed and perform both in the classroom and in all school programs and activities. For example:

2. A 504 plan for a hearing-impaired student may include providing closed captioning on all videos shown in class, providing a microphone or sound system for the classroom, or providing a sign-language interpreter.

3. A 504 plan for a student with diabetes may include the ability for the student to "stop-the-clock" during a timed assessment in school in order to regulate the student's blood sugar.

4. The Americans with Disabilities Act mirrors Section 504 and extends nondiscrimination protection to institutions and businesses that do not receive federal funds.

5. The Individuals with Disabilities Education Act (IDEA) offers further protection for students with disabilities by providing a narrower definition for disability. A student who meets the criteria for services through IDEA also is protected from discrimination by Section 504 and the ADA; however, not all students with disabilities who are protected by Section 504/ADA qualify as children with disabilities under the IDEA.

6. Federal funding is available through the IDEA to support schools in providing students who qualify for special education services with the appropriate special education, related services, accommodations, supports, and modifications they need.

7. Students who qualify as children with disabilities under the IDEA are eligible to receive an individualized education program (IEP).

8. IEPs ensure that students with disabilities receive a free appropriate public education (FAPE).

9. IEPs are individualized to meet the specific needs of students.

10. Under the IDEA, all students with disabilities must be educated in the least restrictive environment (LRE). The default placement for students with disabilities is the regular classroom, where they should be educated with students without disabilities to the greatest extent that is appropriate. They should not be placed in separate learning environments unless the nature and severity of their disabilities demand such a placement in order to achieve FAPE.

Practical Extension

1. An elementary school teacher recently referred one of his students for evaluation. The team concluded that while the student did have a disability (attention deficit hyperactivity disorder), the student did not qualify as having a disability under the IDEA because special education was not required in order to meet the student's identified educational needs. The team then began work on a Section 504 plan. What kind of accommodations might be considered? How should the parents be involved in the development of the plan? How should the plan be communicated to other school staff who work with the student (e.g., music teacher, art teacher, lunch room supervisor)? Whose responsibility is it to implement the 504 plan?

2. A middle school teacher also serves as the school's basketball coach. He learns that three of the members of the team have either a 504 plan or an IEP. What steps should he take to ensure that all students have an equal opportunity to learn basketball and participate on the team?

3. A high school teacher is notified that she will be serving as the "regular class teacher" on an IEP team for a student in her third period algebra class. What steps should she take? In what ways could she contribute to the student's IEP development?

4. After reviewing recent evaluation data for a sixth-grade child with a specific learning disability, the IEP team determines that the child is reading four grade levels below his current grade; however, his listening comprehension is on grade level. The child's general education teacher and special education teacher also note that when materials are read aloud to the child, he is able to understand grade-level content. Based on these present levels of performance and the child's individual strengths and weaknesses, the IEP team determines he should receive specialized instruction to improve his reading fluency. Based on the child's rate of growth during the previous school year, the IEP team estimates that with appropriate specialized instruction, the child could achieve an increase of at least 1.5 grade levels in reading fluency. The team acknowledges the effect of his disability on reading also affects his performance in other academic subjects (e.g., science and social studies). As the team constructs the IEP, what should they consider with respect to those subjects? What curricular adaptations and supports should be considered? Given the extent of his learning disability,

should the specialized instruction or even placement in a special education classroom be considered for content areas other than reading? How would you handle this situation?

Chapter 8

IEPs, Least Restrictive Environment, and Placement

Jean B. Crockett and Mitchell L. Yell

Introduction

The Individuals with Disabilities Education Act (IDEA),[1] which originally became law as the Education for All Handicapped Children Act (EAHCA) in 1975,[2] sought to remedy the exclusion of millions of children from public instruction based solely upon their disabilities. The IDEA affirms the guarantee of a free appropriate public education (FAPE) through an individualized education program (IEP) for each eligible student with a disability.[3] From its enactment to its most recent reauthorization, the law has required that decisions about special education programming and placements be team-based and child-centered. The least restrictive environment (LRE) principle guides placement decisions so that students can be taught in regular classes, to the maximum extent appropriate to their individual needs, or in alternative settings when teams of parents and professionals determine that students cannot make satisfactory progress in regular classes, even with specialized supports.[4]

Although legal procedures guide its delivery, special education is not about law; it is about educating students with disabilities in specialized ways that build upon their strengths and strengthen their weaknesses. Special education is not about *where* students are educated, but about *how* young people are prepared for their futures through farsighted programming and personalized supports. If students with disabilities were just like everyone else, there would be no need for special education. If schools were not accountable for the learning of every student, there would be less urgency to treat some students differently in order to ensure their success. Special education continues to rely on law because justice has not been blind to students whose learning needs are exceptional, or to the extraordinary efforts required by school systems in providing their education.[5]

---

[1] The Individuals with Disabilities Education Improvement Act of 2004, Pub. L. No. 108-446, 118 Stat. 2647 (2004) (codified at 20 U.S.C. §§ 1400-1482 (2012)).
[2] Pub. L. No. 94-142, 89 Stat. 773 (1975).
[3] 20 U.S.C. § 1412(A)(1) (2012) (defining FAPE); 20 U.S.C. § 1414 (d) (2012) (setting forth requirements for IEPs).
[4] See 20 U.S.C. § 1412(a)(5)(A) (2012) (setting forth the statutory LRE language).
[5] See B.H. v. West Clermont Bd. of Educ., 788 F. Supp. 2d 682 (S.D. Ohio 2011) for an illustration of this principle.

In this chapter, the interplay among IEPs, the LRE, and placements is explained and illustrated, with examples drawn from the IDEA Amendments of 2004,[6] the 2006 Federal Regulations,[7] and relevant case law. References are made to guidance from the U.S. Supreme Court addressing IEP disputes, as well as the shared responsibility of school officials and parents to improve outcomes for students with disabilities.

Legal Issues

Teachers are critical to ensuring effective special education in schools. Moreover, teachers are challenged to provide all students with a high-quality education in accordance with their state's academic content standards, as required by the Every Student Succeeds Act (ESSA).[8] Additionally, according to the ESSA, most students with disabilities are to be taught the same challenging academic content as nondisabled students.[9] The IDEA 2004, although aligned with ESSA, expects educators to teach special education students differently, and sometimes to teach them different things, using teaching methods that specifically address each student's needs, all of which is outlined in a personalized IEP. Some educators and members of society prefer that students with disabilities perform in the same way as typically developing students, even though allowing students with disabilities to do things differently could lead to more efficient performance.[10] Special education, by contrast, addresses the individual differences of students with disabilities head-on, providing students who learn differently with more intensive and specialized instruction so they can learn appropriately and gain skills to participate in their communities.

Defining Special Education and the Purpose of the IDEA

According to the statute, the purpose of the IDEA is clear: "to ensure that all children with disabilities have available to them a free appropriate public education that emphasizes special education and related services designed to meet their unique needs, and prepare them for further education, employment and independent living."[11] All children with disabilities ages 3-21 who need special education have the right to FAPE, including children with disabilities who have been suspended or expelled from school, as well as children who

---

[6] Pub. L. No. 108-446, 118 Stat. 2647 (2004) (codified at 20 U.S.C. §§ 1400-1482 (2012)).
[7] *See* 34 C.F.R., Subt. B, Chpt. III, Pt. 300 (2016).
[8] Every Student Succeeds Act, Pub. L. No. 114-95, 129 Stat 1802 (2015).
[9] Every Student Succeeds Act, Pub. L. No. 114-95, § 1111(b)(2)(B)(vii)(II), 129 Stat. 1802 (2015).
[10] Thomas Hehir, NEW DIRECTIONS IN SPECIAL EDUCATION: ELIMINATING ABLEISM IN POLICY AND PRACTICE 14 (2005) (asserting that able-ism, or preferring students with disabilities to do things the same way as their nondisabled peers, can result in unintentional discrimination).
[11] 20 U.S.C. § 1400(d)(1)(A) (2012). In the 2004 Amendments to IDEA, Congress added new wording to include further education as an outcome along with employment and independent living. *See* Pub. L. No. 108-446, § 682(d)(1)(A), 118 Stat. 2647 (2004).

are advancing from grade to grade, or who have not failed or been retained in a course or grade.[12]

The provision of FAPE, in the wording of the purpose statement, emphasizes special education and related services. As defined in the statute, special education has an instructional mission, having been defined as "specially designed *instruction*, at no cost to parents, to meet the unique needs of a child with a disability, including ... instruction conducted in the classroom, in the home, in hospitals and institutions, and in other settings...."[13] *Specially designed instruction* refers to more than academic instruction and extends to meeting students' social, emotional, behavioral, physical, and vocational needs.[14] The term was defined for the first time in the 1999 regulations to the IDEA Amendments of 1997.[15] The current regulations defined "specially designed instruction" as follows:

> Specially-designed instruction means adapting, as appropriate to the needs of an eligible child under this part, the content, methodology, or delivery of instruction
>> i. To address the unique needs of the child that result from the child's disability; and
>> ii. To ensure access of the child to the general curriculum, so that he or she can meet the educational standards within the jurisdiction of the public agency that apply to all children.[16]

The sequence of these requirements indicates that ensuring genuine access to the general curriculum depends upon first addressing a student's unique needs. The primary imperative for school officials is to provide special education—specially designed instruction—that addresses the specific disability-related needs of each student. Special education, with its related services and specialized supports, is the vehicle through which the IDEA delivers the individualized interventions designed "to minimize the impact of disability and maximize the opportunities for children with disabilities to participate in general education in their natural community."[17] When appropriate techniques are delivered effectively, the likelihood is increased that each student will benefit and be able to adjust to the demands of the schoolhouse.

The purpose of the secondary imperative is to ensure that special education students have access to the general curriculum. School officials must ensure that all students have access to the same opportunities because, if appropriate special education is being provided to them, more students with disabilities should be able to learn challenging academic content successfully. This, in turn, should help them be better prepared to participate in and contribute to

---

[12] 20 U.S.C. § 1412(a)(1) (2012); 34 C.F.R. § 300.101(c) (2016).
[13] 20 U.S.C. § 1401(29)(A) (2012) (emphasis added).
[14] County of San Diego v. Cal. Sp. Educ. Hrg. Office, 93 F.3d 1458 (9th Cir. 1996) (emphasis added).
[15] *See* 64 Fed. Reg. 12,406, 12,425 (Mar. 12, 1999).
[16] 34 C.F.R. § 300.39(b)(3) (2016).
[17] *See* Hehir, *supra* note 10 for discussion of the purpose of special education.

society, and live as independently and productively as they can.[18] It would be a serious mistake, however, for school teachers and leaders to misunderstand this imperative as somehow requiring that students with disabilities receive the *same* curriculum as do general education students. In fact, in a November 2015 "Dear Colleague" Letter, the Office of Special Education and Rehabilitative Services (OSERS) of the U.S. Department of Education warned that this imperative should guide "but not replace the individualized decision-making required in the IEP process."[19] Clearly, the IDEA's focus on the individual needs of each child with a disability remains the primary imperative.

It is also important to note that participation in the general curriculum does not mean the same thing as inclusion in general education classes. "Inclusion in a regular classroom concerns the setting where a student with a disability is educated... Participation in the general curriculum concerns what a student learns."[20] The IDEA has never required that students receive inclusive instruction, but the law expects that students for whom the LRE is not the general classroom will be taught the general curriculum to the maximum extent appropriate to their learning needs, wherever they receive instruction.

In providing students with FAPE, the IDEA requires school personnel to follow a proper sequence: finding a student eligible to receive special education; conducting an assessment to determine a student's unique educational needs; developing a student's IEP; and then determining the instructional placement that, for this particular student, constitutes the LRE.[21] In order to ensure educational benefit for individual students and to protect their educational rights in the process, decisions regarding IEPs and instructional placement must never be made by one individual, either a parent or a school official. Instead, programming and placement decisions are to be made by the consensus of a team comprised of the child's parents and school personnel.

IDEA stipulates that IEP teams must include the following members: (1) the parents of the child; (2) at least one general education teacher (if the child is, or may be, participating in the general education environment); (3) at least one special education teacher of the child, or, if appropriate, at least one special education provider of the child; (4) a representative of the public agency who is qualified to provide, or supervise the provision of, specially designed instruction to meet the unique needs of children with disabilities, is knowledgeable about the general curriculum, and is knowledgeable about the availability of resources

---

[18] H. Rutherford Turnbull, III, Matthew J. Stowe & Nancy E. Huerta, Free Appropriate Public Education, The Law And Children With Disabilities 36 (2007) (addressing the findings and purposes of the IDEA).

[19] *See* Michael K. Yudin & Melody Musgrove, Dear Colleague Letter, U.S. Dep't. of Educ. 4 (Nov. 17, 2015), https://www2.ed.gov/policy/speced/guid/idea/memosdcltrs/guidance-on-fape-11-17-2015.pdf.

[20] Karen Glasser Sharp, & Vicki M. Pitasky, The Current Legal Status of Inclusion (2002).

[21] 20 U.S.C. § 1414 *et. seq.* (2012). For an extended discussion of special education programming and placements, *see* Barbara D. Bateman & Mary Anne Linden, Better IEPs: How to develop legally correct and educationally appropriate programs (2012).

of the public agency; (5) an individual who can interpret the instructional implications of evaluation results, who may already be a member of the team; (6) at the discretion of the parent or the agency, other individuals who have knowledge or special expertise regarding the child, including related services personnel as appropriate; and (7) if appropriate, the child.[22]

IEPs: Prescribing an Appropriate Education

A FAPE remains the centerpiece of the IDEA, and the concept of FAPE is assured through the IEP process. A FAPE is defined as special education and related services that are provided at public expense, under public direction, and that meet the standards set by the state's department of education.[23] Schools must provide FAPE across the grade levels for school-aged youth in preschools, elementary schools, and secondary schools, and the special education and related services students receive must be provided in conformity with their IEPs.[24] In general, an IEP is a written document that describes a child's educational needs, details the special education and related services the district will provide to meet those needs, and stipulates the goals that will serve to assess whether the student's needs were, indeed, met.[25]

Failure to develop and implement an IEP correctly is a denial of FAPE and a violation of law.[26] Although formats will vary across school systems, each IEP must include the following information, for the following reasons:

Performance Data. The IDEA directs that an IEP must address the student's "present levels of academic achievement and functional performance."[27] This description must include how the disability affects the student's participation and progress in the general curriculum (or, for preschoolers, appropriate activities). This statement provides the starting point from which progress will be assessed, and it is recommended that performance data be stated measurably.

Measurable Annual Goals. Measurable annual goals are required in IEPs. The IDEA reauthorization of 2004 required the inclusion of measurable academic and functional goals,[28] eliminating mandatory short-term objectives for most students. A description of benchmarks or short-term objectives must be included only for students with the most significant cognitive disabilities taking off-level assessments, or what the statute refers to as "alternate assessments aligned to alternate achievement standards."[29] Even though federal law no longer requires that all eligible students with disabilities have short-term objectives, states may still mandate that they must be included in all students'

---

[22] 20 U.S.C. § 1414(d)(1)(B) (2012); 34 C.F.R. § 300.321(a) (2016).
[23] 20 U.S.C. § 1401(9) (2012); 34 C.F.R. §300.17 (2016).
[24] 20 U.S.C. § 1414(d) (2012).
[25] This document is developed, reviewed, and revised in a meeting in accordance with 34 C.F.R. §§ 300.320-300.324 (2016); 20 U.S.C. § 1414(d)(1)(A)(i) (2012).
[26] 458 U.S. 176 (1982).
[27] 20 U.S.C. § 1414(d)(1)(A)(i)(I) (2012); 34 C.F.R. § 300.320(a)(1) (2016).
[28] 20 U.S.C. § 1414(d)(1)(A)(II) (2012).
[29] 20 U.S.C. § 1414(d)(1)(A)(i)(I)(cc) (2012); 34 C.F.R. § 300.320(a)(2)(B)(ii) (2016).

IEPs; thus, it is important to check with individual state laws and regulations to determinate if short-term objectives are required.[30] Traditionally, benchmarks or short-term objectives were included in IEPs so that personnel would know how to meet the student's disability-related needs and how to enable involvement and progress in the general curriculum. Measurable goals have always been required so that the effectiveness of the district services could be evaluated.[31] Goals should focus on what a student needs to learn both within and beyond the general education curriculum, because students with disabilities often need intensive instruction in curricular areas not addressed by the general education curriculum such as social skills, self-advocacy, cognitive strategies, and independent living.[32]

A Means to Measure Progress. A statement is required to show how the child's progress toward the annual goals will be measured. The IDEA 2004 allows school systems to use "quarterly or other periodic reports, concurrent with the issuance of report cards" that delineate the progress the child is making toward meeting the annual goals.[33] The parents of special education students should be informed about progress at least as often as parents of nondisabled children, so that they might evaluate the extent to which the progress is sufficient to enable their child to achieve the goals by the end of the IEP period.[34]

Services and Modifications. A statement must address the special education, related services, and supplementary aids and services that are to be provided to the student. The IDEA 2004 requires that these practices be "based on peer-reviewed research to the extent practicable."[35] The statement must also address specific program modifications or supports for personnel, so that the student can progress toward annual goals, progress in the general curriculum, and be educated and participate in extracurricular and nonacademic activities with other students, both those with disabilities and those without disabilities.[36] The regular education teacher on the IEP team is expected to help in determin-

---

[30] MITCHELL L. YELL, THE LAW AND SPECIAL EDUCATION 223 (2019) (the author advises that at least one goal be written for each area of academic or non-academic need).

[31] 20 U.S.C. § 1414(d)(1)(A)(i)(III) (2012); Bateman & Linden, supra note 21, (the authors advise districts against dropping short-term objectives because they serve a progress monitoring function).

[32] MITCHELL L. YELL, THE LAW AND SPECIAL EDUCATION 223 (2019) (the author advises that at least one goal be written for each area of academic or nonacademic need).

[33] 20 U.S.C. § 1414(d)(1)(A)(i)(III) (2012).

[34] 34 C.F.R. § 300.320(a)(3) (2016). See Yell, *supra* note 32,(the author advises that using appropriate means for evaluating and reporting regularly on the progress toward annual goals is essential to determining success or failure of the district's efforts to provide FAPE).

[35] 20 U.S.C. § 1414(d)(1)(A)(i)(IV) (2012).

[36] 20 U.S.C. § 1414(d)(1)(A)(i)(V) (2012); 34 C.F.R. § 300.320(a)(4) (2016). Bateman & Linden, *supra* note 21, at 15-16 (the authors advise against cluttering a student's IEP with detailed goals and services for the content standards in the general education curriculum. Instead, the IEP must indicate goals, accommodations, and adjustments focusing on how professionals will enable the student to acquire the access skills necessary to address the standards considered by the team to be most relevant to the student).

ing the appropriate classroom services and modifications necessary for teaching the student appropriately.[37]

Instructional Placement. The IEP document must contain an explanation regarding the extent, if any, to which the student will not participate with nondisabled students in regular classes and in nonacademic activities.[38] As a result, the percentage of time a student spends in special settings for special purposes can be linked directly to the measurable goals, services, and modifications that the IEP team determined to be most appropriate for the student. This practice prevents teams from determining placements by disability category, or by administrative convenience, and promotes placements that foster the delivery of appropriate instruction.[39]

Individually Appropriate Testing Accommodations. The IDEA 2004 addresses test administration and accountability for results, requiring a statement of "any individual appropriate accommodations that are necessary to measure the academic achievement and functional performance of the child on State and district-wide assessments."[40] If the IEP team determines that the student will take an alternate assessment of achievement, a statement must address why he or she cannot participate in the regular assessment, and why the alternate assessment is individually appropriate.[41]

Initiation Date and Service Delivery Details. The IEP also must include the projected date for the beginning of the services and modifications prescribed for the student, as well as the anticipated frequency, location, and duration of those services and modifications.[42] No services are to be provided to a student prior to the initiation date of the IEP.[43]

Transition Services. The IDEA 2004 emphasizes accountability for transition services promoting post-school employment or education for students with disabilities. New provisions require that a statement of appropriate, measurable, postsecondary goals and transition services be formulated no later than

---

[37] 20 U.S.C. § 1414(d)(3)(C) (2012); 34 C.F.R. § 300.324(a)(3) (2016). Section 1414(d)(3)(C) is a statutory provision that specifically addresses the role of the regular education teacher. The regular education teacher on the IEP team is to assist in the development, review, and revision of the IEP, with particular attention to the appropriate positive behavioral interventions and strategies for the child, as well as the supplementary aids and services, program modifications, or supports for school personnel that will be provided for the child to be successful in meeting individual goals, accessing the general curriculum, and being educated and participating with other students with and without disabilities.

[38] 20 U.S.C. § 1414(d)(1)(A)(i)(V) (2012); 34 C.F.R. § 300.320(a)(5) (2016).

[39] 20 U.S.C. § 1414(d)(1)(A)(i)(V) (2012); 34 C.F.R. § 300.320(a)(5) (2016). Bateman & Linden, *supra* note 21, (the authors advise that decisions about the extent of a student's participation in the general classroom depend on the needs identified in the student's evaluation and the student's IEP).

[40] 20 U.S.C. § 1414(d)(1)(A)(i)(VI)(aa) (2012); 34 C.F.R. § 300.320(a)(6) (2016).

[41] 20 U.S.C. § 1414(d)(1)(A)(i)(VI)(bb) (2012); 34 C.F.R. § 300.320(a)(6) (2016).

[42] 20 U.S.C. § 1414(d)(1)(A)(i)(VII) (2012); 34 C.F.R. § 300.320(a)(7) (2016).

[43] 20 U.S.C. § 1414(d)(1)(A)(i)(VII) (2012); 34 C.F.R. § 300.320(a)(7) (2016). *See* Yell, *supra* note 32 (the author advises that the IEP must be implemented as soon as possible after it is written).

the first IEP in effect when a student turns 16 years old, and then be updated annually.[44] Specific, measurable goals must be based upon age-appropriate transition assessments related to training, education, and employment, and, when appropriate, independent living skills. The transition services to be provided (including the prescribed courses of study) must be necessary to assist the student in reaching those goals.[45] At least one year before the student reaches the age of majority under state law, a statement must be included in the IEP signifying that the student has been informed of the rights that would transfer to him or her upon reaching the age of majority.[46]

In addition to the more specific requirements described above, the IDEA sets forth a number of additional factors that a student's IEP team must consider.[47] Teams must consider the strengths of the student[48] and the parents' concerns for enhancing the education of their child.[49] Individualization is an essential component of transition services.[50] The IEP team also must consider the results of the initial or most recent evaluation of the student and, as appropriate, the results of the student's performance on any general state or district-wide assessment programs.[51] Finally, the team is required to consider both the academic and the functional needs of the child.[52]

In certain circumstances, special factors must be considered by the team and documented in the IEP.[53] In the case of a student whose behavior impedes his or her learning or that of others, IEP teams must consider, if appropriate, strategies to address that behavior, including positive behavioral interventions, strategies, and supports.[54] It is important to note that this requirement is not just for students with emotional disturbance. In the case of students with limited English proficiency, IEP teams must consider language needs as they relate to the IEP.[55] For students who are blind or visually impaired, IEP teams must provide for instruction in Braille and the use of Braille unless the team deter-

---

[44] 20 U.S.C. § 1414(d)(1)(A)(i)(VIII)(aa) (2012); 34 C.F.R. § 300.320(b)(1) (2016).
[45] 20 U.S.C. § 1414(d)(1)(A)(i)(VIII)(bb) (2012); 34 C.F.R. § 300.320(b)(2) (2016).
[46] 20 U.S.C. § 1414(d)(1)(A)(i)(VIII)(cc) (2012); 34 C.F.R. § 300.320(c) (2016).
[47] 20 U.S.C. § 1414(d)(3)(A)(i)-(iv) (2012).
[48] 20 U.S.C. § 1414(d)(3)(A)(i) (2012).
[49] 20 U.S.C. § 1414(d)(3)(A)(ii) (2012); see also 34 C.F.R. § 300.322 (2016) (detailing requirement of parental participation in the IEP process).
[50] See Yell, supra note 32, (the author advises that transition services included in an IEP must address instruction, community services, employment, and other objectives of adult living. If any of these required services are not included, an explanatory note must detail the reasons for the exclusion).
[51] 20 U.S.C. § 1414(d)(3)(A)(iii) (2012); 34 C.F.R. § 300.324 (2007).
[52] 20 U.S.C. § 1414(d)(3)(A)(iv) (2012).
[53] 20 U.S.C. § 1414(d)((4)(B)(i)-(v) (2012); 34 C.F.R. § 300.324(a)(2)(i)-(v) (2016).
[54] 20 U.S.C. § 1414(d)(4)(B)(i) (2012).
[55] 20 U.S.C. § 1414 (d)(4)(B)(ii) (2012); 34 C.F.R. § 300.324(a)(2)(ii) (2016).

mines, after an evaluation of the student's reading and writing skills and needs, that instruction in Braille or the use of Braille is not individually appropriate.[56]

IEP teams must also consider the communication needs of students. In the case of a student who is deaf or hard of hearing, the team must consider language and communication needs; opportunities for direct communications with peers and professional personnel in the student's language and communication mode; academic level; and full range of needs, including opportunities for direct instruction in the student's language and communication mode.[57] IEP teams must consider whether students require assistive technology devices and services.[58] If, in considering any of these special factors, the team determines that a student needs a particular device or service (including an intervention, accommodation, or other program modification) in order to receive FAPE, the team must include a statement to that effect in the student's IEP.[59]

The IDEA 2004 included provisions designed to reduce the number of meetings and the amount of paperwork associated with IEPs. These provisions address attendance at meetings, changes to the IEP, and programming for transfer students. The IDEA now requires school systems to ensure FAPE to students with IEPs transferring from other states within the same academic year.[60] Services comparable to those in the IEP developed in the other state must be provided, in consultation with parents, until the school system conducts an evaluation and, if appropriate, develops a new IEP.[61] A student with an IEP who transfers within the same state within the same academic year also is to be provided with comparable services to the IEP developed by the prior district, until the receiving school system either adopts the prior IEP or develops and implements a new one.[62]

IDEA 2004 modified the requirements for team members to attend IEP meetings. When parents agree in writing, members may be excused who have provided input into the IEP prior to the meeting, or whose areas of curriculum or related services are not being modified or discussed at the meeting.[63] The IDEA does require that school systems invite appropriate early intervention service providers to initial IEP meetings if requested by parents to smooth the transition from preschool.[64] Parents and professionals may also agree to meet using alternative means, such as telephone and video conferences.[65]

---

[56] 20 U.S.C. § 1414(d)(4)(B)(iii) 2012); 34 C.F.R. § 300.324(a)(2)(iii) (2016). Teams must also evaluate the appropriate reading and writing media for the student, including an evaluation of the student's future needs for instruction in Braille or the use of Braille.
[57] 20 U.S.C. § 1414(d)(4)(B)(iv) (2012).
[58] 20 U.S.C. § 1414(d)(4)(B)(v) (2012).
[59] *Id.*; 34 C.F.R. § 300.320(a)(6)(i) (2016).
[60] 20 U.S.C. § 1414(d)(2)(C) (2012).
[61] 20 U.S.C. § 1414(d)(2)(C)(i)(II) (2012).
[62] 20 U.S.C. § 1414(d)(2)(C)(I) (2012); 34 C.F.R. § 300.323(e) (2016)4(a)(4).
[63] 20 U.S.C. § 1414 (d)(1)(c) (2012).
[64] 20 U.S.C. §1414 (d)(1)(D) (2012); 34 C.F.R. § 300.321(f) (2016).
[65] 34 C.F.R. § 300.328 (2016).

In reviewing the critical components and special factors to be included in developing IEPs, it becomes clear how the IEP document is intended to carry out the stated purpose of the IDEA. An IEP is not a simple plan of action; an IEP is a specific program designed to achieve results for a specific student. Educational programs of any kind are designed to address learning targets by setting measurable goals and developing ways to evaluate whether the services provided to the recipients were sufficient to meet the goals. Individualized education programs are no exception. To address the kinds of educational benefit a student might receive, the IEP process must rely on an analysis of performance data enhanced by the thoughtful consideration of the transition supports necessary to guide a special education student toward his or her future.

Determining the Extent of Educational Benefit

School teachers might well question what is the proper measure of educational benefit for special education students in this era of standards-based reform[66] The basic right to learn is the centerpiece of the accountability movement, and the proof of learning is now assumed to rest in positive results, not perfectly executed procedures. Program improvements and educational progress for typically developing students are being assessed against standard measures. However, assessing the progress of special education students is complicated by the nature of the disability and the type of assessments used by most states. Accommodations can conflict with the construct validity of tests, and research has yet to provide assurance that these assessments are accurately measuring what students really know and are able to do.[67] There are also major concerns with whether these assessments are broad enough to capture the various ways that special education students demonstrate their capabilities rather than their disabilities.[68]

A fixed standard of *appropriate* has never been set by Congress nor established by the courts.[69] In a landmark special education decision issued in 1982, titled *Board of Education of Hendrick Hudson Central School District v. Rowley*,[70] the U.S. Supreme Court determined that *appropriate* meant tailored to a child's individual needs, not to the needs of the school system; however, the Court also found that a child's IEP provided an "appropriate" education so long as it was reasonably designed to enable the child to obtain educational benefit, and not

---

[66] Scott F. Johnson, *Reexamining Rowley: A New Focus in Special Education Law*, 2003 B.Y.U. Educ. & L.J. 561, 585 (2003). Johnson argued that the concept of FAPE is newly aligned with high expectations established in state education standards, although school systems must address more than academic needs. *Id.* at 561.

[67] See the website for the National Center for Educational Outcomes, funded by the U.S. Department of Education's Office of Special Education Programs, at https://www.osepideasthatwork.org/node/114, addressing frequently asked questions about accommodations for students with disabilities.

[68] Hehir, *supra* note 10.

[69] *See* Perry A. Zirkel, *Is it Time for Elevating the Standard for FAPE under the IDEA?* 79 Exceptional Children 497-508 (2013).

[70] 458 U.S. 176 (1982).

a higher standard that would require the IEP to maximize a child's educational potential.[71] Since the *Rowley* decision, cases addressing a FAPE have hinged on the provision of an IEP that was reasonably calculated to address a student's unique educational needs and provide educational benefit. Educational benefit was not substantively defined by the Court as an opportunity equal to that of nondisabled children, nor did the justices establish a test that would determine the adequacy of the benefits special education students should receive.[72] However, the Court provided guidance in the form of a two-part inquiry to determine if the programming designed for a student was appropriate. First, has the program embodied in the IEP been developed by the school system in a manner procedurally consistent with the law? Second, is the IEP based on a student's unique educational needs and reasonably calculated to confer educational benefit? If this two-part analysis has been met, the school system has complied with the obligations imposed by Congress and "the courts can require no more."[73]

Most states define an appropriate education according to the federal standard set by the Supreme Court and, in some cases, courts have used colorful language to illustrate its meaning. For example, the federal Sixth Circuit Court of Appeals used an automotive metaphor in noting that school systems are required to provide "the educational equivalent of a serviceable Chevrolet" to each student, rather than a Cadillac.[74] The court noted that "the Chevrolet offered to [the student] is in fact a much nicer model than that offered to the average student," suggesting that a customized model offers special value in driving students with special needs toward successful outcomes.[75] This last concept is important to note because the benefit conferred by an IEP must be more than de minimis, or trivial.[76] And yet, the courts struggle to be more

---

[71] *Id.* at 200.
[72] *Id.* at 202. In fact the Court expressly declined to "attempt today to establish any one test for determining the adequacy of educational benefits," noting that the standard will vary greatly by child and disability. *Id.*
[73] *Id.* at 206-07.
[74] Doe v. Bd. of Educ. of Tullahoma City Sch., 9 F.3d 455, 459 (6th Cir. 1993).
[75] *Id.* at 459-60.
[76] *See., e.g.,* Thompson R2-J Sch. Dist. v. Luke P., 540 F.3d 1143 (10th Cir. 2008) (educational benefit must be more than de minimus).

explicit in relating the concept of appropriateness to an individual student's needs, taking into consideration the child's capacity to learn.[77]

In recent years, the concept of *appropriate* has been linked to the contents of the IEP with empirical data about student outcomes.[78] Increased attention to academic performance, especially for students with learning disabilities, characterizes some decisions in which passing grades in regular classes were seen as indicators of FAPE for students pursuing a regular high school diploma.[79] Good grades may provide some evidence of compliance with the IDEA, but as a matter of law, they do not determine whether a school district provided FAPE.[80] In some cases, good report card grades were seen as encouragements rather than as achievements reflecting a student's progress.[81] In *Hall v. Vance County Board of Education*,[82] the Fourth Circuit Court of Appeals discounted grades and turned to standardized test scores and independent evaluations to determine that a student with severe learning disabilities had been denied FAPE, despite passing grades and promotion to the next grade level. The Supreme Court in *Florence County School District Four v. Carter*[83] referred to the *Rowley* decision in noting the appropriate amount of regular education progress depends upon the abilities of each individual special education student. In this case, the IEP goals for Shannon Carter, a student with specific learning disabilities, were determined to be insufficient considering her capability for achieving more than four months growth over one year's time. In other cases, some students,

---

[77] In *Polk v. Central Susquehanna Intermediate Unit 16*, 853 F.2d 171, 182-184 (3d Cir. 1988), the Third Circuit held that an IEP must be calculated to offer "meaningful benefit" by providing educational services in a way that a student can best achieve success in learning. In *Hall v. Vance County Board of Education*, 774 F.2d 629, 636 (4th Cir. 1985), the Fourth Circuit allowed courts to make decisions regarding the substantive standard of an appropriate IEP on a case-by-case basis, taking into consideration the child's capacity to learn. In *J.S.K. v. Hendry County School Board*, 941 F.2d 1563, 1573 (11th Cir. 1991), the Eleventh Circuit required public schools to provide educational benefit greater than a trifle and defined an appropriate education in terms of "making measurable and adequate gains in the classroom" based on the child's needs, potential, and efforts. Other circuit decisions in which a somewhat higher standard of meaningful benefit seems to have been used include *Deal ex rel. Deal v. Hamilton County Board of Education*, 392 F.3d 840 (6th Cir. 2004); and *Adam J. v. Keller Independent School District*, 328 F.3d 804 (5th Cir. 2003).

[78] *See* Mitchell Yell, Jean Crockett, James Shriner, & Michael Rozalski, *Free Appropriate Public Education*, in HANDBOOK OF SPEC. EDUC. (J. Kauffman & D. Hallahan eds. 2017) for extended discussion of FAPE.

[79] Frank G. v. Bd. of Educ. of Hyde Park, 459 F.3d 356, 364 (2d Cir. 2006) ("Grades, test scores, and regular advancement may provide evidence that a child is receiving educational benefit...").

[80] In *Rowley*, the Supreme Court noted that "We do not hold today that every handicapped child who is advancing from grade to grade in a regular public school system is automatically receiving a 'free appropriate public education.'" 458 U.S. at 203 n.25.

[81] D.B. v. Bedford Cnty. Sch. Bd., 708 F. Supp. 2d 564, 584 (W.D. Va. 2010) (noting that the child's promotion from grade to grade every year was, "at best, a sad case of social promotion"); Fayetteville-Perry Local Sch. Dist., 20 IDELR 1289 (SEA Ohio 1994); Tucson Unified Sch. Dist., 30 IDELR 478 (SEA Ariz. 1999).

[82] 774 F.2d 629 (4th Cir. 1985).

[83] Florence Cnty. Sch. Dist. Four v. Carter, 510 U.S. 7 (1993).

because of the extent of their disabilities, will not be able to perform at grade level or will take more time than typical to do so.

It is important to note that, if a student is denied FAPE, a school district may be required to reimburse parents for private school tuition. In the case of *Burlington School Committee of the Town of Burlington v. Department of Education of Massachusetts*,[84] the U.S. Supreme Court ruled that tuition reimbursement could be awarded to parents who had to unilaterally place their child in a private school when the child's public school had failed to provide the child with a FAPE as required by the IDEA. Chief Justice Rehnquist, writing for the majority, asserted that the IDEA gave courts broad discretion in fashioning relief and to deny relief, when appropriate, would deny the parents meaningful input into the development of their child's FAPE. According to Justice Rehnquist, tuition reimbursement did not constitute a damage award, but rather required the school district to "belatedly pay expenses that it should have paid all along and would have borne in the first instance had it developed an appropriate IEP[85]."

In the case of *Cypress-Fairbanks Independent School District v. Michael F.*,[86] the Fifth Circuit Court of Appeals determined that an appropriate IEP must provide educational benefits that are likely to produce meaningful progress for a student, rather than regression or minimal educational advancement. In finding that the school system's IEP provided an appropriate education to Michael, a student with attention deficit hyperactivity disorder (ADHD) and Tourette syndrome, the court considered four factors: (1) was the program individualized on the basis of the student's assessment and performance; (2) was the program administered in the least restrictive environment; (3) were the services provided in a coordinated and collaborative manner by the key stakeholders; and (4) were positive academic and nonacademic benefits demonstrated.[87]

The Fifth Circuit further determined that Michael's IEP was specifically designed to address his individual needs, and that he had been placed in the least restrictive educational environment consistent with those needs.[88] The court relied on testimony provided by individuals who had direct and frequent contact with Michael, including personnel who coordinated his academic and behavioral services when he attended district schools.[89] Accordingly, Michael was achieving passing grades in classes, as well as managing his behavior well enough to eat lunch and travel through the building without a chaperone.[90]

---

[84] Burlington Sch. Comm. of the Town of Burlington v. Dept. of Educ. of Mass., 471 U.S. 359 (1985).
[85] *Id.* at 370-317.
[86] Cypress-Fairbanks Indep. Sch. Dist. v. Michael F., 118 F.3d 245 (5th Cir. 1997).
[87] *Id.* at 253. The court noted that each of the four factors comports with the federal regulations implementing IDEA. *See* 34 C.F.R. §300.324 (academic and functional needs); 34 C.F.R. §§ 300.114-120 (least restrictive environment); 34 C.F.R. § 300.321 (team approach); and 34 C.F.R. § 300.320 (demonstrated outcomes).
[88] Cypress-Fairbanks Indep. Sch. Dist., 118 F.3d at 256.
[89] *Id.* at 253-54.
[90] *Id.* at 251.

Using the four-point test, the court determined that the IEP "was reasonably calculated to, and in fact did, produce meaningful educational benefits both academically and behaviorally."[91] For these reasons, the court denied tuition reimbursement to Michael's parents for enrolling him in private school because the district had met its obligation to provide an appropriate IEP.[92] The court also ordered his parents to pay certain of the district's costs, but not attorney fees.[93]

The Fifth Circuit similarly defined *appropriate* as being demonstrated by student outcome data in the case of *Houston Independent School District v. Bobby R.*,[94] in which parents were also denied reimbursement for their son's private school tuition. In deciding whether the IEP for Caius, a student with dyslexia and attention deficit disorder, had conferred demonstrable academic and nonacademic benefits, the court again applied the four factors outlined in the *Michael F.* case.[95] In this case, the court used grade-level test scores from the Woodcock-Johnson cognitive and achievement test batteries as objective evidence of Caius's progress. In explaining its decision, the court made several things clear:

- A student's academic and nonacademic development should be measured against that individual student's prior performance and not by his relation to the rest of the class.[96]
- Declining percentile scores do not necessarily represent a lack of educational benefit, but rather the student's inability to maintain the same level of academic progress achieved by his nondisabled peers in regular classes.[97]
- It is not necessary for the student to improve in every area in order to obtain educational benefits from the IEP.[98]

The party challenging the IEP must show more than a trivial failure to implement all elements of the IEP, and instead must demonstrate that the school system failed to implement substantial or significant provisions of the IEP.[99]

The Fifth Circuit referred to the Supreme Court's decision in *Rowley* in stating that the question of whether the student might have received a greater benefit under different circumstances was not relevant, because the IDEA does not require maximization of a disabled student's educational potential.[100] The

---

[91] *Id.* at 254.
[92] *Id.* at 258.
[93] *Id.* This action was filed before the 2004 Amendments to the IDEA, which amended the IDEA to allow courts to award attorney fees to a prevailing school board against parents, if the court determines that the action was filed for an improper purpose such as to harass, unnecessarily delay, or needlessly increase the cost of litigation. *See* 20 U.S.C. § 1415(i)(3)(B)(i)(III) (2012); 34 C.F.R. § 300.517(a)(1)(iii) (2016).
[94] 200 F.3d 341 (5th Cir. 2000).
[95] *Id.* at 347-48.
[96] *Id.* at 349.
[97] *Id.*
[98] *Id.*
[99] *Id.*
[100] *Id.*

court noted that although school officials have some flexibility in implementing IEPs, they are held accountable for material failures and for providing a child with meaningful educational benefits.

After more than three decades since deciding *Rowley*, the Supreme Court again addressed the meaning of the word "appropriate" and, in particular, the means by which an "educational benefit" is measured. In 2015, the Tenth Circuit Court of Appeals decided a case, *Endrew F. v. Douglas City School District RE-1*,[101] in which it examined the means to determine whether a student's IEP was reasonably calculated to provide education benefit. The case involved an appeal of an administrative law judge's (ALJ) decision with regard to a due process complaint filed by the child's parents.[102] The student's parents contended that the school district had not provided a FAPE and sought tuition reimbursement because they had placed him in a private school.[103] The ALJ had ruled that the Douglas City School District had provided a FAPE, and thus denied reimbursement.[104] The student's parents then filed in federal district court and, after the district court affirmed the ALJ's decision, filed an appeal with the Tenth Circuit.[105]

That court, applying the first part of the *Rowley* test, found that the school district had not committed any procedural errors that would result in the denial of a FAPE.[106] Then addressing the parents' contention that the IEP was substantively inadequate because it did not provide meaningful educational benefit, the Tenth Circuit court found that the school district's IEP had met the second part of the *Rowley* test because the IEP did provide "some educational benefit," even as it acknowledged that other federal appellate courts have applied a higher standard of "meaningful educational benefit."[107] According to the court, to meet the test of providing FAPE, a school district only had to provide an education that conferred a little more than de minimis, or trivial, educational benefit to the student in question.

On December 22, 2015, the parents filed a petition for a writ of certiorari with the U.S. Supreme Court.[108] The parents' petition posed the following question for the Court's review: "What is the level of educational benefit that school districts must confer on children with disabilities to provide them with a free appropriate public education guaranteed by the Individuals with Disabilities

---

[101] Endrew F. v. Douglas Cnty. Sch. Dist. RE-1, 798 F.3d. 1329 (10th Cir. 2015).

[102] Parents who disagree with the educational decisions regarding their child have the ability to file a "due process" complaint. *See* 20 U.S.C. § 1415(b)(6) (2012). In some states, special education due process complaints are decided by administrative law judges.

[103] 798 F.3d at 1333.

[104] *Id.*

[105] *Id.*

[106] *Id.*

[107] *Id.*

[108] *See* Endrew F. v. Douglas Cnty. Sch. Dist. RE-1, Petition for Writ of Certiorari, No. 15-827 (U.S.) (filed Dec. 22, 2015), http://www.scotusblog.com/wp-content/uploads/2016/05/15-827-Petition-for-Certiorari.pdf.

Education Act?"[109] On August 18, 2016, the U.S. Solicitor General filed an amicus brief in which the government urged the Supreme Court to grant the petition.[110] The Supreme Court granted the parents' petition on September 29, 2016, thus agreeing to hear the case.[111] Oral arguments in the case were heard January 11, 2017; on March 22, 2017, the High Court announced its decision in *Endrew*.[112]

Chief Justice John Roberts wrote the opinion for the unanimous Court. In the decision, he stated that for a school district "to meet its substantive obligation under the IDEA, a school must offer an IEP reasonably calculated to enable a child to make progress appropriate in light of the child's circumstances."[113] Justice Roberts also noted that the new standard that the justices developed was "markedly more demanding than the 'merely more than de minimis' test applied by the Tenth Circuit,"[114] and that "(a) substantive standard not focused on student progress would do little to remedy the pervasive and tragic academic stagnation that prompted Congress to act" in 1975.[115]

The Supreme Court's new educational benefit standard requires that schools offer an IEP reasonably calculated to enable a child to make appropriate progress in light of the child's circumstances. Justice Roberts noted that the new standard was not a formula and that although the new educational benefit standard was clearly higher than the de minimis educational benefit standard, it was not a prescription for hearing officers and judges to follow when determining if a school district has conferred educational benefit. Rather, the decision means that hearing officers and judges will need to focus on the appropriateness of an IEP on a case-by-case basis and judge the adequacy of the IEP vis a vis "the unique circumstances of the child for whom it was created."[116] As Justice Roberts wrote:

> A reviewing court may fairly expect (school officials) to be able to offer a cogent and responsive explanation for their decisions that shows the IEP is reasonably calculated to enable the child to make progress appropriate in light of his (or her) circumstances.[117] (*Endrew*, 2017, p. 16).

---

[109] *Id.*

[110] *See* Endrew F. v. Douglas Cnty. Sch. Dist. RE-1, Brief of the United States As Amicus Curiae, No. 15-827 (U.S.) (filed Aug. 18, 2016), http://www.scotusblog.com/wp-content/uploads/2016/08/15-827-US-Amicus.pdf.

[111] *See* Endrew F. v. Douglas Cnty. Sch. Dist. RE-1, No. 15-827, 2016 WL 5416228 (U.S. Sept. 29, 2016). For updates on the case, visit http://www.scotusblog.com/case-files/cases/endrew-f-v-douglas-county-school-district/.

[112] Endrew F. v. Douglas County School District, 137 S.Ct. 988 (2017). A pdf of the *Endrew* decision is available at https://www.supremecourt.gov/opinions/16pdf/15-827_0pm1.pdf.

[113] *Id.*

[114] *Id.*

[115] *Id.*

[116] *Id.*

[117] *Id.*

The two-part test developed by the U.S. Supreme Court in the *Board of Education of Hendrick Hudson Central School District v. Rowley*[118] decision divided school districts' responsibility into procedural and substantive elements. The first part of the test was procedural: Has the [school] complied with the procedural requirements of the IDEA? The second part of the test was substantive: Was a student's IEP reasonably calculated to enable the student to receive educational benefits? The U.S. Supreme Court, in *Endrew F. v. Douglas City School District RE-1*,[119] elevated the educational benefit standard by requiring that for a school district to meet the substantive standard of FAPE under the IDEA, a student's IEP must be reasonably calculated to enable a student to make progress appropriate in light of his or her circumstances. Thus, to meet the U.S. Supreme Court's FAPE standard, a school district must meet both the procedural and substantive standards. The substantive standard "focuses on the adequacy of the IEP in terms of its likely or actual results."[120]

In the IDEA reauthorization of 2004, Congress codified the procedural/substantive distinction when it required that a hearing officer who rules on a FAPE case must make the ruling "on substantive grounds based on a determination of whether the child received a free appropriate public education."[121] "In matters alleging a procedural violation, a hearing officer may find that a child did not receive a free appropriate public education only if the procedural inadequacies" resulted in substantive harm."[122] Moreover, according to the statute, such a procedural inadequacy must have"[I] impeded the child's rights to a free appropriate public education; [II] significantly impeded the parents' opportunity to participate in the decision-making process regarding the provision of a free appropriate public education to the parents' child; or [III] caused a deprivation of educational benefits."[123] The most serious procedural violation involves school personnel's actions or inaction that results in a student not having full and meaningful involvement in the special education decision-making process.[124] The absolute importance of parental involvement, which the judges on the U.S. Court of Appeals for the Ninth Circuit referred to as the "very essence of the IDEA,"[125] has been confirmed repeatedly by the U.S. Supreme Court.[126]

---

[118] Bd. of Educ. of the Hendrick Hudson Sch. Dist. v. Rowley, 458 U.S. 176 (1982).

[119] Endrew F. v. Douglas Cnty. Sch. Dist. RE-1, 798 F.3d. 1329 (10th Cir. 2015).

[120] Perry A. Zirkel, *Failure to Implement the IEP: The Third Dimension of FAPE Under the IDEA*, 28 J. DISABILITY POLICY STUDIES 174 (2017).

[121] 20 U.S.C. § 1415(f)(3)(E)(i).

[122] 20 U.S.C. § 1415(f)(3)(E)(ii).

[123] 20 U.S.C. § 1415(f)(3)(E)(ii)(I, II, III).

[124] Mitchell L. Yell, Terrye Conroy, Antonis Katsiyannis, & Tim Conroy, *Individualized Education Programs and Special Education Programming for Students with Disabilities in Urban Schools*, 41 FORDHAM L. REV. 681 (2013).

[125] Amanda J. v. Clark Cnty Sch Dist, 267 F.3d 877 892 (9th Cir. 2001).

[126] *See generally,* Bd. of Educ. v. Rowley, 458 U.S. 176 (1982); Burlington Sch. Comm. of the Town of Burlington v. Dept. of Educ., 471 U.S. 359 (1985); Endrew F. v. Douglas Cnty. Sch. Dist. RE-1, 137 S.Ct., 988 (2017).

Implementation of a Student's IEP

Another dimension of FAPE involves school district personnel's accuracy or fidelity when implementing an IEP.[127] The failure to implement a student's IEP could be a denial of FAPE, and thus violate the IDEA. Past litigation has indicated that it likely would take a material or substantial failure to implement a student's IEP before that deficiency rises to the level of a possible FAPE violation.[128] According to the Ninth Circuit, a material failure to implement "occurs when there is more than a minor discrepancy between the services a school provides to a disabled child and the services required by the child's IEP."[135] In a dissent to this 2–1 ruling, one of the judges asserted that failure to implement aspects of a student's IEP should be an automatic denial of FAPE.[129] Moreover, in his dissent it was noted that judges should not be second-guessing parents and school district personnel's decisions by deciding which sections of an IEP are material or not. The importance of accurate implementation was aptly summed up in another decision of the U.S. Court of Appeals for the Ninth Circuit as follows: "An IEP, like a contract ...embodies a binding commitment and provides notice to both parties as to what services will be provided to the student during the period covered by the IEP.[130]

Selection of Educational Methodologies for Particular Students

The *Rowley* and the *Endrew* courts clarified that once an IEP has been determined to be appropriate, deference is to be extended to professionals, and courts are not to substitute their judgments for those of experts with regard to educational methodologies.[131] However, recent increases in litigation addressing private school tuition reimbursement, particularly cases involving students with autism, suggest that methodology is not escaping scrutiny as relevant to FAPE.[132] In *Nein v. Greater Clark County School Corporation*,[133] the federal district court determined that Lucas, an illiterate 12-year-old with severe learning disabilities and a full-scale IQ of 95, was making insufficient

---

[127] Mitchell L. Yell, David Bateman, & James G. Shriner, *Developing and Implementing Educationally Meaningful and Legally Sound IEPs: Bringing It All Together*, 52 TEACHING EXCEPTIONAL CHILDREN 344, 346 (2020).
[128] *Id.* at 346.
[129] *Id.* at 827.
[130] M.C. v. Antelope Valley Union High, 858 F.3d 1189 1197 (9th Cir. 2017).
[131] 458 U.S. at 207-08.
[132] *See* DIXIE SNOW HUEFNER & CYNTHIA M. HERR, NAVIGATING SPECIAL EDUCATION LAW AND POLICY 132 (2012). IDEA's emphasis on adapting the content, methodology, or delivery of instruction has prompted the interest of the courts in different methodologies and the need for educators to select teaching methods responsive to a student's unique educational needs. If a student needs a particular device, service, intervention, accommodation, or modification, then that information must be placed in the IEP. If FAPE can be provided without using a specific method, then the decision to include methodology on the IEP rests with the IEP team.
[133] Nein v. Greater Clark County Sch. Corp., 95 F. Supp. 2d 961 (S.D. Ind. 2000).

progress in the county's Milestones reading program.[134] Even though he was being promoted and making good grades, Lucas could not even read restroom signs.[135] The court drew on the Sixth Circuit's metaphor, finding that the county's insufficiently intensive reading instruction from grades 1-4 provided him "a Chevrolet without a transmission—even if the engine might run, no power ever reached the wheels."[136]

While school systems are entitled to deference in selecting educational methodologies, the school system nonetheless must evaluate a teaching method proposed by the child's parents and cannot "predetermine" to reject that proposed methodology. In *Deal v. Hamilton Board of Education*,[137] the Sixth Circuit held that the federal district court had erred in substituting his own judgment on teaching methodology for that of the administrative hearing officer, who had determined that the school district had violated IDEA by summarily rejecting the parents' proposed teaching methodology.[138] In so holding, the Sixth Circuit noted that, when different methodologies result in vastly different outcomes for the student, providing a lesser program could result in a denial of FAPE.[139] In its decision issued after the Sixth Circuit remanded the case, the federal district court determined that the school district's proposed IEP, together with its proposed teaching methodology, had provided a FAPE.[140] Quoting *J.P. v. West Clark Community Schools*,[141] the federal district court in *Deal* clarified that "whether an approach used in any particular case 'qualifies' as a sound educational practice is fact-specific."[142]

The *J.P.* case also involved a student with autism.[143] In the case, the court determined that, when confronted with a dispute involving competing educational approaches, the court must consider the following criteria: (a) whether school officials can explain the specific benefits of using the methods with the particular child; (b) whether local educators have the experience and expertise to use them successfully; and (c) whether qualified educational experts consider the methods to be at least adequate under the circumstances.[144] In the

---

[134] *Id.*
[135] *Id.*
[136] *Id.*
[137] Deal *ex rel.* Deal v. Hamilton Cnty. Bd. of Educ., 392 F.3d 840 (6th Cir. 2004).
[138] *Id.*
[139] *Id.* at 861-62. Some commentators have suggested that the Sixth Circuit lacked the expertise to recognize or assess the various instructional practices, noting that the Sixth Circuit characterized the parents' teaching method—known as the "Lovaas method"—as having shown "extraordinary results," 392 F.3d at 845, n.2, even though it was not peer-reviewed and other experts questioned the rigor of the design. *See* Tessie E. Rose & Perry Zirkel, *Orton-Gillingham Methodology for Students with Reading Disabilities: 30 Years of Case Law,* 184 J. SPECIAL EDUC. 171, 184 (2007).
[140] Deal *ex rel.* Deal v. Hamilton Cnty. Dep't of Educ., 2006 WL 5667836, 46 IDELR 45 (E.D. Tenn., Apr. 3, 2006).
[141] J.P. v. West Clark Cmty. Sch., 230 F. Supp. 2d 910 (S.D. Ind. 2002).
[142] Deal *ex rel.* Deal v. Hamilton Cnty. Dep't of Educ., 2006 WL 5667836 at *24, 46 IDELR 45, 72 (E.D. Tenn., Apr. 3, 2006).
[143] J.P. v. West Clark Cmty. Sch., 230 F. Supp. 2d 910 (S.D. Ind. 2002).
[144] *Id.*

J.P. case, the court found that the district had provided sufficient answers to questions about methodology and that evidence, along with the judgment of the hearing officer, was sufficient for the court to determine that a FAPE had been provided.[145]

The validity of selected practices is a serious concern in providing FAPE.[146] Provisions in the IDEA 2004 require IEPs to include "a statement of the special education and related services and supplementary aids and services, based on peer-reviewed research to the extent practicable, to be provided to the child, or on behalf of the child" to enable appropriate advancement toward annual goals, as well as participation and progress in the general curriculum.[147] The requirement is intended to strengthen the effectiveness of methods used by school districts, increasing the probability that a given approach "works" and is reasonably calculated to result in educational benefit.[148] In science, researchers enhance their credibility when their work is reviewed by other experts and published in scholarly journals. In schools, educators enhance their effectiveness when they use validated methods in the ways they were intended and with the group of students for whom they were designed.

With regard to whether parents or school districts bear the burden of proving that an IEP provides an appropriate education (or FAPE), the IDEA is silent, but in *Schaffer v. Weast*,[149] the Supreme Court decided that the burden of persuasion rests with the party seeking relief. In effect, this means that parents who challenge an IEP must prove to a hearing officer that the district denied their child FAPE, unless state laws suggest otherwise.[150] In the pro-parent decision of *Winkelman v. Parma City School District*,[151] the Court held that the IDEA grants parents independent, enforceable rights, not limited to procedural and reimbursement-related matters, but extending to the substantive formulation of their child's educational program. Collectively, these Supreme Court decisions underscore the shared responsibility throughout the IEP process for professional diligence in meeting a child's individual needs, and parental vigilance in ensuring that those needs are met appropriately.

---

[145] *Id.*

[146] *See* Bateman & Linden, *supra* note 21, at 138 (advising school officials to carefully and critically review claims for the research base of publishers' curricular materials; pursue guidance from professional development; provide practitioner journals that publish practical articles for teachers and related service providers; consult personnel at state departments of education; and utilize professional websites that publish valid data on evidence-based practices). Additionally, the authors advise educators to shop with a critical eye because "snake oil is more readily available than research-validated remedies."

[147] 20 U.S.C. § 1414(d)(1)(A)(i)(IV) (2012); 34 C.F.R. § 300.320(a)(4) (2016).

[148] Congress did not define peer-reviewed research, but usage of the term is consistent with *scientifically-based instruction* in NCLB, as practices tested and validated through systematic, rigorous, and objective methods. *See* 34 C.F.R. § 300.35 (2016).

[149] Schaffer v. Weast, 546 U.S. 49 (2005).

[150] For an extended discussion of this decision, *see* Charles J. Russo, & Allan G. Osborne, *The Supreme Court Clarifies the Burden of Proof in Special Education Due Process Hearings*: Schaffer ex rel. Schaffer v. Weast, 208 Educ. L. Rep. 705-717 (2006).

[151] Winkelman by Winkelman v. Parma City Sch. Dist., 550 U.S. 516 (2007).

The IEP was referred to by the Supreme Court in *Rowley* as a "written record of reasonable expectations."[152] However, educators have too often focused IEPs on expectations for what a student will achieve, including lengthy lists of goals, instead of emphasizing expectations for what the school system will provide. From the perspective of distributed leadership, IEPs are tools that communicate to members across various professional communities what needs to be done, specifically and intensively, to help a child learn.[153] From the perspective of law, IEPs secure the right to an individually appropriate education, prompting one advocate to remark, "you can fight over placement all you want, but if you want to win, you need to control the content of the IEP."[154]

COVID-19 and FAPE

Schools have found the COVID-19 pandemic challenging, especially with respect to students who are eligible for special education services under the IDEA. In passing the IDEA, Congress never anticipated that special education teachers would need to educate their students through means other than face-to-face interactions. Because of school closures all over America, however, that is precisely what teachers are doing. Policy statements[155] from the U.S. Department of Education have clarified school districts' responsibilities to these students. Both letters recognized the strain school district personnel were under during the pandemic and sought to dispel the notion that school districts were unable to alter instruction for students with disabilities because of the pandemic. Department officials wrote: "As school districts nationwide take necessary steps to protect the health and safety of their students, many are moving to virtual or online education (distance instruction). Some educators, however, have been reluctant to provide any distance instruction because they believe that federal disability law presents insurmountable barriers to remote education. *This is simply not true.*"[156] Additionally, Department officials wrote: "(t)o be clear: ensuring compliance with the Individuals with Disabilities Education Act (IDEA), Section 504 of the Rehabilitation Act (Section 504), and Title

---

[152] 458 U.S. at 208-09, quoting Sen. Conf. Rep. No. 94-445, at 30 (1975).

[153] For a discussion of how the tools used by educators are more than representative of intentions but are constitutive of their practice, see James P. Spillane, Richard Halverson, & John B. Diamond, *Investigating School Leadership Practice: A Distributed Perspective*, 30 EDUC. RESEARCHER 23-28 (2001).

[154] Jeffrey Champagne, "*LRE: Decisions in Sequence*," Symposium at the Annual Conference of the National Association of Private Schools for Exceptional Children, 14 (1992).

[155] *See* Questions and Answers on Providing Services to Children with Disabilities During the Coronavirus Disease 2019 Outbreak (https://sites.ed.gov/idea/files/qa-covid-19-03-12-2020.pdf), Supplemental Fact Sheet: Addressing the Risk of COVID-19 in Preschool, Elementary, and Secondary Schools While Serving Students with Disabilities (https://www2.ed.gov/about/offices/list/ocr/frontpage/faq/rr/policyguidance/Supple%20Fact%20Sheet%203.21%20 FINAL.pdf), U.S. DEP'T OF EDUC. (March 21, 2020).

[156] *Id.*, Supplemental Fact Sheet at 1.

II of the Americans with Disabilities Act should not prevent any school from offering educational programs through distance instruction."[157]

Both statements stressed the importance of school personnel engaging in creative collaboration with parents to deliver IEP or 504 services technologically, with the understanding that effective individualization is often feasible by using online or distance technology such as distance instruction; teletherapy and tele-intervention; meetings held on digital platforms; online options for data tracking and documentation; and low-tech strategies such as curriculum-based resources, instructional packets, projects, and written assignments.[158] Nonetheless, the Department of Education clearly noted that school districts had an obligation to continue to provide a FAPE to students with IEPs.[159]

LRE: Utilizing the Principle of the Least Restrictive Environment

Not all cases determining the appropriateness of an IEP involve disputes over placement, but all disputes over placement are determined by the appropriateness of an IEP. The most contentious of these disputes have centered on issues of placement in the LRE. The LRE requirements of the IDEA set out the factors to consider in educating students with and without disabilities together to the maximum extent that is appropriate.[160] In the language of law, the LRE principle is considered to be a rebuttable presumption. In other words, the law presumes that the least restrictive placement for any student to receive appropriate instruction is the regular education classroom. Presumptive placement in the regular education classroom is rebutted by convincing evidence that a particular student would receive an appropriate education in an alternative placement. For this reason, school officials are legally required to make a full continuum of alternative learning environments available across the system that range from regular classes, special classes, separate schools, residential facilities, hospitals, to home settings.[161]

The IDEA's federal regulations set out the requirements that school officials must follow in order to prevent the troubling practice of placing special education students in general education classes without regard to their specific learning needs. The IDEA regulations set out fact-specific guidelines stipulating that placement decisions must be made by a group of people, including the student's parents and others who are knowledgeable about the child, the meaning of the evaluation data, and the placement options.[162] Placement decisions are also to

---

[157] *Id.*, Supplemental Fact Sheet at 1.
[158] *Id.*, Supplemental Fact Sheet at 1.
[159] *Id.*, Supplemental Fact Sheet at 1
[160] 20 U.S.C. § 1412(a)(5) (2012).
[161] 34 C.F.R. § 300.115 (2016).
[162] 34 C.F.R. § 300.327 (2016); 34 C.F.R. § 300.501(c) (2016).

be made in conformity with the LRE provisions.[163] Placement decisions must be made annually, must be based on the IEP, and must give consideration to any potential harmful effect on the child or to the quality of the required services.[164] Unless their IEPs require otherwise, students with disabilities are expected to attend a school as close to home as possible or the school they would attend if they were not disabled.[165] A special education student must not be removed from education in age-appropriate regular classrooms solely because of needed modifications in the general curriculum.[166] Indeed, the IDEA expressly provides that, for some students with disabilities, the appropriate placement may be in a private school, with the tuition being paid for by the public school system.[167]

Under the IDEA, the LRE is not a specific location but the outcome of a procedural process in which, when determining placement, greater weight is given to the requirement of FAPE than to other factors, such as an interest in integrating students with disabilities across instructional settings. In making placement decisions, courts should carefully compare the FAPE requirement that the student obtain educational benefit with the statute's overall preference for placement in the regular classroom. Parents and professionals, less familiar with the law's presumptive language, often confuse the terms mainstreaming, inclusion, and LRE, but these terms do not have interchangeable meanings.[168] Mainstreaming implies that special education and general education students will be educated together as appropriate, but not exclusively.[169] Full inclusion implies that students with disabilities have an absolute right to regular class placement.[170] The term LRE is not synonymous with inclusion, but rather requires that placement decisions for students be made on the basis of an appropriate IEP.[171] In other words, the LRE is the least restrictive (most inclusive) education setting in which the student can obtain the educational benefits sought by the student's IEP. The IDEA does not require the practices of mainstreaming and inclusion;[172] rather, educators often see them as strategies that can be used to

---

[163] The IDEA regulations set out fact-specific guidelines stipulating that placement decisions must be made by a group of people, including the student's parents and others who are knowledgeable about the child, the meaning of the evaluation data, and the placement options. Placement decisions are also to be made in conformity with the LRE provisions of the federal regulations at 34 C.F.R §§ 300.114-120 (2016).

[164] 34 C.F.R. § 300.116(b)(1)-(2) (2016).

[165] 34 C.F.R. § 300.116(b)(3) (2016) (requirement that placement be as close to home as possible); 34 C.F.R. § 300.116(c) (2016) (requirement that school be the same one that the child would attend if not disabled, unless the IEP requires some other arrangement).

[166] 34 C.F.R. § 300.116(e) (2016).

[167] 20 U.S.C. § 1412(a)(10)(B) (2012).

[168] *See, e.g.,* Stacey Gordon, *Making Sense of the Inclusion Debate under IDEA*, 2006 B.Y.U. EDUC. & L.J. 189, 198-99 (2006).

[169] *Id.*

[170] *Id.*

[171] 34 C.F.R. § 300.116(b) (2016) (a student's placement "must be based on the child's IEP").

[172] Roncker v. Walter, 700 F.2d 1058, 1063 (6th Cir. 1983) ("The Act does not require mainstreaming in every case but its requirement that mainstreaming be provided to the *maximum* extent appropriate indicates a very strong congressional preference").

operationalize the LRE principle in schools. The concept of LRE means that, when school officials cannot provide a beneficial education to a student with disabilities in the same way they do for typically developing students, they must meet their obligation to provide FAPE using the *least* restrictive alternative to usual practices.[173]

In making LRE placement decisions, school officials should keep the issue of place in perspective by remembering that *where* a student receives instruction is only one component of an appropriate education. Some students may need instruction that cannot be provided in regular classes because they need to learn something different than general education students, such as Braille, American Sign Language, or specific technologies that are more efficiently taught in other settings. Some students may need to learn things differently, such as students with severe learning disabilities who need intensive reading instruction in more private learning environments, or students with cognitive disabilities whose job training and life skills curriculum requires them to spend time in community-based settings. The LRE requirement compels school systems to make a continuum of options possible so that IEP teams can make appropriate student-centered placement decisions across a range of viable alternatives.[174]

In making legally correct placement decisions, what might be *possible* for the system to provide should not be construed as synonymous with what would actually be *appropriate* for a particular student to receive, because some possibilities can cause harm. For this reason, school officials need to tally the benefits of regular classes for each special education student, but also calculate the risks. Educational harm can result when decisions about students are based on stereotypes instead of individual strengths; when students are misplaced and left in separate settings that do not match their needs; or when they are included in regular classes without receiving services that comport with their IEPs. The word *harm* is mentioned only once in the IDEA, and that is in the LRE requirements of the federal regulations.[175]

Placement: Determining Appropriate Educational Settings

Currently, there is no national framework employed by courts in making placement decisions. The Supreme Court has not decided any cases involving placement, so each federal appellate circuit court uses its preferred framework to resolve cases related to LRE.[176] Several circuit courts have devised judicial

---

[173] *See* Crockett & Kauffman, The Least Restrictive Environment: Its Origins and Interpretations in Special Education (1999), for a full discussion of the origins and interpretations of the LRE principle in special education.

[174] Jean B. Crockett, *The Least Restrictive Environment and the 1997 IDEA Amendments and Federal Regulations*, 28 J. L. & Educ. 543 (1999); 34 C.F.R. § 300.115 (2016).

[175] 34 C.F.R. § 300.116(d) (2016) ("In selecting the LRE, consideration must be given to any potential harmful effect on the child or on the quality of services that he or she needs.").

[176] The federal circuit courts of appeal have jurisdictions over various regions of the United States. A map that depicts the jurisdictional boundaries of each circuit court of appeal can be found at http://www2.fjc.gov/sites/default/files/2012/IJR00007.pdf.

tests, or analytic frameworks, to evaluate whether a school system has complied with the LRE requirement such that the student with disabilities who is in a regular class placement is achieving satisfactory educational benefit.[177] Circuits not relying on analytic frameworks balance the benefit of special education and general education in determining if a student can be educated satisfactorily in regular classes. These judicial tests illustrate critical components to consider in making placement decisions.

One such framework was developed by the Sixth Circuit Court of Appeals in its 1983 decision in *Roncker v. Walter*,[178] in which the court addressed the fundamental question whether a student should be educated in a general education setting as opposed to a segregated setting. This framework uses a feasibility test, or a portability test, to determine whether services that make a specialized or segregated placement superior could be feasibly provided in a regular education setting.[179] Feasibility is defined by whether any marginal benefits of typical settings are outweighed by the benefits of the special setting; whether the student is disruptive in a typical setting; and whether the costs of serving one student in a typical setting are excessive, depriving other students from getting the services they need.[180] This analytic framework requires school systems to be proactive by considering if specialized services might be transported to typical educational settings. If it is feasible to replicate services that are critical to an individual student's appropriate education, then the special setting is not the LRE.[181] The Eighth Circuit Court of Appeals also has adopted this feasibility test.[182]

In contrast, the Fifth Circuit Court of Appeals devised a different framework in its 1989 case of *Daniel R. R. v. State Board of Education*.[183] This framework considers the benefits of supplementary aids and services, and the nonacademic as well as academic benefits of a general education placement. In this case, the Fifth Circuit rejected the *Roncker* portability standard, viewing the feasibility of transporting services to more integrated settings as dependent on contextual circumstances and reliant on the judgments of school officials, not of courts.

---

[177] The major frameworks include the *Roncker* standard, the *Daniel R. R.* two-pronged test, the four-pronged *Holland* test, and the *DeVries* three-part test. *See* Roncker v. Walter, 700 F.2d 1058 (6th Cir. 1983); Daniel R.R. v. State Bd. of Educ., 874 F 2d. 1036 (5th Cir. 1989); Sacramento City Unified Sch. Dist. v. Rachel H., 14 F.3d 1398 (9th Cir. 1994); DeVries v. Fairfax Cnty. Sch. Bd., 882 F.2d 876 (4th Cir. 1989).

[178] Roncker v. Walter, 700 F.2d 1058 (6th Cir. 1983). This test also is used in the Eighth Circuit. *See* A.W. v. Northwest R-1 Sch. Dist., 813 F.2d 158 (8th Cir. 1987).

[179] 700 F.2d at 1063.

[180] *Id.*

[181] In developing the feasibility standard, the Sixth Circuit acknowledged that a student's need for an appropriate education might conflict with preferences for integration and that certain factors, including marginal benefits, disruption, and cost, could be considered in determining whether education in regular settings could be provided satisfactorily. *Id.*

[182] A.W. v. Northwest R-1 Sch. Dist., 813 F.2d 158 (8th Cir. 1987).

[183] Daniel R.R. v. State Bd. of Educ., 874 F 2d. 1036 (5th Cir. 1989). This test is used in the Second, Third, Fifth, Tenth, and Eleventh Circuits.

The *Daniel R.R.* framework requires a child-centered and fact-specific inquiry that asks two questions: (1) whether education in the regular classroom, with the use of supplementary aids and services, can be achieved satisfactorily for a given student, and if not, (2) whether the school has included the student to the maximum extent appropriate.[184] In making this determination, school officials must balance whether the student can benefit more from general or from special education. In doing so, school officials must consider more than token attempts at modifying instruction, but they need not offer every conceivable service nor completely alter the standard program. Undue teacher time and undue curricular modification are not required. According to the court, this inquiry focuses on the student's ability to grasp the essential elements of the general curriculum. As in the *Roncker* analysis, school officials can consider the effect this child will have on other children and the quality of their education.[185] The Second, Third, Tenth and Eleventh Circuit Courts of Appeal have adopted the *Daniel R.R.* framework.[186]

In the 1994 case of *Sacramento City Unified School District v. Rachel H.* (the "*Holland*" case),[187] the Ninth Circuit Court of Appeals outlined a framework that is clearly related to the previous two frameworks. However, the *Holland* test differs from the others by not balancing the benefits of special or general education, but considering only if a student can receive education satisfactorily in regular classes.[188] This analysis addresses four issues: (1) the educational benefits of placing the student in a full-time regular education program; (2) the nonacademic benefits of such a placement; (3) the effect the student would have on the teacher and other students in the regular classroom; and (4) the costs associated with this placement.[189]

In 1994, yet another federal court, the Fourth Circuit Court of Appeals, decided the case of *DeVries v. Fairfax County School Board*,[190] in which a fourth framework was established. The court noted that Congress had expressed a strong preference for students with disabilities to be educated in the mainstream, but also stated that mainstream placements would not be appropriate for every student with a disability.[191] The court cited portions of both the

---

[184] *Id.*

[185] The *Daniel R. R.* two-pronged analytic framework influenced the 1997 amendments to the IDEA and has had a broad impact on courts deliberating placements in the LRE. This framework requires school systems to consider more than academic achievement in placement decisions and to ensure that access to general education settings will not be denied solely because the progress of the special education student will not equal that of a general education student.

[186] Greer v. Rome City Sch. Dist., 950 F.2d 688 (11th Cir. 1991), L.B. and J.B. *ex rel.* K.B. v. Nebo Sch. Dist., 379 F.3d 966 (10th Cir. 2004), Oberti v. Bd. of Educ. of the Borough of Clementon Sch. Dist., 995 F.2d 1204 (3d Cir. 1993), P. v. Newington Bd. of Educ., 546 F.3d 111 (2d Cir. 2008).

[187] Sacramento City Unified Sch. Dist. v. Rachel H., 14 F.3d 1398 (9th Cir. 1994). This test is used in the Ninth Circuit.

[188] 874 F.2d at 1048.

[189] 14 F.3d at 1404.

[190] DeVries v. Fairfax Cnty. Sch. Bd., 882 F.2d 876 (4th Cir. 1989).

[191] *Id.*

Roncker and *Daniel R.R.* tests and fashioned its own three-part test. According to the *Devries* test, mainstreaming is not required when (a) a student with a disability would not receive educational benefit from mainstreaming in a general education class; (b) any marginal benefit from mainstreaming would be significantly outweighed by benefits that could feasibly be obtained only in a separate instructional setting; or (c) the student is a disruptive force in the general education classroom.[192]

Although the circumstances surrounding each student were different in these cases, the analytical frameworks used to determine placements for them continue to guide school officials and to inform judges in making decisions that comport with both the standard of FAPE and the principle of LRE.

For example, the *Roncker* and *Daniel R. R.* frameworks were put to the test in a case addressing the disputed placement of Beth, a 13-year-old student with Rett syndrome, a rare neurological condition that severely impairs both cognitive and physical functioning. In *Beth B. v. Van Clay*,[193] the federal district court in Illinois noted that neither the Supreme Court nor the Seventh Circuit has indicated a preference among the various judicial tests. Before applying its analysis, the court discussed the merits of each framework, finding the *Daniel R. R.* test superior to the others in tracking the statutory language of the IDEA.[194] In addition, the court determined that the standard of feasibility in the *Roncker* analysis placed too much emphasis on what services could be delivered, but not enough on what the student actually learned.[195]

The district court first analyzed Beth's current regular class placement using the *Daniel R.R.* test. It examined the central question of whether Beth could be satisfactorily educated in the general education classroom. The court noted that the school system made many attempts to accommodate her in the general education setting, including the individualized services of two teacher-aides, an inclusion facilitator, and a customized curriculum using laminated books with embossed pictures and modified text.[196] The district also provided a variety of assistive technologies and trained personnel and other students how to use these technologies in communicating with Beth. Although these were described by her parents as inadequate and by the school system as "Herculean" efforts, the court determined that Beth's progress in the inclusive regular class setting was best described as inconsistent.[197]

In applying the *Daniel R. R.* test, the court noted that the IDEA does not require changes so extensive that the standard curriculum becomes unrecognizable.[198] Significant alterations were made in the seventh-grade classroom to

---

[192] *Id.*
[193] Beth B. v. Van Clay, 211 F. Supp. 2d 1020 (N.D. Ill. 2001), *aff'd*, 282 F.3d 493 (7th Cir. 2002), *cert denied*, 537 U.S. 948 (2002).
[194] *Id.*
[195] *Id.*
[196] *Id.*
[197] *Id.*
[198] *Id.*

adjust to Beth's severe cognitive delays and other issues. Because of her disability, Beth frequently dozed in school, took 20- to 30-minute scheduled toilet breaks, and was absent frequently. Thus, even though she remained in the general education classroom, she was not learning the same or even slightly modified material. In addition, as Beth advanced in grade levels, her interactions with other class members diminished.

The court next considered Beth's effect on both students and teachers in the learning environment, finding that only on occasion were her outbursts or needs distracting to other students.[199] However, Beth's teachers could not work with her and with other students simultaneously because of the significantly modified nature of her curriculum. For these reasons, the court determined that Beth could not be educated satisfactorily in a regular classroom.

The court next turned to the second prong of the *Daniel R. R.* analysis, finding the district's plans for reverse mainstreaming—and for inclusion in nonacademic activities including art, music, lunch, and field trips—acceptable opportunities for social integration. Using the *Daniel R. R.* analytical framework, the court determined that the statutory presumption for regular class placement was overcome.

The court next analyzed Beth's placement using the *Roncker* test. The court first found that the specialized programming was superior to regular programming for Beth. The specialized setting provided her with more direct contact with teachers who were trained and experienced in educating students with cognitive disabilities. In the smaller, more specialized setting, Beth could receive close attention from the teacher without detracting from other students. Not only were the teachers specially trained to work with students like Beth, but the program's administrator also had previous experience with students with Rett syndrome. Although other personnel could be trained to communicate with Beth, such training was not viewed as equivalent to the specialized preparation and experience of special education teachers. According to the court, "special education is also more conducive to systematic instruction. Rather than attempting to keep pace, even in modified form, with her non-disabled classmates' lessons, Beth can repeat skills until she learns them."[200] Thus, the court found that the specialized setting was superior to placement in the general education setting. Finally, the court found that these advantages could not feasibly be duplicated in a regular education setting.

Beth's parents appealed the decision and invoked the IDEA's stay-put provision[201] allowing Beth to remain in the regular class pending the resolution of the placement dispute. Upholding the judgment of the lower court, the Seventh Circuit Court expressly addressed the argument of Beth's parents that placement in the regular education classroom was mandated under LRE because she had obtained some educational benefit in the regular education classroom, thus satisfying the *Rowley* test to determine a FAPE. The Seventh

---

[199] *Id.*
[200] *Id.*
[201] 282 F.3d 493.

Circuit characterized the FAPE-IEP determination as being the threshold for any placement inquiry.[202] It first considered the appropriateness of the IEP in terms of educational benefit and determined that the FAPE mandate was not at issue. Warning that "the FAPE provision and LRE provision are two sides of the same IEP coin,"[203] the court rejected the concept that so long as a child obtains *some* educational benefit in the regular class, the school could not remove her from the setting. The court instructed that "the *Rowley* holding applies only to the school district's responsibility to provide a FAPE—a requirement that analyzes the appropriateness of the district's placement—not the appropriateness of its alternative, in this case, the regular setting."[204] Indeed, misapplying the *Rowley* standard to placement decisions instead of correctly applying it to decisions about an appropriate IEP would "turn the 'some educational benefit' language on its head."[205]

The court declined to adopt a formal framework for use in the Seventh Circuit, but relied on a fact-specific inquiry in finding that the school system's placement represented "an acceptable point along the continuum of services between total integration and complete segregation."[206] As long as the special program included opportunities for interaction with nondisabled peers, the placement satisfied the requirement that Beth be mainstreamed to the maximum extent appropriate. The Supreme Court denied Beth's parents' petition for a writ of certiorari.[207]

Although the Supreme Court established the standard of appropriateness in 1982, the attendant principle of instructional placement in the LRE continues to be left to members of the professional community and the courts to decide. Over the past few decades, legal analysts have developed sets of questions to

---

[202] *Id.*
[203] *Id.*
[204] *Id.*
[205] *Id.*
[206] *Id.*
[207] *Id.*

guide LRE decision making[208] and established sequenced formats to ensure full consideration of the LRE placement requirements.[209] Although the IDEA prefers inclusion, it does not require inclusion; however, courts give careful scrutiny to decisions that place students in more restrictive settings. Placement decisions require thoughtful analysis because the law acknowledges a rational basis for determining, on a case-by-case basis, that a child's FAPE might be provided in specialized settings using differing treatments. School principals need to understand, when IEP teams are determining a student's placement, that the primary consideration must be the unique individual needs of a student and the placement in which these needs can best be met. Moreover, "when there is uncertainty about the appropriate placement for a student, the IEP team should make a documented diligent and good-faith effort to educate the student in the least restrictive environment before considering, much less proposing, a more restrictive one."[210]

Changing Placements and Protecting Individual Rights

Fiscal resources and due process protections support the special education process, and the assurance of both funding and civil rights commands the attention of school administrators. FAPE is at risk when inadequate funding threatens the provision of costly, but appropriate, services. The IDEA places the fiscal burden for educating students with disabilities on school systems, and cost

---

[208] *See* MITCHELL L. YELL, THE LAW AND SPECIAL EDUCATION 284 (2019). The following questions address the components embodied in the LRE frameworks and rely on student-centered data collected throughout the LRE determination process:
(1) Has the school taken steps to maintain the child in the general education class? What supplementary aides and services were used? What interventions were attempted?
(2) What are the benefits of placement in a general education setting with supplementary aids and services versus the benefits of placement in a special education setting? What are the academic benefits? What are the nonacademic benefits, such as social communication and interactions?
(3) What are the effects on the education of other students? If the student is disruptive, is the education of other students adversely affected? Does the student require an inordinate amount of attention from the teacher, and, as a result, adversely affect the education of others?
(4) If a student is being educated in a setting other than the general education classroom, are there integrated experiences with nondisabled peers to the maximum extent appropriate? In what academic settings is the student integrated with nondisabled students? In what nonacademic settings is the child integrated with nondisabled students?
(5) Is the entire continuum of alternative services available from which to choose an appropriate placement?
[209] Decisions about placement can be addressed by using a sequential format that begins by considering whether the appropriate educational services written in the IEP can be delivered in the regular class if modified through the use of supplementary aids and services. If the answer is yes, then the regular class is the primary placement. If not, the team would move along the continuum of alternative placements one step at a time—from regular class, to resource room, to separate class, to separate school, residential setting, hospital, or home—considering whether the appropriate educational services might be delivered with appropriate supports until the answer *yes* is obtained.
[210] STEPHEN E. LAKE, SLIPPERY SLOPE! THE IEP MISSTEPS EVERY TEAM MUST KNOW AND HOW TO AVOID THEM (2007).

may not be a factor in providing a particular student with needed services. In a few cases, usually related to placements, where an appropriate education can be provided in more than one setting, school officials are permitted to select the less-expensive option.[211]

FAPE is also at risk when inadequate safeguards fail to ensure a student's right to receive an individually appropriate education. The IDEA is a child-centered law, and procedural protections surround decisions about IEPs, LRE, and placements. Parents, on behalf of their child, and students at the age of majority have the right to receive prior written notice and to participate in all meetings regarding identification, evaluation, programming, or placement. Informed consent is only required for an initial evaluation to determine if services are necessary, and then only to initiate those services if the child is found eligible to receive special education. Some states have additional requirements for parents to sign annual IEPs before services for the year can begin. If parents whose children are receiving special education refuse to sign consent at any point, school officials may seek an order from a hearing officer to proceed without consent, if that action seems to be in the student's best interests. Dangers arise when school officials appease parents at the child's expense—keeping the peace, but abandoning the child's best interests.

Prior written notice is also required when school officials propose any change in educational placement, including the proposal of a student's graduation with a regular education diploma.[212] In addition, the IDEA allows parents to pursue a due process hearing when they contest a change in placement for their child. However, courts are hesitant to grant hearings in cases where parents seek to prevent school officials from making organizational or fiscal decisions that affect more than their own child, such as closing or consolidating schools.[213] In these instances, it is important for school officials and for parents to understand the differences in meaning between a "program" and a "placement" under the IDEA. Students with disabilities can be transferred from schools or classes without these transfers being regarded as changes in placement, as long as the educational program offered in each setting is comparable and equally appropriate. Only when the services prescribed in a student's current IEP cannot be implemented in the new setting has a change in placement occurred that substantially affects a student's rights to an appropriate education.

Educating students in placements that support the delivery of appropriate instruction is a critical component of the IDEA. The percentage of time indicated on a student's IEP for the receipt of special education and related services outside the regular class is presumed to result from procedures that were legally correct and considerations that were student-specific. Educational placements that result from team-based decisions are presumed to comport with the delivery of services required by the IEP. Consequently, the IDEA's

---

[211] *See* Letter from Patricia J. Guard to Paul Veazey, U.S. DEP'T. OF EDUC. (Nov. 26, 2001), http://www2.ed.gov/policy/speced/guid/idea/letters/2001-4/veazey112601place.pdf.

[212] 20 USC 1415(b)(1)(C) (2012); 34 C.F.R. § 300.503 (2016).

[213] Powell v. Studstill, 441 S.E.2d 52 (Ga. 1994).

"stay-put" provision prevents school officials from disrupting the provision of FAPE by removing students from placements over parental objections, pending the resolution of due process review proceedings.[214] In the case of *Hale v. Poplar Bluff R-I School District*,[215] the Eighth Circuit held that the stay-put provision is to be rigorously enforced to stop schools from using the unilateral authority they once employed to exclude students with disabilities from school. In *Bell v. Education in the Unorganized Territories*, a district court in Maine relied on the stay-put provision in determining that graduation was grounds for a disputed change in placement. In this case, the parents of Jesse Bell, a student with autism, challenged the district's proposal that their son graduate from high school with his class. Finding that the district failed to overcome the law's strong preference for preserving the educational status quo, the court determined that the student remain in his current placement, attending to the curriculum prescribed in the previous year's IEP, during the pendency of further proceedings. The decision in *C.P. v. Leon County School Board*[216] clarified for states in the Eleventh Circuit that the stay-put provision does not require annual updating of an IEP.

Suspension and Expulsion

The only exception to the stay-put provision occurs when a hearing officer finds substantial evidence to indicate that it would be dangerous for the student to remain in the current placement.[217] The IDEA permits school officials to remove students who inflict serious bodily injury to another person while at school, and students who bring weapons or illegal drugs to school or to school functions, for 45 days if they attend an interim alternative educational setting. The discipline setting, not the pre-dispute setting, will be the stay-put placement during contested disciplinary actions.[218] With regard to suspension and expulsion, the IDEA again employs the legal strategy of a rebuttable presumption, favoring the student's placement in the present setting, but allowing the presumption to be overcome by evidence that harm or danger might ensue. Suspending special education students for more than 10 consecutive days, or expelling them from school, both represent changes of placement that trigger the use of procedural safeguards. Additionally, suspensions that total over 10 cumulative days in a school year can also be a change in placement if the removals constitute a pattern.[219]

---

[214] 34 C.F.R. § 300.518 (2016).
[215] Hale v. Poplar Bluff R-I Sch. Dist., 280 F. 3d 831 (8th Cir. 2002).
[216] C.P. v. Leon Cnty. Sch. Bd., 483 F.3d 1151 (11th Cir. 2007).
[217] 34 C.F.R. § 300.530 (2016).
[218] 20 U.S.C. § 1415(k)(1)(G) (2012); 34 C.F.R. § 300.533 (2016).
[219] To determine if suspensions in excess of 10 cumulative school days, the school principal and a student's IEP team should, on a case-by-case basis, examine such factors as: (a) were the student's behaviors that led to the suspension similar to the student's behavior in previous incidences, (b) the length of each removal, (c) the total amount of time the student has been removed, and (d) the proximity of the removals to one another. 34 C.F.R. § 300.536(a-d) (2016).

In these cases, the IDEA is clear: there is to be no cessation of educational services when students are suspended or removed to alternative settings.[220] Suspending or removing a student with a disability to an alternative setting for 10 cumulative days in the same school year does not require educational services. On the eleventh cumulative school day of removal, and all subsequent days, educational services must be provided.[221] FAPE cannot be denied once it has been guaranteed through eligibility and initiated through an IEP. School officials must continue to provide services that allow special education students to have access to the general curriculum and to make progress toward their goals.

Although the disciplinary procedures of the IDEA affect student placement, they are essentially issues related to the principle of zero-reject, which stipulates that a student who has a disability cannot be denied an equitable educational opportunity.[222] The IDEA's requirements that IEPs for students whose behaviors impede their learning include behavioral intervention plans are essentially issues related to the provision of an appropriate education.[223] The U.S. Department of Education has provided strong guidance to school officials, recommending that proactive measures be taken to address misconduct as soon as it appears to prevent more drastic measures from being taken at a later point.[224] Functional behavioral assessments could be conducted to determine if the present programming for a student who engages in misconduct is sufficiently specialized to provide appropriate support.[225] But, consideration of proactive measures to address the misconduct of students through the IEP process,[226] ensuring that individuals with disabilities are educated appropriately, brings this discussion of IEPs, LRE, and placement full circle.

Recommendations for Practice

In making IEP and placement decisions for students with disabilities, there is no substitute for implementing the IDEA with integrity. In making decisions with confidence, schools should anchor their actions in the law's conceptual foundations. The following recommendations are grounded in the trinity of FAPE, LRE, and validated practices so that schools might guide the delivery of effective special education in their schools.

1. Make ethical and legally defensible decisions. Promote professional behavior that pays more than lip-service to providing equity, quality, and

---

[220] 34 C.F.R. § 300.530 (2016). A special education student removed from the current placement for more than 10 consecutive days must continue to receive educational services and behavioral interventions whether or not the offending behavior is a manifestation of the disability.

[221] STEVEN E. LAKE, WHAT DO I DO WHEN—: THE ANSWER BOOK ON SPECIAL EDUCATION PRACTICE AND PROCEDURES 5.7 (2d ed. 2014).

[222] Turnbull, Stowe, & Huerta, *supra* note 18.

[223] 34 C.F.R. § 300.324(a)(2)(i) (2016).

[224] Sue Swenson & Ruth Ryder, Dear Colleague Letter, U.S. DEP'T. OF EDUC. (Aug. 1, 2016), http://www2.ed.gov/policy/gen/guid/school-discipline/files/dcl-on-pbis-in-ieps--08-01-2016.pdf.

[225] 34 C.F.R. § 300.530 (2016).

[226] 34 C.F.R. § 300.324(a)(IV)(2)(i) (2016).

opportunity for all learners. Schools are now enrolling record numbers of students whose learning differences once would have excluded them from receiving a public education. But, for some special education students, functional exclusion is still a reality when schools fail to deliver specially designed instruction or teachers fail to follow the prescriptions of an IEP. As a result, these students "experience a different kind of segregation—the exclusion from the basic right to learn."[227]

2. Directly address individuality and exceptionality in learning. School leaders are in strong positions to articulate that special education is for students with disabilities who need to learn something different, or who need to learn the same thing as everyone else but in a different way. Special education is not for any student who fails in the general curriculum, but for students who, because of the extent of their disability-related needs, require different ways to learn and to demonstrate what they know in order to meet with school success. Special education, with its guarantee of an appropriate public education in the LRE, is for individuals whose disabilities threaten to handicap their future if left unnoticed and unaddressed.

3. Ensure the delivery of special education that is legally correct and educationally meaningful. Communicate to stakeholders the statutory purpose of the IDEA and the legal meanings of its critical components, including a FAPE and placements made in accordance with the principle of the LRE. Although these are familiar terms to most educators, they are often used incorrectly, leading to imprecision, which, in turn, leads to violation of the law and nullification of FAPE.

4. Provide IEPs that address the procedural and substantive requirements of the IDEA. Courts have viewed serious procedural errors as violations of FAPE if they result in harmful disruption to the delivery of appropriate instruction and educational services. Moreover, to meet the substantive requirements of the law ensure that full, individualized, and relevant assessments are conducted of every student who is eligible for special education under the IDEA, develop meaningful and measurable annual goals, determine and implement the necessary special education and related services, and monitor student progress.

5. Develop IEPs that are reasonably calculated to enable a child to make progress that is appropriate in light of the child's circumstances. To confer educational benefit, students' IEPs must (a) be based on relevant and meaningful assessments; (b) include ambitious, but reasonable, measurable annual goals; (c) be comprised of special education and related services that are designed to confer benefit; and (d) involve the collection of relevant and meaningful data to monitor student progress.

---

[227] Jean S. Schumm et al., *General Education Teacher Planning: What Can Students with Learning Disabilities Expect?* 61 EXCEPTIONAL CHILDREN 335 (1995).

6. If an IEP is challenged in a hearing or in court as failing to provide FAPE, be able to provide a cogent and responsive explanation for school personnel's decisions which shows that a student's IEP is reasonably calculated to enable the child to make progress that is appropriate in light of his or her circumstances.

7. Develop IEPs that rely on current and relevant data about the unique educational needs of each student, not on the prerogatives of the school system or on the availability of services.

8. Avoid filling IEPs with details about content standards. Focus, instead, on the necessary adjustments to be made in providing intensive and specific instruction in academics and desirable behavior, so that students can appropriately access and participate in the general curriculum and meet their disability-related goals.

9. Policies of "full inclusion" should not be allowed to substitute for the IDEA's requirement that school systems make available a full continuum of alternative placements. Use student-specific IEP data, not philosophical arguments about inclusion, in making legally correct decisions about placements that constitute the LRE for each student. Remember that providing a student with a special education program that provides educational benefit, thus conferring FAPE, is the primary mandate of the IDEA. Determining the LRE in which a student will receive a FAPE is a secondary mandate that is made after the IEP is developed.

10. If a student exhibits problem behavior, the IEP team must determine if the behavior is to be addressed in the IEP; if the team does so, IDEA requires consideration of positive behavioral interventions and supports.[228] When possible, disciplinary procedures that employ in-school procedures, such as in-school suspension, should be used. Remember that services to students are not to cease because of suspension or expulsion from school. Any change of placement, for any reason, requires that parents be notified of the school's intent to remove their child from the current setting. Remember, too, that the IDEA has a strong preference for the placement that represents the status quo.

11. Support high expectations for positive results. Ensure that professionals use effective instructional methodologies and assessment systems that have a demonstrated record of being successful for students with disabilities. Ensure that special and general educators balance a student's need to be successful in the general curriculum with the need to learn from a specialized curriculum in other areas.

12. Establish productive partnerships with parents. Notify parents in writing before taking any action regarding their child's programming or placement. Give parents a copy of procedural safeguards before IEP meetings and provide them with genuine opportunities to participate in any meetings

---

[228] 20 U.S.C. § 1414(d)(3)(B)(i) (2012).

regarding their child. Involve parents as full partners, but do not appease them by forsaking professional judgment about the best interests of their child.

13. Remember that schools have the best hope for meeting state standards and national goals adequately when they are vigilant in meeting the needs of their students with disabilities appropriately.

Case List

A.W. v. Northwest R-1 Sch. Dist.
Adam J. v. Keller Indep. Sch.Dist.
Amanda J. v. Clark Cnty. Sch. Dist.
B.H. v. West Clermont Bd. of Educ.
Beth B. v. Van Clay
Bd. of Educ. of the Hendrick Hudson Sch. Dist. v. Rowley
Burlington Sch. Comm. of the Town of Burlington v. Dept. of Educ. of Mass.
C.P. v. Leon Cnty. Sch. Bd.
County of San Diego v. Cal. Sp. Educ. Hrg. Office
Cypress-Fairbanks Indep. Sch. Dist. v. Michael F.
D.B. v. Bedford Cnty. Sch. Bd.
Daniel R.R. v. State Bd. of Educ.
Deal *ex rel.* Deal v. Hamilton Cnty. Dep't of Educ.
DeVries v. Fairfax Cnty. Sch. Bd.
Doe v. Bd. of Educ. of Tullahoma City Sch.
Endrew F. v. Douglas Cnty. Sch. Dist. RE-1
Fayetteville-Perry Local Sch. Dist.
Florence Cnty. Sch. Dist. Four v. Carter
Frank G. v. Bd. of Educ. of Hyde Park
Greer v. Rome City Sch. Dist.
Hale v. Poplar Bluff R-I Sch. Dist.
Hall v. Vance Cnty. Bd. of Educ.
J.P. v. West Clark Cmty. Sch.
J.S.K. v. Hendry Cnty. Sch. Bd.
L.B. and J.B. *ex rel.* K.B. v. Nebo Sch. Dist.
M.C. v. Antelope Valley Union High
Nein v. Greater Clark Cnty. Sch. Corp.
Oberti v. Bd. of Educ. of the Bor. of Clementon Sch. Dist.
P. v. Newington Bd. of Educ.
Polk v. Cent. Susquehanna Intermed. Unit 16
Powell v. Studstill
Roncker v. Walter
Sacramento City Unified Sch. Dist. v. Rachel H.
Schaffer v. Weast
Thompson R2-J Sch. Dist. v. Luke P.
Tucson Unified Sch. Dist.

Van Duyn v. Baker Sch. Dist.
Winkelman by Winkelman v. Parma City Sch. Dist.

Key Words

age of majority
assessing and reporting progress
best interest
burden of proof
communication needs
continuum of options
de minimis
Education for All Handicapped Children Act
educational benefit
educational placement
educational settings
Every Student Succeeds Act
expulsion
extracurricular activities
fiscal burden
free appropriate public education (FAPE)
general curriculum
hearings
inclusion
individualized education program (IEP)
Individuals with Disabilities Education Act (IDEA)
integration
learning disabilities
least restrictive environment (LRE)
mainstreaming
measurable annual goals
partnership with parents
placement decisions
problem behavior
procedural safeguards
program versus placement
reasonable expectations
special education and related services
specially designed instruction
stay-put provision
student outcomes
suspension
testing accommodations
transition services

Takeaways

1. The goal of IDEA is to ensure that all students with disabilities receive FAPE so that they are prepared for the future.
2. Under the IDEA, students with disabilities, ages 3-21, are entitled to receive FAPE.
3. In order to provide FAPE to students with disabilities, instruction must be individualized to meet the diverse needs of the learners with disabilities.
4. An IEP is a specific program designed for a specific student with a disability to support their success in school.
5. Under IDEA, students with disabilities should be placed in the LRE to the maximum extent possible. While the least restrictive environment for most students is the general education classroom, it is not an appropriate setting for all students with disabilities; therefore, the IEP team determines what constitutes the LRE for each individual student to ensure FAPE.
6. Together, IDEA and ESSA ensure that students with disabilities receive a high-quality and challenging education that is fair, appropriate, and meets their diverse learning needs.
7. Under the ESSA, most students with disabilities are to be taught the same challenging academic content as nondisabled students.
8. A student's IEP requires teachers to deliver the challenging academic content to a student with a disability in a different way to meet the needs of the student.
9. Under IDEA, public schools that are unable to provide a student with a disability a free and appropriate public education are responsible for paying private school tuition for the student.
10. Schools are legally obligated to develop and implement IEPs appropriately; failure to do so is considered a violation of FAPE and a violation of the law. It is imperative that teachers understand why and how IEPs are created, what IEPs cover, and their obligation to implement each IEP correctly.
11. Students with IEPs who are suspended more than 10 school days are entitled to receive educational services on the eleventh cumulative day of suspension. Regardless of the reason for their suspension, the school is obligated to provide the student with FAPE as per IDEA.

Practical Extension

1. A parent contacts a student's English teacher about providing additional accommodations that are not included in the child's most recent IEP. The parent requests that her child receive 100% extended time (instead of the 50% that is prescribed in the student's IEP), as well as use of a word bank on vocabulary assessments. How should the teacher proceed?

2. In this digital age, there is greater access to online educational tools and programs to support learners in the classroom. Consider ways that general education teachers may use technology to differentiate instruction, modify curriculum, and support the diverse learning needs of students with disabilities in their classrooms in accordance with students' IEPs.

Chapter 9

Disciplining Students with Disabilities

Mark A. Paige

Introduction

Appropriately handling behavioral and discipline issues of students with disabilities is an important part of special education. It raises significant legal questions, in addition to questions of practice. As discussed in more detail below, the IDEA (the Individuals with Disabilities Education Act) and its implementing regulations provide comprehensive rules that govern this issue. Similarly, court cases provide important guidance for school administrators. Within the overall subject of special education discipline, particular areas that require careful attention of school administrators include removal of students with disabilities, as well as the restraint and seclusion of these students, among others. These areas are given particular attention in the following pages.

Context matters in understanding the law and rules governing student discipline. It is important to understand that special education law on the topic of discipline attempts to balance competing interests. On the one hand, the IDEA is meant to protect the individual rights of students with disabilities. Given the history of treatment of such students in public schools, this is understandable. Unfortunately, children with disabilities were completely excluded from public education until the courts intervened to ensure that their right to a free appropriate public education was delivered. In this regard, the law rightly expresses a concern for disciplinary action that could exclude or diminish the educational opportunities afforded to students with disabilities.

The law must also consider rights of all students, with or without disabilities. In this respect, all students have a right to an orderly and safe school environment as part of their right to equal educational opportunity. Thus, the law seeks both to ensure the rights of students with disabilities and to permit school officials the discretion to effectively manage schools. The day-to-day balancing and operationalization of these interests, in the end, is in the hands of school administrators. This chapter will outline important elements of the law and provide information to assist school officials in their work.

The chapter is organized as follows: (1) It delivers a brief overview of the general concepts of discipline in the special education context; (2) It highlights key considerations regarding discipline of students with disabilities that flow from the pertinent regulations under IDEA and case law, with particular attention to the concept of "change in placement" that can be triggered in certain circumstances; (3) It discusses the several categories of removal that may be helpful in complying with the law—short-term (less than 10-day) removals, long-term removals (including change of placements), and interim alternative educational settings (IAES). The chapter also discusses the legal issues surrounding restraint and seclusion.

Discipline and the IEP

Several principles concerning development of an individualized education program (IEP) deserve review before taking a deep dive into the rules governing the discipline of children with disabilities. To begin with, IEP teams should always carefully consider the behavioral needs of a student as they generate an IEP, regardless of whether these needs interfere with a student's learning. Creating the educational structure and services that are tailored to the child's needs simply reflects best practices, at a minimum, and helps ensure the proper development of an IEP.

With that said, there are times when good practice is required practice in the context of an IEP. An IEP team must consider the behavioral needs of a student when they develop an IEP, if that behavior impedes the child's learning.[1] In these cases, the team should consider positive behavioral interventions and other supports that address the problematic behavior.[2] It has been the long history of special education law that behavior should be addressed proactively in a student's IEP.[3] In this way, it is important to recall that all members of the IEP team play an important role in assessing the impact of a student's behavior and developing appropriate responses. For instance, the student's regular education teacher plays an important role in developing interventions meant to address behavior that impedes a student's learning, and should be central to this process.[4] As the old saying goes "an ounce of prevention is worth a pound of cure"—in this case, when an IEP team takes a proactive step in addressing behavioral needs for children with disabilities, it reduces the risk of encountering the legal issues noted below.

---

[1] 34 C.F.R. § 300.324(a)(2) (2016).
[2] 20 U.S.C. §1414(d)(3)(B)(i) (2012).
[3] *See e.g.*, Neosho R-V Sch. Dist. v. Clark, 315 F.3d 1022 (8th Cir. 2003) (holding that failure to offer behavioral services amounted to denial of FAPE). *But compare with* C.J.N. v. Minneapolis Pub. Schs., 323 F.3d 630, 642 (8th Cir. 2003) (noting that failure to adopt a behavioral intervention plan did not amount to denial of FAPE where mother disagreed with components of the proposed plan and refused to sign it.); *see also* Lathrop R-II Sch. Dist. v. Gray, 611 F.3d 419 (8th Cir. 2010) (noting that IEP need not have specific goals related to behavior).
[4] 34 C.F.R. § 300.324(a)(3) (2016) (regulation requiring that the regular education teacher of a child with a disability as a member of the IEP Team must participate in developing of the IEP of the child, including behavioral interventions).

General Disciplinary Authority and Short-Term Removals

The seminal Supreme Court case of *Honig v. Doe*[5] continues to provide the basis for discipline of special education students. Under *Honig*, a school district may remove a student who violates the school disciplinary code for no more than ten consecutive school days.[6] Calculating the ten days set forth under *Honig* does require careful attention, in some circumstances. Moreover, it should be noted that schools are not prohibited from enforcing their typical school procedures regarding discipline of students with disabilities when those students threaten themselves or others.[7] This principle means that, in the most straightforward case (e.g., suspension up to ten days for school disciplinary code violation), a school district does not have additional duties owed to the student. By way of federal law, the IEP team does not have to meet, services do not need to be provided, nor must a functional behavioral assessment be provided.

However, practitioners in different jurisdictions should be aware of applicable state laws. State laws can, and many do, impose additional duties on school officials that reach beyond the procedures codified in federal law. For instance, Massachusetts law imposes several procedural and substantive requirements when a school seeks to suspend a student, regardless of classification (e.g., whether the student qualifies for special education or not).[8] Indeed, given the shift in education policy away from removal of students from an educational setting, it is quite likely that your state or district may have policies governing student removal that should supplement these materials. It is important to mention that school principals may be the focal point for enforcement and oversight of these rules, thus highlighting the significance of school leaders in this area.[9]

Long-Term Removal: More than Ten Days in Total over Time

When a suspension exceeds ten days, school officials must satisfy several obligations.[10] Sometimes this triggering event occurs somewhat unexpectedly. Indeed, a student may be suspended on numerous occasions for shorter duration, such as two- or three-day suspensions. It is conceivable that these multiple

---

[5] 484 U.S. 305, 325 (1988) (defining that a "change of placement" occurs when a student is suspended in excess of ten days).

[6] 34 C.F.R. § 300.530(b)(1) (2016).

[7] *Honig*, 484 U.S. at 325; *see also* 71 Fed. Reg. 46540, 46715 (Aug. 14, 2006) (noting that the disciplinary measures should be applied to children with disabilities to the extent that they are applied to children without disabilities, stating "[a] primary intent of Congress in revising the [IDEA] was to provide for a uniform and fair way of disciplining all children – both for those children with disabilities and those children without disabilities").

[8] *See, e.g.,* 603 Mass. Code Regs. 53.13 (West 2016) (imposing numerous requirements on school officials to provide educational opportunities for all students when suspensions of any length or expulsions are issued).

[9] *Id.* The Massachusetts regulations impose the oversight and enforcement of its rules governing student removal on principals in many instances.

[10] The additional topic of "change of placement" is considered elsewhere in this chapter.

"short" suspensions could accrue to exceed the ten-day threshold under *Honig*. Speaking hypothetically, this might occur when a student is suspended on four separate occasions for unrelated infractions, with a three-day suspension for each infraction—thus, the student has been suspended for a total of twelve days. If these recurring suspensions are considered a pattern of removal, the student may have been subjected to a change in educational placement, which would trigger additional protections as discussed below.[11] If, however, the suspensions do not amount to a "pattern" of removal that might be considered a change of placement, no additional proceedings are necessary.

However, even while suspended, the student with disabilities must continue to receive educational services to be able to continue to participate in the general curriculum and make progress toward the IEP goals.[12] If appropriate, behavioral interventions—e.g., functional behavioral assessment (FBA), or behavioral intervention plan (BIP)—designed to address the underlying behavior must also be delivered to the student to prevent a recurrence of the violation.[13] School personnel and at least one of the child's teachers determine the services needed to enable the child to participate in the general education curriculum.[14]

Long-term Removal: Change of Placement

The concept of "change in placement" is an important legal term that deserves careful attention. Many of the remedies the IDEA seeks to impose relate to the idea that a school district cannot unilaterally change the placement of a student, something that was the central piece of the *Honig* litigation.[15] In *Honig*, students with disabilities had been summarily expelled or excluded from school without any procedures to guard against arbitrary government action. Subsequent to this case, special education law imposes additional duties on school officials when a change in placement occurs. But, what constitutes a "change in placement"? If there are shorter-term suspensions that do not, individually, exceed the ten-day threshold, do they trigger a change of placement?

The regulations give some guidance to help understand how the concept of change in placement relates to many forms of possible removal of a student (e.g., half-day suspension). First, a change of placement occurs when a child with a disability is removed for more than ten consecutive school days.[16] This example is the more straightforward case. Removal for more than ten consecutive days triggers the numerous procedural and substantive obligations discussed below.

Second, a change of placement for disciplinary reasons occurs when a series of removals constitutes a "pattern." Of course, understanding what equates with a pattern is important for administrators and teachers. This type of change of placement—one that occurs through a pattern—poses a significant risk for

---

[11] 34 C.F.R. § 300.536 (2016).
[12] 34 C.F.R. § 300.530(b)(2) (2016); 34 C.F.R. § 300.530(d)(i) (2016).
[13] 34 C.F.R. § 300.530(d)(ii) (2016).
[14] 34 C.F.R. § 300.530(d)(4) (2016).
[15] *See Honig, supra* note 7.
[16] 34 C.F.R. § 300.536(a)(1) (2016).

an IDEA violation. In this instance, the law acknowledges that removal of a child for periods that exceed ten days for "substantially similar" behavior may create a "pattern" that is the legal equivalent of a "change of placement." Put another way, a pattern, as defined below, also triggers specific procedural and substantive protections.

The federal regulations relating to IDEA speak to what will be considered a "pattern" of removal constituting a change of placement, reading as follows:

> The child has been subjected to a series of removals that constitute a pattern—
> a. Because the series of removals total more than ten school days in a school year;
> b. Because the child's behavior is substantially similar to the child's behavior in previous incidents that resulted in the series of removals; and
> c. Because of such additional factors as the length of each removal, the total amount of time the child has been removed, and the proximity of the removals to one another.[17]

What constitutes a pattern of removal (and therefore a change of placement) is not always easy or obvious. In fact, if school officials do not refer back to the prior incidents, they may completely overlook any analysis as to whether a pattern has emerged. It is quite possible that many administrators may simply refer back to the *Honig* standard of ten consecutive days. To be sure, the regulations provide some guidance, but no clear "test" as to how to understand what amounts to a pattern of removal. Importantly, the law recognizes that each case is different, and the determination of whether removals amount to a pattern and, therefore, a change of placement, is determined on a "case-by-case" basis.[18] To some extent, the nature of the infraction and timing of removal may be two variables that can assist in this determination. If, for example, the conduct is similar and the removals are close in timing, then an argument is strengthened that a pattern exists (assuming the ten-day threshold is satisfied).[19] Importantly, schools that operate under a zero-tolerance policy should also be aware that this raises a conflict with the "case-by-case" requirement. While the regulations place great deference to administrators' judgment as to whether a pattern has occurred, in the end, such a decision can be contested through special education due process proceedings and litigation.[20]

Schools should be consistent and should develop some uniform practice of assessing whether a behavioral pattern exists. They should be attentive—and have some organized system in place—to alert them as to whether a pattern is emerging or has emerged. Moreover, they should attempt to discern the nature of the underlying behavior and its timing. Consistent and thorough

---

[17] 34 C.F.R. § 300.536(a)(2)(i)-(iii) (2016) (emphasis added).
[18] 34 C.F.R. § 300.536(b)(1) (2016).
[19] 34 C.F.R. § 300.536(a)(2)(ii) and (iii) (2016) (noting specifically that the behavior must be "substantially similar" and the "proximity of removals to one another").
[20] 34 C.F.R. § 300.536(b)(2) (2016).

record keeping and communication among the special education team may assist in this effort.

Duties of School District when Change of Placement Occurs

As discussed, assessing whether a change in placement has occurred is simply one in an important series of steps in the analysis for school administrators. Importantly, significant procedural and substantive duties are triggered if a change of placement occurs. To begin with, within ten school days of the decision to change the placement, the IEP team must meet.[21] On the date that the decision to change placement is made, parents must be notified and receive a procedural safeguards notice.[22]

Substantive obligations are triggered if a change of placement occurs (e.g., the continuation of providing educational services).[23] Specifically, the child must continue to receive education services so as to "participate" in the general curriculum and "progress" toward IEP goals.[24] The IEP team is charged with determining the services that are needed to provide a free appropriate public education (FAPE).[25] Moreover, the regulations require, if appropriate, a functional behavioral assessment (FBA) and behavioral interventions designed to prevent a recurrence of the behavior.[26]

Services a student receives during a removal need not be precisely the services a student would receive in school;[27] services have to be determined on a case-by-case basis.[28] Of course, with this "case-by-case" standard, it makes it impossible for districts to develop a bright-line rule. They must pay careful attention to the specific needs of the child so as to develop the services to be applied during the removal that will continue to allow the child to "participate." The nature of the student's needs should be the starting point for determining the services that must be offered out of school. Students with more sophisticated IEPs and greater needs likely will need more involved coordination of services for out-of-school suspensions. Conversely, students with more marginal needs

---

[21] 20 U.S.C. § 1415(k)(1)(E)(i) (2012).
[22] 34 C.F.R. § 300.530(h) (2016).
[23] 34 C.F.R. § 300.530(d) (2016).
[24] 34 C.F.R. § 300.530(d)(1) (2016).
[25] 34 C.F.R. § 300.530(d)(5) (2016); See, e.g., M.M. v. Special Sch. Dist. No. 1, 512 F.3d 455 (8th Cir. 2008) (holding that offer of homebound services was sufficient even though parents rejected that offer); Troy City Bd. of Educ., 27 IDELR 555 (AL 1998) (affirming district's provision of four hours of homebound tutoring per week to properly expelled middle school-aged student with a disability as consistent with the provision of FAPE).
[26] 34 C.F.R. § 300.530(d) (2016).
[27] 71 Fed. Reg. *supra* note 7, at 46716 (Aug. 14, 2006) (requiring school district to provide services so that the student can "participate" does not mean that the district must "replicate" every service a child would receive in the normal classroom).
[28] 34 C.F.R. § 300.530(d)(5) (2016) (in cases where the removal is a change of placement the IEP Team determines "appropriate" services.); *see also* Farrin v. Maine Sch. Admin. Dist. No. 59, 165 F. Supp. 2d 37 (D. Me. 2001); 71 Fed. Reg., *supra* note 7, at 46720 ("[D]ecisions regarding the manifestation determination must be made on a case-by-case basis.").

(but still requiring special education) may need less to be able to continue to progress, notwithstanding their removal.

Importantly, a manifestation determination review (MDR) must occur in order to determine whether the misbehavior was, in fact, caused by the child's disability in cases involving a change of placement.[29] A meeting to make this determination must take place within ten school days of the decision to change placement due to a disciplinary code violation. Regulations require the LEA, parent, and "relevant members" of the IEP team to attend.[30] Significantly, administrators should note that this group is not the child's entire IEP team. School officials should be careful to convene this configuration for the manifestation determination unless state law or regulation dictates otherwise.

The attendees must determine the following:
- If the conduct in question was caused by, or had a direct relationship to, the child's disability; or
- If the conduct in question was the direct result of the LEA's failure to implement the IEP.[31]

If either of the above conditions is met, then the conduct is determined to be a manifestation of the child's disability.[32] Under those circumstances, the child cannot be subject to further school discipline. Further, if the manifestation was a result of the failure to implement the IEP, then the IEP team must "take immediate" steps to remedy the deficiencies. In making this determination, the manifestation determination should consider all relevant information in the child's file, including the IEP, teacher observations, and relevant information from parents.[33] When there is direct evidence linking the misconduct and the disability, then a conclusion that the behavior was a manifestation may follow.[34]

Additional obligations arise if the behavior was a manifestation of the disability. The IEP team (note that this is different than the manifestation determination group) must do either of the following: (1) Conduct a FBA (unless they had already done so before the behavior that resulted in the change of placement) and implement a behavioral intervention plan; or (2) If a BIP has been developed, review and modify it to address the behavior.[35]

Even if the conduct was not a manifestation of the disability and the removal occurs, school districts cannot discontinue services.[36] Courts appear divided in their assessment of whether conduct was a particular manifestation

---

[29] It is worth repeating that manifestation determinations are only required removals that constitute a "change of placement." 71 Fed. Reg. *supra* note 7, at 46720.
[30] 34 C.F.R. § 300.530(e) (2016).
[31] *Id.*
[32] *Id.*
[33] 34 C.F.R. § 300.530(e) (2016). This list is not exhaustive, however. *See* San Diego Unified Sch. Dist., 52 IDELR 301 (SEA CA 2009).
[34] *See, e.g.,* Swansea Public Sch., 47 IDELR 278 (SEA MA 2007) (child's emotional and oppositional behavior resulted when administrator violated the terms of the BIP).
[35] 34 C.F.R. § 300.530(f) (2016).
[36] 34 C.F.R. § 300.530(d)(1)(i) (2016).

of a disability.[37] However, school administrators that follow the process above and assess the situation in a fair and balanced manner stand a greater chance of having their decision upheld, should the matter ever come before the courts.[38]

Several cases provide some guidance about situations when administrative bodies have concluded that the behavior was not a manifestation of the disability. For instance, where a student exercises behavior that can be characterized as poor judgment, a manifestation may not be found.[39] Yet, in at least one case, a student's role in a drug distribution ring was, in fact, determined to be a manifestation of his disability.[40]

Unfortunately, there seems to be little guidance (from courts, at least) about what satisfactory behavioral intervention plans look like. Indeed, courts and hearing officers have declined to create standards to assess the appropriateness of such plans.[41] In the absence of specific guidelines, school officials should be sure to closely follow the procedural requirements and exercise their considered and professional judgment regarding the appropriateness of a behavioral plan.

The regulations speak to placement of the child following a manifestation determination. Indeed, unless there is an agreement between the parent and the LEA, the student must return to the placement from which the removal was made.[42] A school district may challenge the return of the student to a placement, however. Here, the school district must demonstrate that there is a "substantial likelihood" of injury to the child, or others, if the student remains in the placement.[43] Presumably, the school would request an expedited hearing or seek injunctive relief.[44] During this appeal process, the student's stay-put placement is in the interim placement.[45]

---

[37] *Compare* Randy M. v. Texas City Ind. Sch. Dist., 93 F. Supp. 2d 1310 (S.D. Tex. 2000) *with* Jonathan G. v. Caddo Parish Sch. Bd., 875 F. Supp. 352 (W.D. La. 1994).

[38] *See, e.g.,* Rowley v. Bd. of Educ. of Hendrick Hudson Cent. Sch. Dist., 458 U.S. 176 (1982) (noting, in dicta, that courts must be careful to avoid imposing their educational judgment on local education agencies).

[39] *See, e.g.,* Fitzgerald v. Fairfax Cnty. Sch. Bd., 50 556 F. Supp. 2d 543 (E.D. Va. 2008); *see also* Lewellyn v. Sarasota Cnty. Bd. of Educ., 2009 WL 5214983 (M.D. Fla. 2016) (Dec. 29, 2009) (unreported decision).

[40] Sch. Bd. of Prince William Cnty. v. Malone, 762 F.2d 1210 (4th Cir. 1985) (affirming lower court decision that student's role in drug distribution was a function of his disability). *But compare with* Lancaster Elementary Sch. Dist., 49 IDELR 53 (SEA CA 2007) (bringing drugs to school was not related to specific learning disability).

[41] *See, e.g.,* Alex R. v. Forrestville Valley Cmty. Sch. Dist. #221, 375 F.3d 603 (7th Cir. 2004). *See also* Susan C. Bon & Allan G. Osborne, Jr., *Does the Failure to Conduct an FBA or Develop a BIP Result in a Denial of FAPE under the IDEA?* 307 Educ. L. Rep. 581, 583 (2014) (noting that there are no substantive requirements for such plans).

[42] 34 C.F.R. § 300.530(f)(2) (2016).

[43] 34 C.F.R. § 300.532(a) (2016).

[44] 34 C.F.R. § 300.532(c) (2016).

[45] 34 C.F.R. § 300.533 (2016).

Discipline Other than Out-of-School Suspension

Schools have a variety of means for disciplining a student through suspension. In-school suspension is certainly one of these and is used frequently. This means of discipline allows the school to maintain oversight and education of the student, yet at the same time prevents the student from being disruptive to others' education. However, the question arises as to the relationship between in-school suspensions and removal, as that term is understood in special education law. To what extent, if any, does in-school suspension count toward the ten days of suspension referenced under the IDEA's regulation? Here, the Department of Education takes the position that an in-school suspension does not count toward the ten days of suspension, under certain conditions,[46] as follows: the child must be afforded the opportunity to appropriately participate in the curriculum, receive the services under the IEP, and continue to participate with nondisabled students to the extent that the current placement directs.[47] Given this guidance from the Department of Education, teachers should be aware of their continued role in delivering the curriculum and continuing to serve the child who is removed to an in-school suspension setting.

As one can imagine, the school bus can be the site of misconduct, and a student may be removed from bus transportation to prevent the behavior. Here, the question arises: Does a bus suspension count toward the ten days under the regulations? It depends, but it is helpful to think about the extent to which the transportation relates to the child's special education. A bus suspension would count toward the removal timeline if bus transportation is a required service under the child's IEP.[48] This reasoning is due to the fact that the service is required for the student to reach the location where the educational services will be delivered;[49] thus, it is a related service incorporated into the programming. If the service was not part of the IEP, then suspension from the bus is not a "suspension" within the meaning of the regulations.[50] In this instance, the parents have the same obligation to transport the student as would the parents of a nondisabled peer similarly disciplined.[51]

Interim Alternative Educational Setting: 45-Day Removal

There are special circumstances where a school district may remove a student without regard to whether the disciplinary violation was a manifestation of the disability. School personnel may move a student to an interim alternative

---

[46] 71 Fed. Reg., *supra* note 7, at 46715; *See* Delaware (OH) City Sch. Dist., 51 IDELR 257 (OCR 2008) (decision of whether in-school suspension counts as removal depends on whether educational and special services were provided during the in-school suspension).

[47] 71 Fed. Reg., *supra* note 7, at 46715.

[48] *Id.*

[49] *Id.*

[50] *Id.*

[51] The Department of Education does not take a position on this matter. *Id.*

educational setting (IAES) for no more than 45 school days in three situations, set forth below.[52] The student's IEP team determines the IAES.[53]

First, if the child brings to school or possesses a dangerous weapon on school premises, or at a school function under the jurisdiction of the LEA or SEA, this option may be available to a district. "Dangerous weapon" is defined as:

> [A] weapon, device, instrument, material, or substance, animate or inanimate, that is used for, or is readily capable of, causing serious death or serious bodily injury, except that term does not include a pocketknife with a blade of less than 2½ inches in length.[54]

Second, a district may remove a child for no more than 45 school days if the child knowingly possess or uses illegal drugs, or sells or solicits the sale of a controlled substance while at school, or on school premises, or at a school function under the jurisdiction of the LEA or SEA.[55] The definition of "controlled substance" simply mirrors the Controlled Substance Act.[56] An "illegal drug" is a controlled substance; however this does not apply to a legally possessed controlled substance or to such a substance being used under the supervision of a licensed health care professional or legally possessed by another authority under the Controlled Substance Act.[57] Thus, school administrators must use their judgment and seek guidance, if there is doubt.

Third, a district may remove a child to an interim alternative setting for up to 45 school days when the child inflicted serious bodily injury upon another person while at school, on school premises, or at a school function under the jurisdiction of the LEA or SEA. Here again, attention must be paid to the critical definitional term of "serious bodily injury," which means:

> [A] bodily injury that involves:
> - A substantial risk of death;
> - Extreme physical pain;
> - Protracted and obvious disfigurement; or protracted loss or impairment of the function of a bodily member, organ, or mental faculty.[58]

A few final notes are in order with respect to the interim alternative educational setting. Schools should still be aware of the procedural duties that arise when they make a change of placement in this or any other setting. There are important procedural notification requirements to follow. Specifically, schools must notify parents of the decision to change placement and give them the

---

[52] 34 C.F.R. § 300.530(g)(1)-(3) (2016).

[53] 34 C.F.R. § 330.531 (2016).

[54] 71 Fed. Reg., *supra* note 7, at 46723; *see also* 18 U.S.C. § 1356(h)(3) (2012) (defining "controlled substance"); 34 C.F.R. § 300.530(i)(4) (2016).

[55] *See* 71 Fed. Reg., *supra* note 7, at 46723 (the definition of controlled substance changes frequently and, therefore, the Department of Education refuses to attempt to offer a definition in their regulations or commentary and simply maps the definition used in the Controlled Substance Act); *see also* 34 C.F.R. § 300.530(i)(1) (2016).

[56] *See* 34 C.F.R. § 300.530(i)(1) (2016).

[57] 34 C.F.R. § 300.530(i)(2) (2016).

[58] *See* 71 Fed. Reg., *supra* note 7, at 46723.

procedural safeguards notice,[59] in addition to the substantive requirements (e.g., review of the IEP, conduct FBA, etc.).

As one can imagine, a parent and school district may not agree to a change of placement based on disciplinary action, and there are routes available to resolve such a disagreement. Indeed, schools may seek injunctive relief to prevent a child from returning to a placement that it deems dangerous.[60] They may also seek review through an expedited hearing process.[61] Likewise, the same expedited appeal process is available to parents to challenge a district's decision.

Non-identified Students and Child Find

School districts must consider their disciplinary actions in relation to students who have not yet been identified as eligible for special education and related services. A key determination here is whether the district "had knowledge" that the student was a student with a disability prior to the disciplinary infraction(s)/behavior. The regulations specify when a school district will be deemed to have the requisite knowledge.

- A district must be considered to have had knowledge that the student was a child with a disability under the following circumstances.
- If prior to the behavior that precipitated the disciplinary action, the parent expressed in writing that the child is in need of special education. The writing could be expressed to "supervisory or administrative personnel" or "a teacher of the child."[62]
- If prior to the behavior that precipitated the disciplinary action, the parent requested an evaluation.[63]
- If prior to the behavior that precipitated the disciplinary action, the teacher or other LEA personnel expressed specific concerns about a pattern of behavior directly to the director of special education or other supervisory personnel.[64]

However, in certain circumstances, schools will not be deemed to have knowledge that a nonidentified student was a student with a disability. Indeed, when the *parent* of the child has not allowed an evaluation to occur,[65] or has refused services,[66] then the district cannot be said to have had knowledge of the disability. Additionally, when the child has been evaluated and determined not to have a disability, the special rules governing disciplinary actions for students

---

[59] 34 C.F.R. § 300.530(h) (2016).
[60] *See Honig v. Doe*, 484 U.S. 305 (1988); 34 C.F.R. §§ 300.532 and 300.533 (2016) (school may seek injunctive relief in court to prevent dangerous student from returning to school).
[61] *See* 34 C.F.R. §§ 300.532(c) and 300.533 (2016) (outlining the appeal process for parents and school districts and requiring student to remain in the interim alternative educational setting during the pendency of the appeal, e.g., stay put).
[62] 20 U.S.C. § 1415(k)(5)(B)(i) (2016).
[63] 20 U.S.C. § 1415(k)(5)(B)(ii) (2016).
[64] *See* 20 U.S.C. § 1415(k)(5)(B)(i) (2016); 34 C.F.R. § 300.534(b)(1)-(3) (2016).
[65] 34 C.F.R. § 300.534(c)(1)(i) (2016).
[66] 34 C.F.R. § 300.534(c)(1)(ii) (2016).

with disabilities will not apply.[67] Under these situations—where there is no basis for knowledge that the child has a disability—the school district may apply the disciplinary procedures it would normally use for nondisabled students.[68] However, in the instance where a district does have knowledge, or should have had knowledge, then the student can assert the procedural protections.

What if a request is made for an evaluation during the time when the child is disciplined under the school's normal procedures—in other words, with an occurrence that may happen frequently, the child is not identified, commits an infraction, is disciplined, and then someone (e.g., a parent) requests an evaluation? In these circumstances, the evaluation must be expedited.[69] Yet, until the evaluation is complete, school authorities have the discretion to determine placement, including expulsion or suspension.[70] During this time, educational services are not required.[71] Of course, if the expedited evaluation and processes reveal that the student is a child with a disability, then the school must provide special education and related services under the IDEA.[72]

Referral to Law Enforcement and Judicial Authorities

Certain in-school behavior may be so serious as to rise to a criminal level. Indeed, the possession of a weapon or drugs is perhaps an all-too-common infraction that illustrates this point. As a result, local law enforcement officials may need to be involved. In such circumstances, the IDEA provides some guidance as to how the discipline provisions in special education interact with behavior that may involve other law enforcement agencies.

It should be clear that the IDEA and its accompanying regulations do not prevent a school district from reporting criminal or suspected criminal behavior to appropriate authorities.[73] Moreover, the discipline sections regarding special education law do not prevent state law enforcement officials from exercising their duties in applying state or federal law.[74]

With that said, school districts reporting crimes do have some obligations with respect to the student's records; namely, the school must ensure that the

---

[67] 34 C.F.R. § 300.534(c)(2) (2016). However, certain circumstances may arise whereby the school district will be deemed to have had knowledge that the child qualified for special education and, therefore, the protections regarding discipline attach. *See, e.g.,* S.W. v. Holbrook Pub. Schs. 221 F. Supp. 2d 222 (D. Mass. 2002); Colvin *ex rel.* Colvin v. Lowndes Cnty. Sch. Dist., 114 F. Supp. 2d 504 (N.D. Miss. 2000) (ruling that the disciplinary protections afforded students with disabilities applied to student where parents had requested student be evaluated but district ignored such requests). And, of course, there are different fact patterns where knowledge will not be imputed to the district. *See, e.g.,* Mr. and Mrs. R. v. West Haven Bd. of Educ., 36 IDELR 211 (D. Conn. 2002) (district did not have knowledge).

[68] 34 C.F.R. § 300.534(d) (2016).
[69] 34 C.F.R. § 300.534(2)(i) (2016).
[70] 34 C.F.R. § 300.534(2)(ii) (2016).
[71] *Id.* But school officials should note that if they provide services to nondisabled peers, then the same practices should follow for a student undergoing evaluation for special education.
[72] 34 C.F.R. § 300.534(2)(iii) (2016).
[73] 34 C.F.R. § 300.535(a) (2016).
[74] *Id.*

student's records are transmitted to the appropriate agency where the crime was reported so that they may be considered.[75] In doing so, the school must comply with the Family Educational Rights and Privacy Act (FERPA).[76] To the extent that school districts coordinate or report to the police, they should be careful to abide by constitutional requirements regarding search and seizure, as well.

Restraint and Seclusion

While this overview regarding the use of restraint and seclusion may be helpful, careful consideration must be afforded to specific state laws.[77] States may, for instance, define "restraint" differently.[78] Each state also may carve out exceptions to that definition that, again, may vary depending on the jurisdiction.[79] However, regardless of jurisdiction, the law generally disfavors physical restraint and seclusion, and that is worth repeating. These concepts are antithetical to basic freedoms and the intent of special education. Accordingly, best practices should avoid their use whenever possible.

Indeed, there have been multiple incidents in which students with disabilities have been seriously injured, or even killed, as a result of a school district's use of restraint and seclusion techniques to control behavior or discipline. Use of restraints or seclusions may raise constitutional or statutory claims by parents; for example, a student who is injured as a result of a restraint may present a viable claim that her substantive due process rights have been violated.[80] The use of physical restraints and seclusion methods is disfavored by the U.S. Department of Education and, in general, the education profession. Most states have adopted specific statutes regarding restraint and seclusion, which requires careful attention on the part of administrators.[81]

Of course, there are times when restraint or seclusion may be warranted, or even required, to prevent further injury of the student or others. Each case is unique, but courts have been called upon to address the use of these methods against claims that the student's constitutional or statutory rights have been violated. In one instance, a court determined that a special education teacher's

---

[75] 34 C.F.R. § 300.535(b) (2016).
[76] 34 C.F.R. §300.535(b)(2) (2016).
[77] For an overview of state laws, see Deanna Arivett, *The Need for Restraints in Public Schools? Keeping Students Safe in the Age of Inclusion*, 40 Dayton L. Rev. 155 (2015) available at:https://udayton.edu/law/_resources/documents/law_review/vol40_no2/402_the_need_for_restraints_in_public_schools.pdf.
[78] *See, e.g.*, N.H. Rev. Stat. Ann. § 126-U:I-IV (2016) (defining restraint as "bodily physical restriction, mechanical devices, or any device that unreasonably limits the freedom of movement. It includes mechanical restraint, physical restraint, and medication restraint used to control behavior in an emergency or any involuntary medication.").
[79] *Id.* (excepting from the definition of restraint actions that constitute "holding a child to calm or comfort").
[80] *See, e.g.*, Brown v. Ramsey, 121 F. Supp. 2d 911 (E.D. Va. 2000) (holding that basket hold restraint did not violate student's substantive due process rights).
[81] For an excellent resource, *see* U.S. Dep't. of Educ., *Restraint and Seclusion: Resource Document*, (May 2012), available at http://www2.ed.gov/policy/seclusion/restraints-and-seclusion-resources.pdf.

use of restraints and seclusion did not violate the student's Fourth Amendment right when the IEP authorized the use of such techniques.[82] Yet, in another instance, a student presented a triable issue as to whether her Fourth Amendment right was violated where a teacher strapped the student in a "restraint chair" almost immediately upon the beginning of the school day.[83]

School districts may establish policies that govern the use of restraint and seclusion as part of their effort to comply with governing statutes and regulations. These are susceptible to court review, as well. In one case, *Hernandez v. Board of Education of Albuquerque Public Schools*, special education students argued that a district's policy violated the Americans with Disabilities Act (ADA), among other claims.[84] The district court upheld the policy. Importantly, the court noted that the policy outlines the use of restraint for all students, not simply students with disabilities; thus, it was not discriminatory against students with disabilities. Moreover, the court found that the district's policy asserted, at multiple instances, that the use of physical restraint or force was a "last resort" and that the district's adoption of the policy was, in part, intended to reduce the use of restraint, rather than promote it vis-a-vis students with disabilities.[85] The express sentiment of the policy, then, was to avoid the use of restraint or seclusion; in other words, it was intended to protect students from abuse of these techniques.

Recommendations for Practice

1. School districts can remove students with disabilities for violation of the disciplinary code for a period of 10 school days without triggering additional duties, such as providing services. Of course, school district should be careful here. If they typically provide services to nondisabled students when they are suspended for 10 or fewer days, then those obligations apply to children with disabilities.

2. Removals that cumulate to 10 days become a change of placement if they form a pattern of removal, in which case additional procedures are triggered just as they are with a 10-consecutive-day removal.

3. Careful attention should be paid to what constitutes a "suspension" and, therefore, contributes to the 10-day maximum. For instance, an in-school suspension may not be a "suspension" within the meaning of the IDEA, if the student has the opportunity to participate appropriately in the general education curriculum and continues to receive services, among other factors.

---

[82] C.N. v. Willmar Public Schs., 591 F.3d 624 (8th Cir. 2010).
[83] A.B. *ex rel*. B.S. v. Adams-Arapahoe Sch. Dist., 831 F. Supp. 2d 1226 (D. Colo. 2011). However, claims involving a violation of Fourth Amendment rights because of a more limited use of a restraint chair by other teachers and a "basket hold" were dismissed. *Id*.
[84] Hernandez v. Bd. of Educ. of Albuquerque Public Sch., 124 F. Supp. 3d 1181 (D.N.M. 2015).
[85] *Id*.

4. There are important timelines that districts should be aware of with respect to removals that amount to change of placement. Perhaps the most important of these relates to the requirement to conduct a manifestation determination. Here, the determination must be made within 10 school days of the decision to change the placement.
5. If the conduct was a manifestation of the child's disability, districts must conduct an FBA or review and modify a behavioral intervention plan, if warranted.
6. In terms of procedure, school districts must notify parents of a change of placement decision on the date that the decision is made. At this time, they must provide parents with information regarding procedural safeguards.
7. Schools have the authority to place students in an IAES for up to 45 school days when the child brings a weapon, sells or possesses drugs, or inflicts serious bodily injury on another.
8. Students who have not been identified as disabled may still be entitled to additional procedural protections, but only when the school district had knowledge that the child may, in fact, have a disability.
9. Nothing in the IDEA prohibits school officials from reporting crimes or suspected crimes to the authorities.
10. The use of restraint and seclusion should be avoided wherever possible. In addition, the rules governing these issues are determined on a state-by-state basis; you should be sure to consult your state laws and regulations on this matter.

Case List

A.B. *ex rel.* B.S. v. Adams-Arapahoe Sch. Dist.
Alex R. v. Forrestville Valley Cmty. Sch. Dist. #221
Brown v. Ramsey
C.J.N. v. Minneapolis Pub. Schs.
C.N. v. Willmar Pub. Schs.
Colvin *ex rel.* Colvin v. Lowndes Cnty. Sch. Dist.
Farrin v. Maine Sch. Admin. Dist. No. 59
Fitzgerald v. Fairfax Cnty. Sch. Bd.
Hernandez v. Bd. of Educ. of Albuquerque Pub. Sch.
Honig v. Doe
Jonathan G. v. Caddo Parish Sch. Bd.
Lancaster Elem. Sch. Dist.
Lathrop R-II Sch. Dist. v. Gray
Lewellyn v. Sarasota Cnty. Bd. of Educ.
M.M. v. Special Sch. Dist. No. 1
Mr. and Mrs. R. v. West Haven Bd. of Educ.
Neosho R-V Sch. Dist. v. Clark

Randy M. v. Texas City Indep. Sch. Dist.
Rowley v. Bd. of Educ. of Hendrick Hudson Cent. Sch. Dist.
S.W. v. Holbrook Pub. Schs.
Sch. Bd. of Prince William Cnty. v. Malone
Troy City Bd. of Educ.

Key Words

Americans with Disabilities Act
behavioral intervention plan (BIP)
bus transportation
change in/of placement
child find
Controlled Substance Act
crimes
cumulative suspensions
dangerous weapons
disciplinary measures
drugs
educational opportunities
evaluation
Family Educational Rights and Privacy Act (FERPA)
Fourth Amendment
free appropriate public education
functional behavioral assessment (FBA)
individualized education plan (IEP)
Individuals with Disabilities Education Act
interim alternative educational setting
interventions
law enforcement
manifestation of disability
non-identified students
pattern of removal
procedural safeguards
removal
restraint
seclusion
serious bodily injury
student rights
suspension
ten-day rule
threaten
timelines
zero tolerance policy

Takeaways

1. When students with IEP plans are suspended for more than 10 school days, the school district is obligated to provide the student with educational services. Students may not be removed from school (more than 10 days is considered removed from school) if the behavior is due to their disability.
2. If a student with disabilities is suspended for more than 10 days, and the behavior is determined to be a manifestation of their disability, the school district must require a functional behavioral assessment (FBA) and modify or review the student's behavioral intervention plan (BIP). A behaviorist may work with the IEP team to determine the best course of action for the student.

Practical Extension

1. Can students with disabilities receive the same discipline as their non-disabled peers?
2. What protection does IDEA offer students with disabilities in terms of discipline in school?
3. What constitutes a "change in placement?"
4. What is the purpose of having a manifestation determination (MDR)? Who should participate in the MDR? What should be determined at the MDR?